TOP 50

REPRODUCIBLE!

Ages 5–10

BIBLE LESSONS ABOUT ORDINARY PEOPLE in GOD'S EXTRAORDINARY PLAN

AMBER PIKE

ROSEKIDZ

The Top 50 Bible Lessons about Ordinary People in God's Extraordinary Plan

Published by RoseKidz®
a division of Tyndale House Ministries
351 Executive Drive
Carol Stream, Illinois 60188 USA
tyndale.com

Author: Amber Pike

Managing Editor: Karen McGraw

Front Cover Design: Drew McCall
Back Cover Design: Karen McGraw
Interior Design: Karen McGraw

ISBN: 978-1-64938-035-7

Printed in the United States of America

34 33 32 31 30 29 28 27 26 25
10 9 8 7 6 5 4 3 2 1

Table of Contents

Preface.......5
Introduction.......6

Chapter 1 David.......7
God can use us even when we sin!

Chapter 2 Paul.......12
God's Spirit changes us!

Chapter 3 Jonah.......17
God wants us to obey!

Chapter 4 Moses.......22
God helps us do what he asks us to do!

Chapter 5 Samson.......27
God gives us strength!

Chapter 6 Peter.......32
God's kingdom grows through faith!

Chapter 7 Jacob.......37
God had a plan for you before you were born!

Chapter 8 Gideon.......42
God will be with you!

Chapter 9 Martha.......47
God shows us what is important!

Chapter 10 Thomas.......52
God rescues us from our doubts!

Chapter 11 Sarah.......57
God keeps his promises, even if we don't believe!

Chapter 12 Zacchaeus.......62
God cares about you, no matter what!

Chapter 13 Eli.......67
God warns us to be faithful.

Chapter 14 Abraham.......72
God doesn't forget his promises.

Chapter 15 Aaron.......77
God can use us to help others!

Chapter 16 Zechariah.......82
God can teach others through us!

Chapter 17 The Woman at the Well.......87
God doesn't let your mistakes get in his way.

Chapter 18 Solomon.......92
God wants us to be wise!

Chapter 19 Elijah.......97
God is the one true God!

Chapter 20 Judah.......102
God's plans are the best plans!

Chapter 21 Rahab.......107
God is to be feared!

Chapter 22 Adam & Eve.......112
God made us in his image!

Chapter 23 The Thief on the Cross.......117
We know Jesus is the Messiah!

Chapter 24 Esther.......122
We can listen to people who follow God!

Chapter 25 Joseph.......127
God can make bad things good.

Chapter 26 Rebekah.......132
God helps us be kind.

Chapter 27 Pharaoh 137
It's important to listen to God's Word.

Chapter 28 King Saul 142
God wants to be our King.

Chapter 29 Ruth 147
God is the ultimate redeemer!

Chapter 30 Samuel.....................................152
We can tell others God's Word!

Chapter 31 Noah...157
God is a fair judge!

Chapter 32 Daniel 162
God is in control!

Chapter 33 The Israelites 167
God shows us the best path.

Chapter 34 Baruch.......................................172
God's Word can't be destroyed.

Chapter 35 Jesus' Disciples 177
God wants you to help him!

Chapter 36 Judas Iscariot 182
God lets us choose to follow him!

Chapter 37 Isaiah..187
God gives us hope!

Chapter 38 King Herod............................. 192
God isn't surprised by our actions!

Chapter 39 Lydia 197
God wants everyone to be in his family!

Chapter 40 Nehemiah................................202
God wants us to work hard!

Chapter 41 Josiah....................................... 207
God gave us his Word to follow!

Chapter 42 Barnabas, Timothy & Silas 212
We can share the good news about Jesus!

Chapter 43 Matthew...................................217
Jesus wants us to follow him!

Chapter 44 The Roman Officer..................222
God offers eternal life through Jesus.

Chapter 45 Nicodemus 227
God loves us!

Chapter 46 John the Baptist......................232
If we repent, God will forgive us.

Chapter 47 Jeremiah 237
God's plans are good.

Chapter 48 Balaam 242
God speaks to us.

Chapter 49 Prison Guard........................... 247
God frees us from sin.

Chapter 50 Mary 252
God chooses ordinary people.

Preface

A Note to Children's Ministry Leaders & Parents

One of the top questions I hear from kids is "How can I hear God speak?" We teach kids that God still speaks to believers today. We teach them that God has a plan for their lives and that he wants to use them for his good and his glory. But they don't always get how. In their walk with Christ, as a child, it's hard to hear God speaking.

Don't just teach boys and girls Bible stories. Teach them **God's extraordinary plan.** Show them that God's Word is alive and that he's still speaking today. Through the stories of the men and women in the Bible, invite boys and girls to see how God was able to use these ordinary people—people just like them! Challenge kids to open up their hearts to allow God to speak to them as well.

> "For all who are led by the Spirit of God are children of God" (Romans 8:14).

As you pour into the kids God has brought into your life and make God's Word come alive for them, remember that you are not just teaching stories. You are teaching about **God's extraordinary plan** and how your kids are a part of that plan.

~Amber Pike

Introduction

Another great title in RoseKidz's best-selling Top 50 series, *Top 50 Bible Lessons about Ordinary People in God's Extraordinary Plan* is an interactive, activity-based lesson book for elementary-aged children. This fun book features strong, Bible-based teachings, interactive activities (that address a variety of learning styles), small-group discussions, and life-application questions and activities.

Children will be learning more about the men and women of the Bible. They'll learn that these Bible people were ordinary people like us! They were not perfect and sometimes really messed up—just like us.

Despite their imperfections, God's love for them never changed and he was able to use them as part of his extraordinary plan. That's true for us, too. If we are listening to God and in relationship with him, we can be used by him to do extraordinary things.

We are a part of God's extraordinary plan.

How to Use This Book

The lessons include:

- ***Memory Verse*** to help kids get God's Word forever in their hearts and minds.
- ***Overview*** will give you some history and prepare you for teaching the lesson.
- The ***Bible Story*** opens God's Word and begins the learning. There is both scripted conversation and passages to be read. You can read the passages aloud, or ask volunteers to read the Scriptures. Use bookmarks or sticky notes to mark passages in Bibles ahead of time.
- Each lesson includes a ***Big Idea*** Bible truth to guide all the activities kids will be engaged in. The Big Idea helps you keep children focused on the main truth being taught from the Bible. It also helps kids see how they fit into God's plan.
- Children love the ***Opening Activity***. This engaging activity introduces kids to the Bible person, the Big Idea, or something connected to the Bible story.
- An ***Object Lesson*** helps them see Bible truths through the use of common everyday items.
- ***Optional Activities*** allow children with different learning styles to get more time with the Bible truth. And they allow you to tailor the lesson to the time you have in your schedule.
- ***Materials*** gives you a list of everything you need to complete each activity.
- ***Step-by-Step Instructions*** tell you what to do.
- ***Guided Conversation*** and ***Life-Application Questions*** help you know what to say. All the scripted conversation is set in **SEMI-BOLD** type.
- Also included are a variety of ***Reproducible Pages***: crafts, games, word searches, crosswords, codes, mazes, coloring pages, etc. Use them as part of your teaching time, as time-fillers, or as take-home papers.

Chapter 1: David

2 Samuel 11

I will exalt you, my God and King, and praise your name forever and ever. I will praise you every day; yes, I will praise you forever. PSALM 145:1–2

Overview

Say: **Everyone who has ever lived is going to disobey God. Scripture tells us this in Romans 3:23. Sin is when we disobey God; we break his laws and commands. God doesn't want us to sin. He wants us to obey him.**

Even though we sin, God still loves us, and he still uses us to do his will. Today, we are going to learn about a man who loved God very much. Although this man loved God, he didn't always follow God. But God still used him to do big things, even when he disobeyed. We will learn today that God can use us even when we sin!

Opening Activity

Worship with Instruments

Preparation: Photocopy Clues #1–3 and cut out.

Materials

- Clue #1: Worship (p. 11)
- Scissors
- Children's worship music and player
- Rhythm instruments (shakers, tambourines, drums, etc.)

Say: **God is all-powerful. He can do anything! Because he can do anything, he doesn't really need us, but he chooses us anyway!**

For the next several weeks, we're going to learn about some of the ordinary people God chose to serve him. The story of each of these people comes from the Bible. Let's see if you can figure out who the person is that we are talking about today. *(Show kids CLUE #1—WORSHIP. Children guess who the person might be. Neither confirm nor deny the guesses.)*

If you're not sure, don't worry. There are a couple more clues to come. I'll explain how all the clues reveal our mystery person after you see the final clue.

Do: Play some upbeat children's worship music while kids sing along and play rhythm instruments.

Bible Story

David and Bathsheba

Read: Psalm 145

Materials

- Clues #2 and #3: Heart and King (p. 11)

Say: **We just worshiped God with music and read a psalm about worshiping God. A *psalm* is a sacred song, or a song about God. There is a whole book of psalms in the Bible. Guess the name of the book.** (*Children respond.*) **That's right! The book of Psalms!**

Does reading a psalm give you a hint as to who our lesson is about? (*Children respond.*) **Here's our next clue.** (*Show kids CLUE #2—HEART. Children guess.*)

In the time of the Old Testament, God's people cried out to him, asking for a king. They wanted to be ruled by a king, just like everyone else.

Through the prophet Samuel, God warned the people what would happen if they had a human king—their possessions, their sons, and daughters would be taken. God warned that the people would cry out asking to not have a king ruling over them. But the people still wanted a king to rule over them.

God answered their cries and selected Saul as the first king of Israel. At first, Saul followed the Lord, but then he started to disobey God. Through the prophet Samuel, God sent King Saul a message.

> ***"How foolish!" Samuel exclaimed. "You have not kept the command the LORD your God gave you. Had you kept it, the LORD would have established your kingdom over Israel forever. But now your kingdom must end, for the LORD has sought out a man after his own heart. The LORD has already appointed him to be the leader of his people, because you have not kept the LORD's command"*** (1 Samuel 13:13–14).

"A man after God's own heart." That's another clue. Do you know who we are talking about yet? We have one final clue. (*Show kids CLUE #3—KING. Children guess.*)

Did you guess that we are talking about King David? David loved the Lord! As a boy, he defeated the Philistine giant, Goliath, and gave God the glory! He wrote many psalms to God and through them taught us what worship looks like.

But God also used David in another really big way. Does anyone know how else God used him and who was in his family? (*Children respond.*)

Read: 2 Samuel 7:11–16

Say: **God promised David that someone from his family would sit on the throne forever. Who was God talking about?** (*Children respond.*) **Jesus! Jesus comes through the line of David!**

Wow! Those are amazing things that the Bible tells us about David. David must have been perfect, right? Or pretty close? Wouldn't he have to be for God to choose him to be the great-great-(*count fourteen* greats *on your fingers.*)**-grandfather of Jesus? Right?**

Uh . . . NO! David, though he was a man after God's heart and was used by God in many big ways, was still an ordinary person. David still messed up sometimes.

In 2 Samuel 11, we read that David stole a man's wife, and then had that man killed. Do you think that was the end of David following the Lord? *(Children respond.)*

Never! David sinned. Romans 3:23 tells us that we ALL sin. Yes, David, who was known as "a man after God's own heart," and the man that God picked to lead his people had sinned. But David still loved God, even though he sinned. And God still used David to accomplish his extraordinary plan, even though David sinned!

When David realized what he had done, and that he was sinning against the Lord, he cried out to God asking for forgiveness. Do you think God forgave David? Murder is a pretty big sin. *(Children respond.)* **Absolutely, God forgave him! Scripture tells us that God will always forgive our sins (1 John 1:9).**

Did God still love David and want to use him to do big things, even though he messed up? *(Children respond.)* **You betcha!**

We all are going to sin and mess up, but God is faithful and just to forgive our sins. And, he will always love us! But like David, when we realize that we have sinned against God, we need to confess our sins, asking God for forgiveness, and to restore our relationship with him once again!

Pray: Give children time to pray silently, asking God to forgive their sins. Close prayer, asking God to use each of them for his extraordinary plan.

Object Lesson

Materials

- Dry-erase board or mirror
- Black permanent marker
- Red dry-erase marker
- Dry-erase eraser

Erasing Sin

Preparation: Write the word *SIN* on the dry-erase board or mirror with permanent marker.

Say: Scripture tells us that, like David, we all sin. We need Jesus to forgive our sins; we can't get rid of sin on our own! *(Try to rub the word* SIN *off with a dry-erase eraser. It won't come off.)*

(While you read the following, color over the permanent maker with red dry-erase marker.) **But when we confess our sins to God and ask for forgiveness, Jesus removes our sins! It's because Jesus was willing to die on a cross to pay the punishment for our sins. It's Jesus' blood that removes the stain of sin from our lives.** *(Erase the word* SIN *with dry-erase eraser.)*

Optional: Children use the dry-erase board or mirror and markers from the object lessons, writing and then erasing sins kids their age might do.

Additional Activity Options

Materials

- Beach ball or soft ball

Optional

- Children's worship music and player

Pop-Up Praise Game

Do: While upbeat praise music plays in the background, children crouch down on the floor and toss around the ball. When they catch the ball, they should pop up and shout a reason to worship God. Player holding the ball when a song ends chooses two or three volunteers to recite the memory verse with them.

Say: No matter what was going on in David's life, good or bad, he worshiped the Lord still. We should be doing the same, worshiping God through the good and the bad in our life!

Stand Up If It's True Bible Review

Say: **Stand up if the answer to the question is true but sit down if it is false. If the answer is false, explain what makes it false.**

1. **David wrote psalms to God.** (True)
2. **David was the first king of Israel.** (False)
3. **Samuel anointed Saul as the first king of Israel.** (True)
4. **Saul followed the Lord until he died.** (False)
5. **David was Saul's son.** (False)
6. **David was known as "a man after God's heart."** (True)
7. **David never messed up.** (False)
8. **The woman David stole was named Bathsheba.** (True)
9. **Bathsheba was not married.** (False)
10. **God still loved David, even though he sinned.** (True)

Discussion Questions

1. What did David do that was wrong? (He stole another man's wife, and then had that man killed.)
2. Stealing a man's wife and then having that man killed seems like a pretty big sin; yet David is known as "a man after God's own heart." How can that be?
3. Does God forgive us, no matter how bad our sins and mistakes are?

King's Crown Craft

Say: **David loved God with all of his heart, but he wasn't perfect. He messed up and needed God's forgiveness. To remind us of King David, we are going to make crowns to wear! As we wear our crowns, we can be reminded that God continues to love us, and God can use us even when we sin!**

Do: Children cut out and tape crowns to wear on their heads. Using markers and decorative materials, they decorate the crowns.

Optional: Children draw hearts on their crown to remind them that David was a man after God's own heart, and we should be, too!

Materials

- Card stock or construction paper
- Scissors
- Tape
- Markers
- Decorative materials (adhesive-backed jewels, stickers, craft-foam shapes)

Songs of Praise

Say: **David loved the Lord, through the good and the bad, through the times when he was obedient to God and even when he was not. As a musician, David wrote all kinds of songs praising our great God, from happy songs to songs of sadness, fear, and repentance. What kind of song can you write to praise God?**

Do: Children, in groups or individually, will write songs of praise to God, just like David!

Materials

- Paper
- Markers

Bible Story Clues

Chapter 2: Paul

Acts 9:1–9

You will receive power when the Holy Spirit comes upon you. And you will be my witnesses, telling people about me everywhere—in Jerusalem, throughout Judea, in Samaria, and to the ends of the earth. **Acts 1:8**

Overview

Say: **Do you think you are really good at noticing changes? If the sky were suddenly green, would you notice? What if I started wearing blue contacts? Would you notice that?**

There was a man in the Bible named Paul. Do you remember who Paul is? *(Children respond.)* **Well, Paul went through a BIG change in his life. His name even changed! It went from Saul to Paul! (Today's Saul is not King Saul from our lesson about David. It's a different Saul.)**

Paul became one of the greatest witnesses for God ever! But he didn't change on his own. In today's Bible lesson, we will learn that just like with Paul, God's Spirit changes us!

Opening Activity

Say: **Let's play a little game to see how well you can spot changes.**

What's Different?

Do: Select a child to be the changer. Everyone else examines the changer closely. After a few seconds, the changer should go out of the room, in a closet, or behind a screen. Changer then subtly changes something about their appearance, such as switching a bracelet to another hand, untucking their shirt, taking out a ponytail, etc.

The rest of the children guess what is different about the person's appearance. Player who guesses correctly becomes the new changer and play continues as time and interest allow.

Say: **Sometimes it was pretty easy to see the change in someone during our game, wasn't it? If the thing that was changed was a smaller, more subtle change, it might have been harder to see.**

Those are just changes in a person's appearance. What about if a person that didn't follow God changes their life and starts following Christ? Would that change be hard or easy to see? If you have been in church since you were born and became a Christian at five years old, people might not be able to see much change in your behavior. You were probably already acting in ways that pleased the Lord.

But what about the actions of a person who HATED God before? Do you think there would be a big change in their behavior after they become a Christian, one that people will notice? *(Children respond.)*

Our Bible person today had one of those BIG CHANGES!

Younger Child Option: Instead of using children for this activity, have a flannelgraph board with characters. Hide or switch out one character each round for children to guess. Or have a variety of objects on a tray. Remove a different item for each round.

Bible Story

The Road to Damascus

As children read the biblical account of Saul's transformation on the road to Damascus, select five volunteers to act out the story.

Say: **Part of our story is going to be read directly from the Bible. In the Bible account, Paul is referred to by his first name Saul. So don't be confused. Just remember, Saul and Paul are the same man!**

Read: Acts 9:1–9

Say: (*Volunteers return to their seats.*) **What happened to Saul on his way to Damascus?** (*Children respond.*) **God stopped Paul in a pretty drastic way! God asked him why he was persecuting him—why he was hurting believers in Christ.**

God also blinded Saul for three whole days in order to get his attention. What kind of a man was Saul that God stopped him like that? Listen to what the Bible tells us about Saul.

> ***Then they put their hands over their ears and began shouting. They rushed at*** **[a follower of Jesus named Stephen]** ***and dragged him out of the city and began to stone him. His accusers took off their coats and laid them at the feet of a young man named Saul.***
>
> ***As they stoned him, Stephen prayed, "Lord Jesus, receive my spirit"*** (Acts 7:57–58).

The people killed Stephen by throwing rocks at him, just for following Jesus. And what role did Saul play? (*Children respond.*) **He held the coats of the people who were stoning Stephen! He was 100-percent OK with killing this man that loved Jesus!**

Saul actually loved God, however. He was a Jewish man. He not only knew the Old Testament Scriptures, he also followed them. He loved God in a big way! He just didn't believe that Jesus was God's one and only Son. So he went around killing, beating, or jailing people that believed in Jesus!

That is why God stopped Saul. He was hurting God by hurting these new members of God's family!

So, Paul was stopped by God on his way to Damascus and blinded for how many days? (*Children respond.*) **For three days. Scripture says that he neither ate nor drank during that time.**

God sent a man named Ananias to come and restore Paul's sight. Paul didn't just get his sight back, though. He received the Holy Spirit as well!

God didn't just heal Saul; he changed him! Saul was soon baptized and began traveling around, preaching that Jesus was the Son of God! This was when he started going by his Greek name, *Paul*, and that's how we usually refer to him.

That's a pretty big turnaround! When we become members of God's family, we can be changed by the Holy Spirit, too! God's Spirit Changes Us!

Pray: Pray with the children, thanking God for sending Jesus to die on the cross for us and that the Holy Spirit changes us when we become members of his family.

Object Lesson

Blindfolded Feeding

In this activity, children have some messy fun, trying to have a snack while being blindfolded.

Preparation: Cover tables with newspapers or plastic tablecloths. Place a similar amount of whipped cream on three to five paper plates.

Do: Choose the same number of volunteers as plates you prepared. Blindfold volunteers and hand each a plastic spoon. Volunteers try to eat all their whipped cream without making a mess!

Materials

- Newspapers or tablecloths
- Paper plates
- Whipped cream
- Plastic spoons
- Blindfolds
- Premoistened wipes or paper towels

Say: **Some of our volunteers did a pretty good job! Imagine how hard it would be if, like Paul in today's Bible story, all of the sudden you were blind. Things we take for granted like brushing our teeth, eating soup, or even fixing our hair would instantly become difficult. You might make a mess or look ridiculous.**

Do you think that's why Paul didn't eat or drink for three days? Just so he wouldn't make a mess on his clothes? *(Children respond.)*

Scripture doesn't tell us what Paul did during those three days that he was blind. What would you be doing if God came to you and told you that you had been hurting him and he also took away your sight? *(Children respond.)* **A lot of us would be praying and asking God not only for healing, but for forgiveness.**

When we do wrong things, God is ready to forgive us. When we become members of God's family, we receive his gift of the Holy Spirit. And God's Spirit changes us!

Additional Activity Options

Blindfold Tag

Materials

- Blindfolds

Do: Select one child to be "It." Place a blindfold securely on "It." "It" tags other children, relying on their sense of hearing, while keeping their blindfold on. Once tagged, players assist "It" be giving instructions where to move. After two or three players have been tagged, "It" and tagged players recite the memory verse, a new "It" is chosen, and play continues.

Say: **Why was tag harder to play wearing a blindfold? How do you think Paul felt being blinded for three days? Even though Paul had to lose his sight for a few days, I'm thankful that God changed him, and made Paul a man he could use in his extraordinary plan. God's Spirit changes us!**

Optical Illusion Spinner

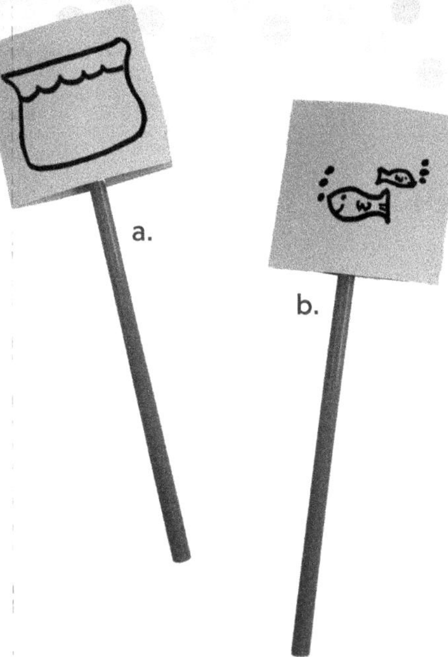

Materials

- White card stock
- Rulers
- Pencils
- Scissors
- Markers
- Plastic straws
- Tape

Preparation: Children cut card stock into two 3-inch squares. In the center of one square, children draw an object something else might go in or on (image a): fish bowl, bird cage, chair, etc. On the other square, children draw something that would go in that object (image b): fish, bird, sitting person, etc.

Hint: Try to place the second image in the center of your sheet so it will look like it's in the center of the first image.

Children tape a straw to the back of one of the squares, and then sandwich the straw with the other square, taping the two squares securely together. Children spin the spinner between their palms, creating a fun optical illusion.

Say: **When you added a second image to your craft, the whole thing changed! Do you think Paul looked different after God changed him on the road to Damascus?** (*Children respond.*) **When the Holy Spirit comes into our life, God's Spirit changes us!**

Fact Face-Off Bible Review

Do: Form two teams. Team members face off against each other, one at a time, answering the questions and earning points for their team.

Changing People Crossword: Photocopy the puzzle on page 16, making one copy for each child plus extras. Kids complete in class or take home.

1. **Did Paul follow the Old Testament or the New Testament?** (Old Testament)
2. **What did he do to Christians?** (Killed them)
3. **Where was Paul headed to?** (Damascus)
4. **What happened to Paul on the way there?** (He was blinded.)
5. **What did God ask him?** (Why he was persecuting him)
6. **How long was Paul blinded?** (Three days)
7. **Did Paul eat or drink during those three days?** (No)
8. **Was Paul Jewish or Greek?** (Jewish)
9. **Did Paul get his sight back?** (Yes)
10. **After God restored Paul's sight, what did Paul do?** (Became a Christian and told others about Jesus)

Discussion Questions

1. **How did the Holy Spirit change Paul?**
2. **How can the Holy Spirit change us today?**
3. **What are ways that people could tell that you are a follower of God?**

Burning Bush Snack

Materials

- Frosted cupcakes
- Candy corn

Do: Children decorate cupcakes with candy corn "flames," and then eat and enjoy their snack.

Say: Our cupcakes with their pretend flames remind us of the burning bush from our story and that God's Spirit changes us!

Changing People Crossword

Paul killed Christians, but God still came to him and changed him. Could the bad things we've done keep God from wanting us as members of his family?

Some people think that they aren't good enough for God to forgive them and love them. They think that they have done too many wrong things and that they need to act better before Jesus can forgive them. Does this sound right? No way!

Complete this crossword by finding people God will forgive. Remember that **God's Spirit changes us!** And when people are forgiven by God and become members of his family, the Holy Spirit changes them.

Hint: The shaded boxes contain one of the letters in today's Big Idea.

Across

3. People who haven't grown up yet
4. People who lead a church
6. People who don't tell the truth
7. People who pick on and hurt others
9. People who have killed other people

Down

1. People who teach others
2. People in your family
4. People who have children
5. People who take things that belong to others
8. All the people in the world

Chapter 3: Jonah

Jonah 1–3

If you love me, obey my commandments. **JOHN 14:15**

God wants us to obey!

Big Idea

Overview

Say: **When mom tells you to clean your room, what are you supposed to do?** *(Children respond.)* **Clean your room, of course! When your teacher tells you which math problems to do for homework, which math problems should you answer?** *(Children respond.)* **The ones your teacher assigned! Moms and dads and teachers all want you to obey their instructions. There are laws and rules throughout life that you are supposed to obey as well!**

But people don't always obey. At some point, all of us have disobeyed a parent. Most adults have broken the law by speeding. When you disobey a parent, you get punished. If you speed, you might get a ticket. There are consequences for disobeying and breaking the rules.

What about disobeying God? The Bible is full of instructions for how we are supposed to live and walk in relationship with God. It's also full of stories and examples of men and women who followed God . . . and some that did not. God's way is the best way, so we should obey his commands and laws. But we don't always do that. The people in the Bible didn't always obey, either. Sometimes God had to punish them, just as he punishes us when we disobey.

As we read about Jonah, and his decision to disobey God, we will see just how much God wants us to obey!

Opening Activity

Materials

- Mystery box and/ or shield
- 6–10 objects that make noise (jingle bell, bike horn, squeaky dog toy, buzzer, cowbell, etc.)

Now Hear This

Do: Use the mystery box or shield to conceal the items from the children. Make each sound one at a time, as children guess what it is.

Alternate Idea: Play this game with two blindfolded contestants, playing for points.

Say: **How well did you listen? Did you guess each sound correctly?** *(Children respond.)* **Maybe you were a good listener in our game, but are you a good listener in life? Not just listening to sounds, but are you a good listener to God?** *(Pause, allowing children to reflect.)*

Younger Child Option: Start out quietly making an animal sound. Once children hear the sound and identify the animal, they should begin moving like that animal.

Bible Story

Jonah Disobeys

Say: In Old Testament times, God spoke to prophets. These were men chosen by God to deliver his messages to people: men like Samuel, Elijah, and Isaiah. Sometimes God would have a good message for his people, like the messages Isaiah told about the Messiah that would one day come. Other times, the prophets would be delivering messages of judgment or warning.

God spoke to the prophet Jonah.

The Lord gave this message to Jonah son of Amittai: "Get up and go to the great city of Nineveh. Announce my judgment against it because I have seen how wicked its people are."

Jonah heard exactly what God said. He just didn't like it.

The people of Nineveh were not nice people and Jonah did not want to go there. So instead of obeying God and going to Nineveh like God commanded, Jonah boarded a ship and sailed off towards Tarsus—the opposite direction.

How do you think God felt about Jonah disobeying him? *Children respond.* Remember, God wants us to obey! And he had given Jonah a job to do, a command that Jonah disobeyed. So . . . God punished Jonah.

The Bible doesn't say that a whale swallowed Jonah. And although it sounds like a whale of a tale, there are actually several animals that would have been capable of swallowing Jonah, allowing him to survive inside for several days.

- **Blue Whale**
- **Sperm Whale**
- **Great White Shark**
- **Whale Shark**
- **Or even an extinct sea creature!**

Read: Jonah 1:7–17

Bible Story Enrichment: While reading (or telling) the account of Jonah, children pretend to be in the boat. As the storm rages, children rock around. You can also use a spray bottle of water and storm sound effects for extra fun!

Say: Because of Jonah's disobedience, God sent a storm as punishment. It was a big storm! It was so big that the men on the boat thought that they were going to die. Jonah realized that the storm was his fault and was a punishment for his disobedience.

He told the men to throw him into the sea so the storm would stop. When Jonah was thrown into the sea, God sent something to get him. What did God send? (*Children respond.*) A great, big fish swam and swallowed Jonah, whole!

Inside the fish, Jonah was safe. It might have been smelly, and it was probably scary, but Jonah realized that he had disobeyed God. For three days and nights, Jonah prayed to God. He asked God for forgiveness, and he praised God for who he is!

After being inside the fish for three days and nights, Jonah chapter 3 verse 10 tells us that God commanded the fish to spit Jonah up on dry land!

Jonah was safe, and he was forgiven. When God spoke to Jonah a second time, again telling him to go to Nineveh, Jonah obeyed. **God wants us to obey him**, too!

Pray: Spend some time in silent prayer, encouraging children to listen and allow God to speak to them.

Object Lesson

Up and Away!

Do: Give each child a mesh tube spring and a Ping-Pong ball. Show them how to press the spring down on the table, using two fingers, while placing the Ping-Pong ball on top.

When you let go of the spring, the Ping-Pong ball will fly up into the air, reminding us of how God commanded the fish to spit Jonah up on dry land.

Materials

- Ping-Pong ball
- Mesh tube spring, one for each child (available online)

Say: What did Jonah do when God told him to go to Nineveh? (He ran away.) **When Jonah disobeyed God, God took some extreme steps to get Jonah to change his mind and obey. What happened to change Jonah's mind?** (God sent a storm and Jonah was thrown out of the boat. A big fish swallowed Jonah.) **God doesn't want to send storms and big fish after us! God wants us to obey. Do you love God? Our memory verse, John 14:15, says that if we love God, we will obey him.**

Additional Activity Options

Pick-a-Side Bible Review

Preparation: Use masking tape, rope, or clothesline to make a line down the center of the playing area.

Materials

- Masking tape, rope, or clothesline

Do: Play begins with children standing along the rope or clothesline.

Say: Choose one of two ways to complete the following statements, *A* or *B*. If you choose *A*, jump to the right side of the line. If you choose *B*, jump to the left side.

1. **Jonah was *A*—a prophet or *B*—a priest.** (*A*—Prophet)
2. **God told Jonah to go to *A*—Tarsus or *B*—Nineveh.** (*B*—Nineveh)
3. **Jonah went the wrong way because he was *A*—confused or *B*—didn't want to go.** (*B*—Didn't want to go)
4. **God sent a *A*—storm or *B*—star.** (*A*—Storm)
5. **Jonah was swallowed by a *A*—whale or *B*—Big fish.** (*B*—Big fish)
6. **In the fish, Jonah *A*—laughed or *B*—prayed.** (*B*—Prayed)
7. **God *A*—did or *B*—did not give Jonah a second chance to obey.** (*A*—Did)
8. **The next time God told Jonah to go to Nineveh, he *A*—obeyed or *B*—did not obey again.** (*A*—Obeyed)
9. **God *A*—does or *B*—doesn't want us to disobey him.** (*A*—Does)
10. **We should obey God because *A*—we don't want to get punished or because *B*—we love him.** (*B*—We love him.)

Discussion Questions

1. **Is there ever a good reason for disobeying God?**
2. **Have you ever disobeyed God? What happened?**
3. **How do you know what God wants you to do? How does he speak to people today?**

Bible Bookmarks

Materials

- Big Fish Bookmark (p. 21)
- Card stock
- Decorating supplies (Crayons or markers, gel pens, stickers, adhesive gems, etc.)

Preparation: On card stock, photocopy Big Fish Bookmarks, making one copy for every two children plus extras.

Do: Children cut out and decorate bookmarks to use while reading their Bibles.

Say: **God doesn't speak to us today in the same way he spoke to Old Testament prophets, but he does still speak to us. When we read our Bibles, we are reading God's message to us! Spending time reading his Word helps us know how to obey him.**

Extra Fun: Children put today's memory verse on their bookmarks as a reminder that **God wants us to obey.**

Go or No Game

Do: Start the game by telling children to begin walking around the room. After a few moments, give a command. The children do the opposite of the spoken command. Give commands faster and faster to see who can keep up until the end!

- Walk = Stop walking
- Turn right = Turn left
- Crouch down = Jump up

And the opposite of each of the above! Make up your own actions, too.

Say: **When God told Jonah to go to Nineveh, Jonah said no! It was important for Jonah to go to Nineveh so that the people there would follow the Lord. It is important for us to obey God, too. God speaks to us through prayer and through the Bible, giving us not just a bunch of rules to follow, but instructions on how to live life in relationship with him. And God wants us to obey!**

Who Is Speaking

Materials

- Blindfold

Do: Blindfold one child. One at a time, other children take turns to disguise their voices with different tones or silly accents. Blindfolded child guesses who is talking. If the blindfolded player guesses correctly, they choose one or two volunteers to recite the memory verse with them. The child identified becomes the new blindfolded listener. If player doesn't guess correctly, another child takes a turn to disguise their voice. Continue play until each child has a turn or as time and interest allow.

Say: **God isn't a silent God! He still speaks to us today. He speaks through his Word and through prayer. But we have to be listening for him, giving him room to speak. How does God speak to us?** *(Children respond.)*

Big Fish Bookmarks

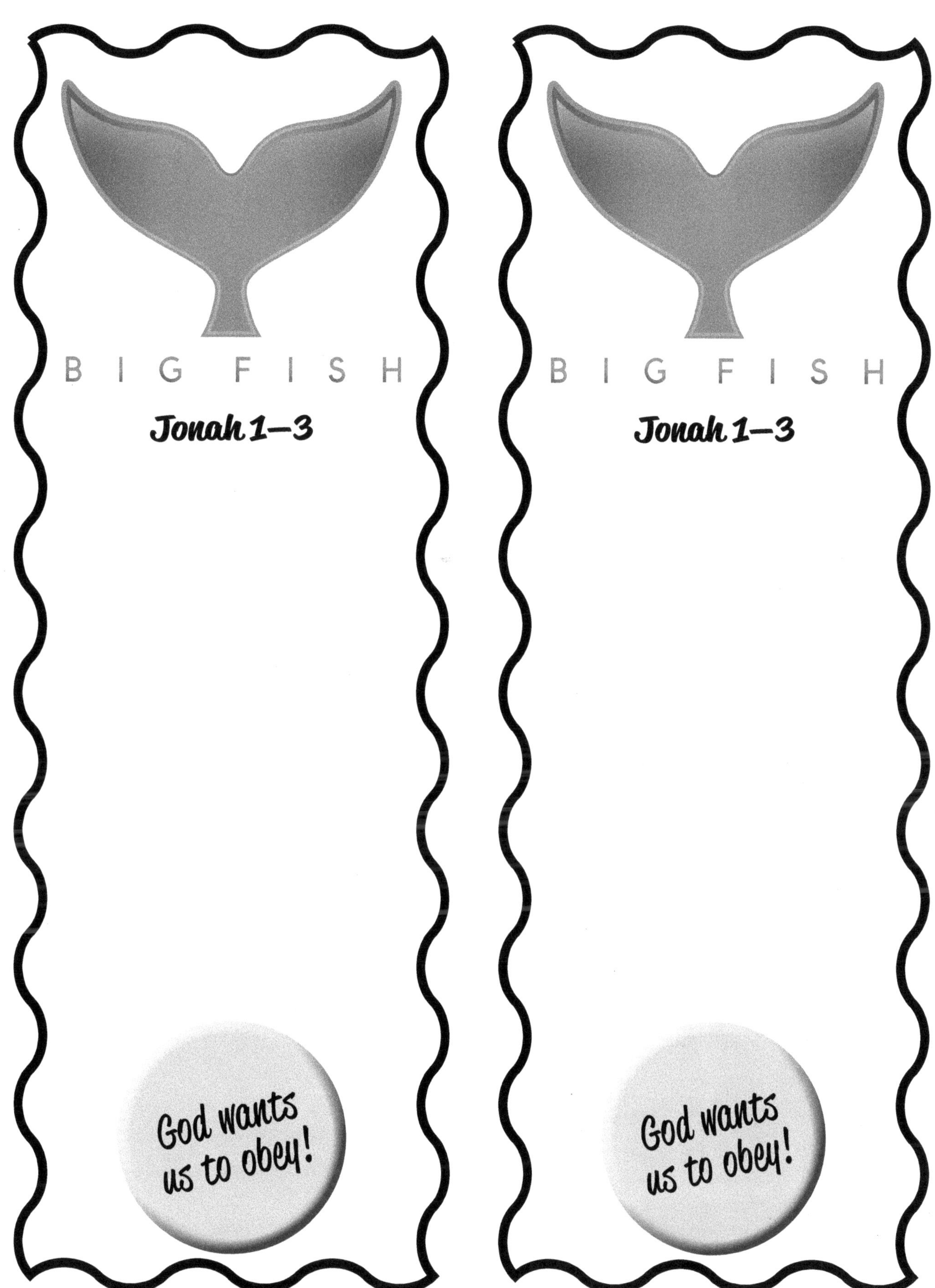

Chapter 4: Moses

Exodus 3—4

For I hold you by your right hand—I the LORD your God. And I say to you "Don't be afraid. I am here to help you." **ISAIAH 41:13**

Overview

Say: **God's chosen people, the Israelites, were living as slaves in the land of Egypt. The king of Egypt, Pharaoh, made life difficult for the Israelites. They were forced to work hard and were treated badly. Because he was afraid that the Israelites would outnumber him and try to take his throne, Pharaoh even ordered that all of the Israelite baby boys be thrown into the Nile River to be killed.**

The Israelites called out to God to save them, and he heard their cry. God had placed a very special man in the position to lead his people to safety—Moses.

Moses was scared he couldn't do the really big job God asked him to do, but God was with him. God equipped Moses with everything he would need to do the job God had for him.

God has a job for each member of his family and he will give us whatever we need to do that job. God helps us do what he asks us to do!

Opening Activity

Pyramid Stack Race

Do: Children divide into equal teams of three or four players. Teams line up. Place a stack of 15 cups an equal distance away from each team line.

Team members take turns to race to the cups, stack them into a pyramid, take them back down into a stack, and then return to tag the next player in line.

The first team to have all of their members stack and unstack a pyramid recites the memory verse.

Play again, forming new teams as time and interest allow.

Materials

- Plastic cups, 15 for each team of three or four players

Younger Child Option: Use only six cups to make a pyramid.

Bible Story

The Burning Bush

Say: Pyramid making was a lot of work, wasn't it? Just imagine if you had to make thousands of big heavy bricks by hand. And then had to use those bricks to build pyramids taller than a football field! Then to top it off, your supervisors were very mean. They would beat you or whip you if you were going too slow.

That's the kind of life God's people, the Israelites, were living in Egypt. They cried out to God to rescue them from the hands of the Egyptians. God heard their cries.

The Israelites were known as God's chosen people. God chose them to love and obey him. He chose them as the people to write and keep his Word, and to be the people from whom the Savior of the world, Jesus, would come.

This all started long before the Israelites were working as slaves in Egypt. God had promised a man named Abraham that he would bless him with many descendants—more descendants than there are stars in the sky. Abraham would be the father of a mighty nation.

One of those descendants was Joseph, who eventually became the second in command of Egypt's Pharaoh. He took his whole family to Egypt and became the Israelites. Joseph had eleven brothers and their families became the twelve tribes of Israel. This is the nation that God promised to Abraham. And it grew very quickly.

> *In time, Joseph and all of his brothers died, ending that entire generation. But their descendants, the Israelites, had many children and grandchildren. In fact, they multiplied so greatly that they became extremely powerful and filled the land* (Exodus 1:6–7).

Say: The land of Egypt was full of Israelites. Later, when a new Pharaoh sat on the throne, he didn't remember Joseph or what he had done for Egypt. He was scared that this large group of people, the Israelites living in his land, would try to take his throne away. This is why Pharaoh made life very hard for God's people.

Say: One day, a man named Moses was out with his sheep in the wilderness. The job of a shepherd is to keep sheep safe. What sort of things would a shepherd be watching out for? (*Children respond.*) You're right! Shepherds would be watching out for predators like wolves or unsafe land conditions like a cliff that the sheep could fall down.

Younger Child Option: Consider creating a visual for the Bible story by creating a burning bush. Use a fake plant and red and yellow tissue paper or purchase an Artificial Flame Lamp and add leaves to make it look like a bush. Have kids pretend to be Moses' sheep. Ask a volunteer to be Moses and lead the sheep to the burning bush visual.

Normally, when a shepherd saw a bush in the wilderness, it wouldn't be a big deal. But Moses saw a bush . . . and it wasn't like any bush like he had ever seen before.

Read: Exodus 3:1–10

Say: **What was so different about the bush that Moses saw?** *(Children respond.)* **It was on fire! The bush was burning, but it wasn't burning up. How is that possible?** (The power of God.)

God then gave Moses the job of going to Pharaoh and telling him to free the Israelites. How do you think Moses felt about being given this big, important job? *(Children respond.)* **Moses really did NOT want to go. He came up with a lot of excuses.**

Read: Exodus 3:11–17

Even after all of that, Moses STILL protested that he wasn't the right man for the job.

Read: Exodus 4:1–17

Moses didn't think he could do the big job that God had for him. But when God asks us to do something, he helps us to do what he asks us to do!

Pray: Pray over the children, asking God to give them confidence to know that he will help them do the things he asks them to do.

Object Lesson

Burning Bushes

Materials

- Paper picture of a bush (drawn, found in a magazine or printed from online)
- Pan or baking dish
- Measuring cups and spoons
- Isopropyl alcohol (91% alcohol)
- Water
- Salt
- Metal tongs
- Lighter

Preparation: In a pan or baking dish, prepare a solution of ½ cup of isopropyl alcohol, ½ cup of water, and ¼ teaspoon salt.

Do: Soak the picture in the solution for a moment. Remove picture and hold with the tongs. Use the lighter to light the picture on fire.

The alcohol will burn off the paper, but because of the water, the paper will not burn.

Say: **Our bush was on fire, but it didn't burn up. This reminds us of the bush Moses saw out in the wilderness. There is a big difference between our bush and the bush Moses saw, though.**

Our bush burned because of a chemistry trick. (The rubbing alcohol burned off, but the water kept the paper from burning up.) **No one soaked the bush Moses saw with rubbing alcohol and water, and it burned for a lot longer than our picture did.**

Moses was worried about the big job God wanted him to do. But he needed to remember that God helps us to do what he asks us to do!

Additional Activity Options

Speak Up Craft

Materials

- Megaphone Patterns (p. 26)
- Card stock
- Decorative materials (crayons, markers, stickers, craft-foam shapes, etc.)
- Scissors
- Tape

Preparation: On card stock, photocopy Megaphone Patterns, making one for each child plus extras.

Do: Children use decorating materials to write the memory verse on and decorate their megaphones. Children cut out decorated megaphones, including the slits as indicated. Children fold megaphones on the lines, slip tabs into the slits, and tape to secure.

Say: **When Moses was worried that everyone would think he wasn't worthy to go make demands of Pharaoh, what did God do?** *(Children respond.)* **God helped Moses! When Moses was worried no one would know who sent him, what did God do?** *(Children respond.)* **God helped Moses! When Moses was worried that he wouldn't be able to speak well enough, what did God do?** *(Children respond.)* **God helped Moses!**

God was sending Moses to do a big job. But he didn't send him alone. God was with him, helping him every step of the way! And God helps us to do what he asks us to do!

Sign-a-Letter Bible Review

Do: Teach children the ASL signs for the letters A and B (see images below).

Say: **Choose one of two ways to complete the following statements, *A* or *B*. If you choose *A*, hold up the ASL sign for *A*. If you choose *B*, hold up the ASL sign for *B*.**

A

1. **God's chosen people were the *A*—Israelites or *B*—Egyptians?** (A—Israelites)
2. **God promised *A*—Jacob or *B*—Abraham that he would bless him with more descendants than there are stars in the sky?** (B—Abraham)
3. **Joseph had *A*—eleven brothers or B—twelve brothers?** (A—Eleven brothers)
4. **Pharaoh *A*—feared or *B*—didn't care about the Israelites living in Egypt?** (A—Feared)
5. **Moses *A*—was or *B*—was not an Israelite?** (A—Was)
6. **The bush Moses saw was *A*—a weird color or *B*—on fire?** (B—On fire)
7. **God wanted Moses to *A*—become the new Pharaoh or *B*—tell Pharaoh to let God's people go?** (B—Tell Pharaoh to let God's people go)
8. **Moses was *A*—worried or *B*—excited to do what God asked him to do?** (A—Worried)
9. **God called himself *A*—the Prince of Peace or *B*—I AM?** (B—I AM)
10. **When God gave Moses a job to do, he *A*—helped him or *B*—told Moses to figure it out on his own?** (A—Helped him)

B

Discussion Questions

1. **What would you think if you saw a bush that was burning but didn't burn up? What would you do if you heard a voice come from the burning bush?**
2. **How did God help Moses do what he asked him to do?**
3. **How does God help you do what he asks you to do?**

I AM Posters

Say: **One of God's names is *I AM*. That name means that God is the one and only God. There is no one like him! Let's fill our posters with things about our amazing God!**

Do: Children divide into groups of two or three. Each group prints "I AM" in big capital letters on the poster board, and then creates a poster telling about our God (God hears us when we pray, he is all powerful, God is love, etc.).

Materials

- Poster board, one sheet for each group of two or three
- Decorative materials (crayons, markers, stickers, craft-foam shapes, etc.)

Megaphone Patterns

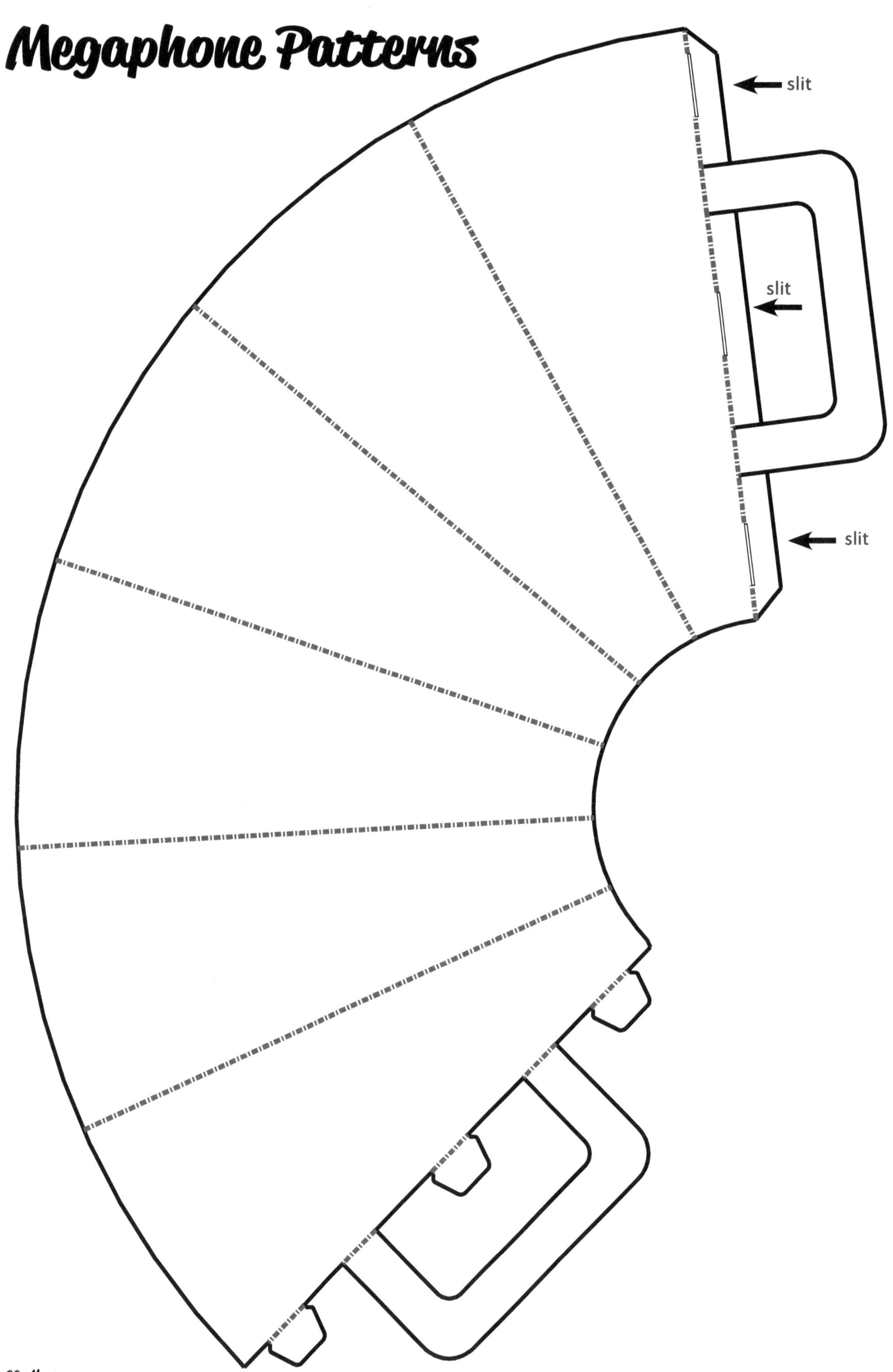

Chapter 5: Samson

Judges 13–16

God is our refuge and strength, always ready to help in times of trouble. PSALM 46:1

Overview

Say: Even before he was born, God set apart Samson. The angel of the Lord appeared to a woman whose name the Bible doesn't tell us. The angel told her that she would give birth to a boy. The angel told the woman that her son would deliver God's people, the Israelites, from the hands of their enemy, the Philistines.

The woman gave birth to a son and named him Samson. Samson was a Nazirite which meant he could never cut his hair. Samson was unusually strong!

God had an extraordinary plan to use Samson to defeat the Philistines. But God used Samson's own power. Because of God, Samson had the power to defeat his enemies. God gives us strength!

Opening Activity

Who's the Strongest Game

Say: Who thinks that you are the strongest person in the world? How about the strongest in our group? *(Children respond.)* **Well, let's see if we can find out.**

Do: The children compete in a strength competition to see who is the strongest.

1. Push Ups
2. Sit Ups
3. Standing on one foot
4. Holding a book in an outstretched hand

Younger Child Option: Consider using simpler actions such as jumping jacks and hopping on one foot and doing them as a group. Try going faster and faster, encouraging silly giggles!

Say: Now that we've had our competition, who is the strongest in our group? *(Children respond.)* **Would you like to be super, super strong? Why or why not?** *(Children respond.)* **Just imagine: If a ball rolled under someone's car, what could you do?** *(Children respond.)* **You could just lift the car with your super strength! What about if the sunlight was shining in the window and making you squint? No worries! You're so strong, you could just move the house!**

OK, maybe we aren't that strong! But there was a man in the Bible that was crazy, super strong!

Bible Story

The Strength of Samson

Read: Judges 13:1–4

The woman was so happy she would have a son! She followed the instructions the angel had given her, and soon a son was born. She named the boy Samson, and he grew healthy and strong.

One day, when Samson was a young man, he and his parents were out walking.

> *As Samson and his parents were going down to Timnah, a young lion suddenly attacked Samson near the vineyards of Timnah. At that moment the Spirit of the LORD came powerfully upon him, and he ripped the lion's jaws apart with his bare hands. He did it as easily as if it were a young goat. But he didn't tell his father or mother about it* (Judges 14:5–6).

Say: Samson was so strong that he tore a lion apart with his hands! But where did his strength come from? *(Children respond.)* God gave Samson strength, so he could defeat Israel's enemies, the Philistines. Over and over again, Samson defeated the Philistines. Once, using only the jawbone of a donkey, he won a fight against 1,000 men!

If one of your enemies keeps defeating you over and over again, how would you feel about that person? *(Children respond.)* You'd probably want to get rid of them! Well, that's exactly the way the Philistines felt about Samson; so, they came up with a plan to destroy him . . . or at least destroy his strength.

Read: Judges 16:4–22

Enrichment Idea: Children act out the Bible story while a leader reads it.

Say: Delilah helped the Philistines destroy Samson. After lots of begging and whining, Samson finally told her that his source of strength was in his hair.

Let's think about something for a minute: Was it actually Samson's hair that made him strong? *(Children respond.)* No! God gave Samson his strength. He didn't have magic hair like Rapunzel or anything crazy like that. As a Nazarite, he was set apart for God and was not supposed to cut his hair. When his enemies cut his hair, Samson's strength left him, because like verse 20 said, the Lord left him.

But that's not the end of Samson's story.

The Philistines that captured Samson were celebrating his capture. They were partying hard and treating Samson badly. They figured they could get away with it because they had already gouged his eyes out and he could not see to stop them.

Then Samson asked a servant to place his hands on the pillars that supported the temple, so that he could lean against them. Then Samson prayed.

> *"Sovereign LORD, remember me again. O God, please strengthen me just one more time. With one blow let me pay back the Philistines for the loss of my two eyes"* (Judges 16:28).

His arms were stretched out between the two pillars. Samson pushed with all of his might . . . and the whole temple came crashing down! Everyone inside was killed, including Samson. He killed more of God's enemies at his death than he did in all of his life.

God gives us strength to do the impossible for him!

Pray: Children spend time in silent prayer, asking God to help them trust in his love and the strength he gives them. Close, thanking God that he gives us strength in times of need.

Object Lesson

Refuge and Strength

Materials

- Paper
- Tape
- Hardcover books

Do: Children attempt to build the strongest structure they can out of a single sheet of paper. The goal is to hold a book for at least 10 seconds before breaking. **Try folding or rolling your sheet of paper!**

Say: **Today's verse, Psalm 46:1, tells us that God is our refuge and strength. A *refuge* is a place of safety. Our verse also promises that God is "always ready to help in times of trouble."**

We get weak. I don't mean just physically weak. When someone at school won't quit being mean to us, we get tired. When we have someone we love facing sickness, we need God's strength to get us through. When life feels rough and it feels like it won't ever get better, God is there to strengthen us! He is there to remind us that he gives us strength!

Additional Activity Options

Power Tower Game

Materials

- Plastic cups, 50–100 for each group of no more than ten players
- Paper

Do: Children divide into groups of no more than ten. Each group works together to build a strong tower.

At your signal, teams wad sheets of paper into paper balls and try to knock down other towers by tossing paper balls at them. The first team to knock down the other team's tower recites the memory verse.

Say: **How did your strong towers hold up?** (*Children respond.*)
If the Bible calls God a strong tower, can he ever fall or be destroyed like a tower? (*Children respond.*) **If he is our source of strength, will he ever get tired?** (*Children respond.*)

No! God will never get tired! He will never run out of strength! He will always be there to strengthen you—an ever-present source of strength and help!

Paper Chains Craft

Preparation: On a large sheet of paper, print the verse: "God is our refuge and strength, always ready to help in times of trouble" (Psalm 46:1). Post paper where children can see it while doing the activity.

Cut construction paper or card stock into strips 1–2 inches thick. Make fifteen strips for each child.)

Do: Children write the memory verse, each word on a separate strip, and the reference on the final strip. Form each strip into a link in a chain, taping them to secure.

Materials

- Large sheet of paper
- Markers
- Scissors or paper cutter
- Construction paper or card stock
- Tape

Say: **God gave Samson strength to break through chains! He gave him the strength to defeat the enemies, even when he had been captured and defeated. Just like he helped Samson, God will give us strength!**

Thumbs Up Thumbs Down Bible Review

Say: **Give a thumbs up if the answer to the question is true. Give a thumbs down if it is false. If the answer is false, explain what makes it false.**

1. **Samson's mom's name was Ruth.** (False)
2. **Samson's mom was already pregnant when the angel of the Lord visited her.** (False)
3. **Samson couldn't cut his hair.** (True)
4. **With his club, Samson could defeat any enemy.** (False)
5. **Samson once killed 1,000 men with a donkey's jawbone.** (True)
6. **Delilah was loyal to Samson.** (False)
7. **Samson's strength was in his hair.** (False)
8. **When the Philistines shaved his head, the Lord left Samson.** (True)
9. **The Philistines arrested Samson, but they treated him well because they were afraid of him.** (False)
10. **God gave Samson strength one more time, and he destroyed the temple and all who were inside.** (True)

Discussion Questions

1. **Why did God want the Philistines destroyed?**
2. **Other than physical strength, like Samson, how does God give you strength?**
3. **Has there ever been a time when God gave you the strength to do something he asked you to do?**

Samson Maze: Photocopy the maze on page 31, making one for each child plus extras. Kids complete in class or take home.

Power Prayers

Do: Give children the time to talk to God about any struggles or troubles they are facing and ask him for strength. Encourage them to spend time listening to God and asking him to lead and guide their lives.

Enrichment Idea: Soft worship music in the background helps create a worshipful environment.

Samson Maze

Help the servant boy guide Samson to the pillars. Along the way, you will find the words to the memory verse. Write them on the appropriate blank line.

____,

____

__________________________ (________ 46:1).

Chapter 6: Peter

Matthew 14:18–33; 16:13–20

Simon Peter answered, "You are the Messiah, the Son of the living God." **MATTHEW 16:16**

Overview

Say: **When Jesus began his earthly ministry, he chose twelve men, his disciples, to travel around with him. Jesus was revealing who he was and what he came to do while he preached, healed, and performed miracles, but the disciples didn't always get it.**

God's people, the Jewish people, knew that God would be sending a Savior, the Messiah, who would become their mightiest leader. They had been waiting on this promised Messiah for a really long time—thousands of years, actually. But when Jesus came, not everyone understood he was the long-awaited Savior. Some people, like the Jewish religious leaders, the Pharisees, who later put Jesus to death, rejected Jesus as the Messiah.

But there were those who accepted who he was and followed him with their lives. One man, Simon Peter, understood who Jesus was—the Messiah and Savior of the world. Because of Peter's faith in Jesus, God used him to build the church.

As we learn about Peter, we will learn that God's kingdom grows through faith!

Opening Activity

Materials

- Rope or masking tape

Fishers of Men Tag

Tell what you wanted to be when you grew up, when you were a child.

Say: **What do you want to be when you grow up?** *(Children respond as time allows.)*

If your dad is a doctor, maybe you want to become a doctor as well. Maybe you want to be a teacher just like your foster mom. Raise your hand if any of you want to do the same job your parents or guardians do.

It sometimes happens today, but it's not as common as it used to be. Back in biblical days, it was extremely common for boys to go into the same job their father did. If your dad was a carpenter, he taught you how to become a carpenter. If your dad owned a fishing business, you and your brothers all went into the fishing business.

In fact, around Jerusalem, where Jesus lived, fishing was a popular profession. There were lots of fishermen. And when Jesus started his ministry as an adult, that's where we find him . . . with fishermen.

Preparation: Use rope or masking tape to make two grids on the floor to serve as nets.

Do: Choose two volunteers to be the fishermen. The fishermen try to tag the other children, who when tagged go to that team's net. The fishermen with the most people in their net at the end of the game wins!

Optional: Have a leader "throw the fish back" and release all children in the net, periodically.

Say: **Nowadays, when you go fishing you can use technology like digital fish finders that tell you where the fish are. But they didn't have those in Jesus' day. They used heavy nets and wooden boats. Catching fish was a lot of work!**

Bible Story

Peter Walks on Water

Read: Matthew 4:18–20

Say: **Jesus saw Peter and his brother Andrew fishing on the Sea of Galilee and told them to follow him. Jesus would teach them how to "fish for people" he said. How do you fish for people?** *(Children respond.)*

Jesus was getting ready to start his ministry. He would go around healing the sick, raising the dead, forgiving people of their sins, and telling them how they will be able to have eternal life. He was telling—and showing—people who he was and what he was going to do!

Peter and Andrew were two of twelve men who became Jesus' disciples. They went everywhere with Jesus and "fished for people," inviting them to make the choice to follow Jesus.

Jesus became really popular after he started his ministry of helping, healing, forgiving, and teaching people about God. He was so popular that wherever he went, crowds followed him! Sometimes Jesus would even try and sneak away, so that he could be with the Father, but the people would search him out and find him!

Late one day, Jesus had just finished preaching and feeding a crowd of over 5,000 men, women, and children. Jesus really wanted to spend some quiet time with God. So Jesus sent the disciples out on the boat ahead of him. He promised to meet up with them later.

Night had fallen, and the disciples were on the boat, when the wind started to blow. The wind caused waves to form. The waves rocked the boat and spilled water into the boat. Then the rain started to fall. *(Lead children to make a scared face.)* **The storm rocked the boat all night. What would you be doing if you were on that boat?** *(Children respond.)*

Around three o'clock in the morning, Jesus went out to his disciples. How do you think he got to where they were? *(Children respond.)* **Jesus walked! He walked on the water!**

The disciples saw him but didn't realize it was Jesus. ***How could a person walk on water?*** **They must have wondered. "It's a ghost," they said. The disciples were terrified.** *(Lead children to look terrified.)*

Jesus called out to the disciples, "Take courage. It is I. Don't be afraid." How do you think it made the disciples feel to know it was Jesus? *(Children respond.)* **Remember, Jesus was walking on water! What would you do if someone you knew was walking on water?** *(Children respond.)* **Peter did something unexpected.**

Read: Matthew 14:28–33

Say: **When Peter kept his eyes on Jesus, he walked on water, too! But as soon as he took his eyes off of him, Peter began to sink. Peter let his fear of the waves be stronger than his faith, or belief, in Jesus.**

Peter was an ordinary man with ordinary fears; and like all of us, he sometimes had doubts. But Peter's faith was strong and grew stronger! Peter went on to reach many people for Jesus. He had an amazing ministry with Jesus, and after Jesus went to heaven, Peter continued to preach and teach about salvation through Jesus. It was part of God's extraordinary plan that Peter be able to help build God's kingdom. God's kingdom grows through faith!

Read: Matthew 16:13–20

Say: **Peter understood who Jesus was, even though at times his faith faltered, like when he took his eyes off of Jesus and began to sink. But Peter knew that Jesus wasn't just a prophet or a man. Jesus was God, the long-awaited Savior of the world, and the one who would forgive our sins. Peter realized this!**

Jesus called him a rock and even told him that he was building his church on him. Jesus didn't mean that he was building a building on top of Peter. Jesus meant the church would be built on Peter's faith, his belief in Jesus.

Because Peter knew Jesus and followed him, Peter traveled around telling people how they too could be forgiven. He was fishing for people! And the Kingdom of God grew. God's kingdom grows through faith!

Pray: Children to pray, asking God to grow their faith and to help them keep their eyes on Jesus.

Object Lesson

Materials

- Fishing pole

Fishers of Men

Do: Show fishing pole to group. Explain how it is used to catch fish. First the line is cast out; then it is reeled in when a fish is caught. Ask different volunteers to use the fishing pole to pretend to catch different kinds of fish: a trout, a whale, a goldfish, etc.

Say: **In Bible times, fishermen like Peter and Andrew didn't use fishing poles to catch fish. They used large, heavy nets. When Jesus told Peter and Andrew that they would be fishers of people, did Jesus mean they would go out and catch people in nets?** (*Children respond.*) **No! What did Jesus mean?** (*Children respond.*)

Additional Activity Options

Rock, Paper, Scissors Showdown

Do: Play a version of Rock, Paper, Scissors. As a group, children stand and play against the leader. The object of the game is NOT to do the same hand gesture as the leader. If a child matches the leader, they sit down for the rest of the round. The last child standing chooses two or more volunteers to recite the memory verse with them. Player then becomes the leader for the next round.

Say: **Jesus told Peter that he was the rock that Jesus would build his church on. What did Jesus mean?** (Discuss how God was able to use the faith of Peter and the other disciples to build the church.)

Foundation Stones Craft

Do: Using permanent markers, children decorate rocks and write "Jesus" on them.

Younger Child Option: Instead of using permanent markers, have younger children paint their rocks. When they are dry, a leader writes "Jesus" on them with a paint marker.

Say: **What happened to Peter when he was walking on the water and he took his eyes off of Jesus.** (*Children respond.*) **Peter fell into the water and started sinking!**

When we take our eyes off of Jesus, we too start to fall. Our decorated rocks will remind us to keep our eyes on Jesus, to continue to spend time with him and grow in our faith, and to keep our foundation rock strong!

Materials

- Flat, smooth rocks
- Permanent markers

Tic-Tac-Trivia Bible Review

Do: Draw a Tic-Tac-Toe grid on a large sheet of paper. Children divide into two teams, the *X*s and Os. Teams take turns answering one of the questions below. If they answer correctly, they write their *X*s or Os in a space on the grid. If they don't answer correctly, the other team has a chance to answer. Draw additional grids as needed.

Materials

- Large sheet of paper
- Marker

1. **What did Peter do for a living?** (He was a fisherman.)
2. **What was Peter's brother's name?** (Andrew)
3. **When Jesus came to Peter and Andrew, what did he ask them?** (To follow him and become fishers of men)
4. **How many disciples/apostles did Jesus have?** (Twelve)
5. **How many people did Jesus feed from one lunch, at the beginning of our Bible lesson?** (More than 5,000 men, women, and children)
6. **What did Jesus do when he sent the disciples away on the boat?** (He went to pray on a mountain.)
7. **What was the weather like while the disciples were on the boat?** (It was storming; there were wind and waves.)
8. **When they saw Jesus walking on the water, what did the disciples think?** (They were terrified. They thought Jesus was a ghost.)
9. **What happened when Peter stepped out of the boat?** (He walked on water, then sunk when he took his eyes off of Jesus.)
10. **What does the name Peter mean and why did Jesus give him that name?** (The rock. Peter would be the rock on which Jesus built his church.)

Discussion Questions

1. **How would you describe Jesus?**
2. **What is faith?**
3. **How can you build your faith on a solid foundation?**

Follow Me Wristlet: On card stock, photocopy page 36, making one copy for each child plus extras. Kids complete in class or take home.

Alternate Activity: Children, in groups or in partners, practice witnessing to each other, giving the gospel. **Jesus told the disciples that they would be fishers of men. Later, before returning to heaven after his death and resurrection, Jesus would give them the command to go to the ends of the earth spreading the gospel message. We are called to spread the good news of the gospel as well—to fish for people!**

Follow Me Wristlet

What you need

• scissors • stringing material (yarn, string, plastic cording, etc.) • hole punch • crayons or markers • tube-shaped tricolor dry pasta, such as penne or elbow macaroni

What you do

1. Cut out the Sandal Pendant and six square beads. Cut a 14-inch piece of stringing material.
2. Punch a hole in the center of each square and two holes in the pair of sandals where indicated.
3. Print "I follow Jesus!" in the center of the sandals.
4. Color the sandals and place them in the center of your bracelet.
5. String the sandals on the yarn, then alternate stringing individual pieces of pasta and square beads on both sides of the sandals.
6. Ask someone to help tie the bracelet loosely around your wrist. The bracelet will remind you of Peter and Andrew, the first disciples to follow Jesus.

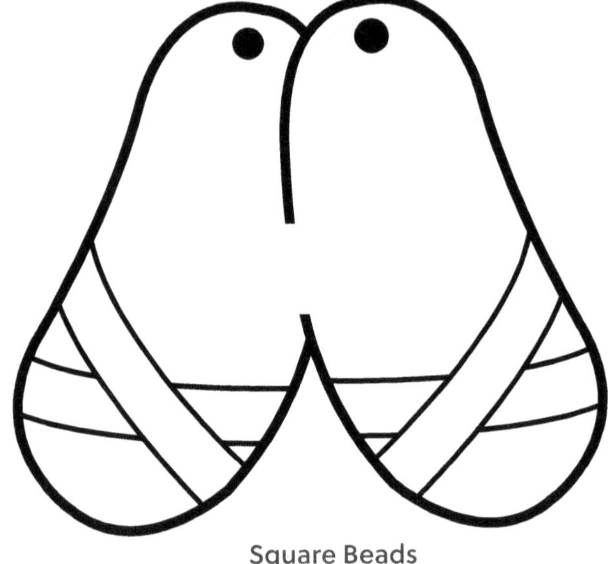

Square Beads

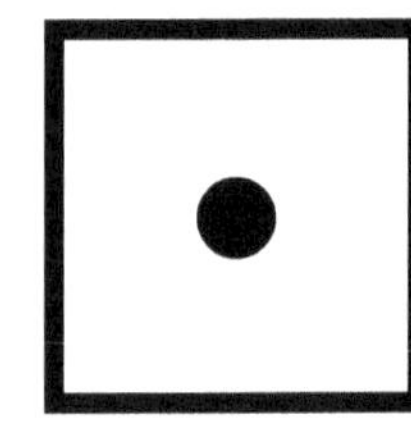
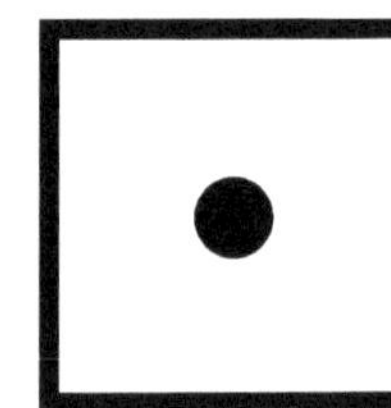
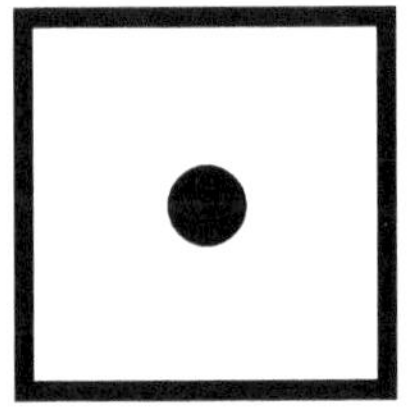
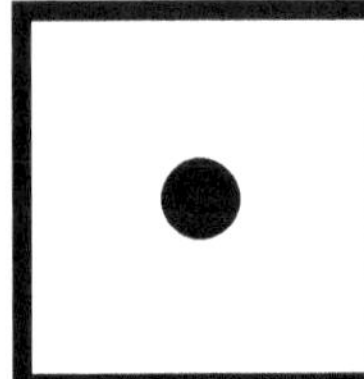

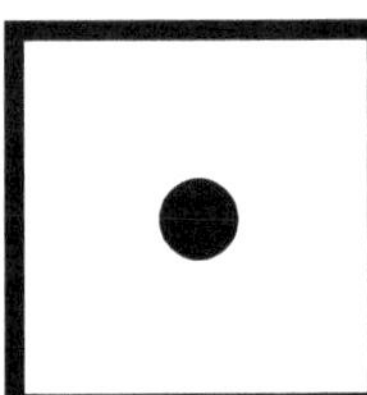
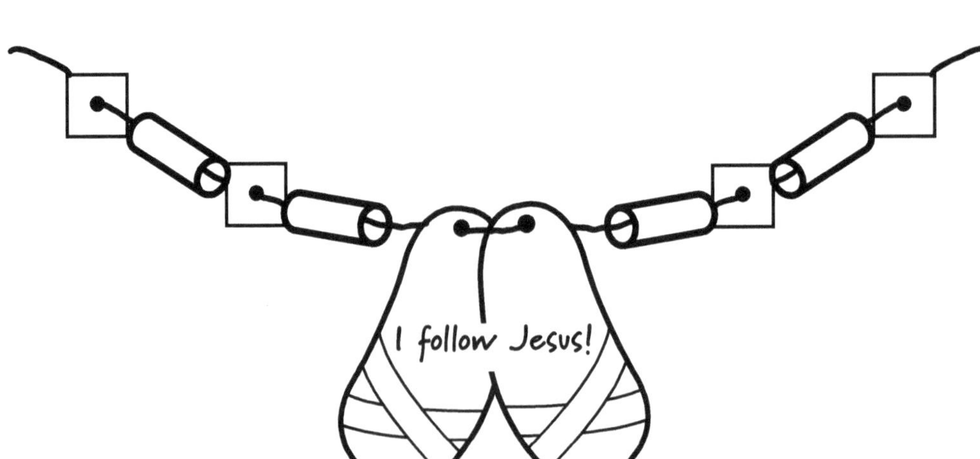

Chapter 7: Jacob

Genesis 25:19–34; 27; 32:22–32

"For I know the plans I have for you," says the LORD. "They are plans for good and not for disaster, to give you a future and a hope." **JEREMIAH 29:11**

Overview

Say: **Some parents, when their baby is born, might hope that the child grows up to be a doctor or a lawyer. Maybe they hope their child will be a world-famous musician. They can put their child in the best schools or have them take music lessons with the very best teachers, but that doesn't guarantee that the child will grow up to be what the parent wanted them to be.**

There's no way for a parent to know what their child will grow up to do for a living or who they will grow up to be.

But God knows.

Before Jacob was born, God had a plan for him. He knew exactly who Jacob would be. God knew that not only would Jacob be a twin, but the younger twin. What God had planned for Jacob was even more unexpected because in Bible times, the first born son would normally received the inheritance and birthright.

Through the story of Jacob, and the promise God will fulfill through him, we will see that just like he did with Jacob, God had a plan for you before you were born.

Opening Activity

Line Up!

Do: Children race to line up in order, based on the commands a leader gives.

Large Group Modification: Separate kids into groups of ten to fifteen that compete to see which group can get lined up first.

- Line up from tallest to shortest.
- Line up in rainbow order according to the colors of their clothes.
- Line up in order of birth months—January to December.
- Line up from the number of pets you have, from least to most.
- Line up according to your grade in school from oldest to youngest.
- Line up from youngest to oldest.

Younger Child Option: Stick with visual prompts, such as tallest to shortest or rainbow colors.

Bible Story

Jacob Tricks Isaac

Preparation: Cut red fake fur into strips three or four inches wide. Poke holes at the top and bottom corners and thread lengths of yarn through the holes to make arm coverings. Make two sets of arm coverings.

Place arm coverings and other props, listed in the box at right, where you can easily reach them as you tell the story. Select four volunteers to play the roles of Isaac, Rebekah, Esau, and Jacob.

Materials

- Red fake fur
- Scissors
- Red yarn
- Red wig
- Toy bow and arrow
- Apron (not feminine or frilly)
- Bowl
- Spoon

Say: **It's fun to go first, isn't it?** *(Children respond.)* **In Old Testament times, the first boy born to a family received the *birthright*. A birthright is like an inheritance, receiving the money and other possessions of someone who has died. But there's more to it. The birthright is also the authority to lead the family.**

Now imagine you lived in Old Testament times and were the oldest son in your family. How you would feel knowing you would inherit everything and be the new head of your family? *(Children respond.)* **Now imagine how you would feel if you didn't get the birthright! How would you feel?** *(Children respond.)*

In Genesis, we read about a man named Isaac. Isaac was the son of Abraham who God promised would be the father of a great nation, with more descendants than there were stars in the sky. Isaac was married to Rebekah. While Rebekah was pregnant with twins, the babies began to jostle each other. She went to God in prayer and listen to what God said.

Read: Genesis 25:23

Say: **Even before the twins were born, God had a plan for them. The firstborn son was red and hairy. Isaac and Rebekah named him Esau.** *(Esau volunteer wears furry arm coverings and red wig.)* **The second son was holding onto his brother's heel when he was born. They named him Jacob. The boys grew up, and Esau became a skilled hunter** *(Give Esau volunteer the bow and arrow prop.)***, while Jacob was a quiet man who stayed at home** *(Give Jacob volunteer the apron, bowl, and spoon props.)*

Read: Genesis 25:28–34 *(Volunteers act out the story as you read.)*

So, Jacob, the younger son, now has his older brother's birthright. But there was one more thing that fathers give to their sons before they die—the blessing. As Isaac neared the end of his life, he wanted to give the blessing to his oldest son.

Read: Genesis 27:1–40 *(Volunteers act out the story as you read. At the appropriate time, give volunteer the second pair of fuzzy red arm coverings.)*

Say: **Jacob has received his father Isaac's blessing and the birthright. Even though he was the younger son, God's promise to Abraham of fathering a great nation would come through Jacob, not Esau. This was all part of God's extraordinary plan. And just like God had a plan for Jacob even before he was born,** **God had a plan for you before you were born,** too.

Evangelical Moment: **The idea of a birthright is used in the New Testament, to explain what Jesus' death on the cross did for us. But instead of only the oldest son receiving the birthright, EVERYONE who becomes a member of God's family receives the same birthright as Jesus—God's one and only Son! The Bible says, "since we are his children, we are his heirs. In fact, together with Christ we are heirs of God's glory"** (Romans 8:17). **If you would like to know more about becoming a member of God's family, see me when our lesson is over.**

Pray: Pray, thanking God for knowing us and having a plan for our lives.

Object Lesson

Soap That Grows

Materials

- Bar of Ivory soap (Note: It must be Ivory soap.)
- Microwave-safe bowl
- Microwave oven

Do: Show children the bar of soap, paying special attention to its size. Then, microwave a bar of Ivory soap for about two minutes. Take it out of the microwave and show children what happened to the soap.

Say: **Look how big one little bar of soap grew! God made a promise to Abraham that he would become a mighty nation, his descendants so many that you wouldn't be able to count them. That promise was passed on to his son Isaac, who passed it on to Jacob when he tricked his dad by pretending to be Esau.**

With Jacob, we begin to see that promise being fulfilled. Just like our small bar of soap grew very big, we can see Abraham's small family begin to grow quickly! Jacob had TWELVE sons: Reuben, Simeon, Levi, Judah, Dan, Naphtali, Gad, Asher, Issachar, Zebulun, Joseph, and Benjamin. His twelve sons went on to have several children who had several children and on and on.

Before Jacob was born, God knew that Jacob, through his twelve sons, would fulfill his promise to Abraham. God is omniscient. In other words, he is all-knowing. Plus, he is sovereign, which means he is in control of all things. God had a plan for Jacob before even Jacob's father was born. And God had a plan for you before you were born, too! Jeremiah 1:5 tells us, "I knew you before I formed you in your mother's womb." God knew us long before we were born, just like he knew Jacob.

Additional Activity Options

Taking the Treasure Game

Materials

- Small foam or plastic balls, 4 or 5 for each child
- Laundry baskets or trash cans, one for each team

Do: Children divide into two teams, assigning each team a laundry basket or trash can. Spread teams out evenly in the playing area, and place the balls in the middle of the playing area.

On your signal, players collect balls for their team's basket. Players may only carry one ball at a time but are allowed to steal balls from the other teams' baskets.

After a few moments, signal players to freeze. Count the balls in each team's basket or trash can. The team with the most balls recites the memory verse. Repeat play as time and interest allow.

Say: **Esau's inheritance was taken away—stolen. Just like in our game, your team's balls could be stolen. When Esau realized that Jacob had taken his blessing, he wasn't very happy! He was so mad, he actually wanted to kill Jacob, his own twin brother!**

Our memory verse tells us that as members of God's family, we too have an inheritance. But the inheritance we receive as joint heirs with Jesus cannot ever be taken away or destroyed!

Self Portrait

Materials

- Self-Portrait Template (p. 41)
- Markers or crayons

Preparation: Photocopy Self-Portrait Template, making one for each child plus extras.

Do: Children draw self-portraits. In the space around each figure, children draw things that remind them of things they like to do or talents and abilities they have.

Say: Before Jacob was born, God knew that he would be the one to fulfill the promise made to Abraham. Not Esau, the rightful heir. Just like with Jacob, **God had a plan for you before you were born,** too! God has given you talents and abilities to help you accomplish the plan he has for you. What are some ways you could use the talents and abilities God has given you to serve God and his people? (*Children respond.*)

Stand Up If It's True Bible Review

Say: Stand up if the answer to the question is true but sit down if it is false. If the answer is false, explain what makes it false.

1. God made a promise to Noah, that he would be a great nation. (False)
2. Abraham's son was Isaac. (True)
3. Isaac had twins—a boy and a girl. (False)
4. Jacob was born first. (False)
5. Esau sold his birthright to Jacob, for a bowl of stew. (True)
6. A birthright wasn't a very big deal, so Esau didn't care. (False)
7. Because Isaac couldn't see well, Jacob was able to pretend to be Esau to receive his blessing. (True)
8. Esau was so mad that Jacob stole his blessing, he tried to kill him. (True)
9. Jacob didn't have any kids. (False)
10. Jacob's name was changed to Israel and his twelve sons became the nation of Israel. (True)

Discussion Questions

1. What was a birthright?
2. What is the birthright for believers?
3. How can God know you and have a plan for you even before you are born?

When I Grow Up

Materials

- Beach ball

Do: Children sit or stand in a circle, tossing a beach ball around the circle. Every time a player catches the ball, they name something they are good at or something they like to do.

If someone drops the ball, discuss how God could use the named talents and abilities to complete his extraordinary plan for their lives. **God had a plan for you before you were born!**

Self-Portrait Template

"For I know the plans I have for you," says the LORD. "They are plans for good and not for disaster, to give you a future and a hope." **JEREMIAH 29:11**

Chapter 8: Gideon

Judges 6–7

Do not be afraid or discouraged, for the LORD will personally go ahead of you. He will be with you; he will neither fail you nor abandon you. **DEUTERONOMY 31:8**

Overview

Say: If a mighty warrior went into battle and came out victorious, you wouldn't be surprised, right? If this warrior was trained in sword fighting and had already fought in several battles, which he had won, you wouldn't be surprised when he won.

But when someone who has never battled before wins, who gets attention? It's then that God can get the glory.

This is what happened with a man named Gideon. God chose Gideon to fight a mighty battle, but he wasn't a warrior. He was the least in his family, from the weakest tribe of Israel. But God chose Gideon, so that he would get the glory.

When God asks us to do things, we have to rely on his strength, so that he is the one getting the glory and the praise. Gideon is a great example of this. God had a big task for Gideon, and he didn't think he could do what God asked him to do. But the great part was that Gideon wasn't alone. He could do what God had planned for him, because God was with him.

And just like he was with Gideon, **God will be with you!**

Opening Activity

When and How?

Read the following situations and have kids discuss how they could know God was with them and how that could help them during the situation.

1. You have to move to a new school in the middle of the year.
2. You are nervous about playing your part in the church play.
3. There is a kid in your class who keeps being mean to you.
4. All of the kids on your team are making fun of someone.
5. You keep fighting with your sibling.

Say: Just like God was with Gideon, **God will be with you**, too!

Bible Story

Gideon Defeats the Midianites

Say: Israel, God's chosen nation of people, was having a rough time. God had promised to protect them and lead them, but the people weren't following God. They were worshiping a false god, Baal. As punishment, God allowed the Midianites to cause problems for the Israelites. The Midianites kept invading the Israelites' land, taking their cattle, and ruining their crops. The people were desperate. They cried out to God, and he heard them.

Read: Judges 6:11–20

Gideon had no idea why God chose him for such an important job. So he asked God to prove it was really him. Gideon asked him to stay there while he went to get an offering to sacrifice. The Lord agreed to stay.

After a bit, Gideon came back with some bread, meat, and broth. The angel of God told him to put everything on a rock. Then the angel touched it with his staff and the whole thing went up in flames! Then the angel disappeared. Gideon knew it really was God, and that God had a plan for him.

But Gideon must have still had his doubts. Because soon after, he had another request for God.

Read: Judges 6:36–40

Say: Gideon had an army of 32,000 men with him to defeat the Midianites. God looked at the army and said that it was too many men. Why wouldn't God want lots of men fighting for Israel? *(Children respond.)* With that many men, when they won, Israel might think that they won because their army was so strong.

So, God made the army smaller. God instructed Gideon to tell any man that trembled with fear to turn around and flee. How many men do you think left? *(Children respond or play a higher or lower guessing game to help children find the number.)* Twenty-two thousand men left! Two thirds of the army just left. Surely, God would think with just ten thousand men fighting, that he would be the one to get the glory.

But God said it was still too many men! This time, God did something different to decide how many men would remain and fight. Let's pretend we are at a river getting a drink of water from the river. You have no cups or containers. Without saying anything, show me how you would get a drink of water. *(Just like Gideon, separate the kids who lap the water like a dog and those that cup the water.)*

That's just what God told Gideon to do. Gideon took his soldiers to the water. And everyone who used their hands to cup water to drink were the warriors who stayed. There were just 300 men left.

But how big was the Midianite army? If it was 300 versus 300, that's not a big deal, right? The Bible tells us that the Midianites settled in the valley were as thick as locusts. And there were as many camels as grains of sand. That's a big army!

Was Gideon fighting for Israel alone? *(Children respond.)* Was it just the army of 300 fighting with Gideon? *(Children respond.)* No! God was with Gideon, just like he promised!

Read: Judges 7:11–22

Just like God used an ordinary man like Gideon to win an extraordinary battle, God can use you to fulfill his plans. And just as God was with Gideon, God will be with you!

Pray: Pray a prayer for encouragement over the children, reminding them that God is always with his children, just as his Word tells us.

Object Lesson

The Trumpet Sound

Materials

- 3–4 items that make loud noises (megaphone, cowbell, air horn, drum, etc.)
- Trumpet (toy or real trumpet, sound effect, kazoo, party blower, etc.)

Say: (*Play a sound.*) **Did that sound scare you so much that you ran away in fear?** (*Children respond.*) **No? OK, how about this one?** (*Play a second sound.*) **No? This one?** (*Play additional sounds, playing the trumpet sound last.*)

Sounds, loud sounds especially, might startle you, but they probably won't scare you so much that you run away screaming. But that is exactly what happened in the battle between Gideon's army (of 300 men) and the Midianites.

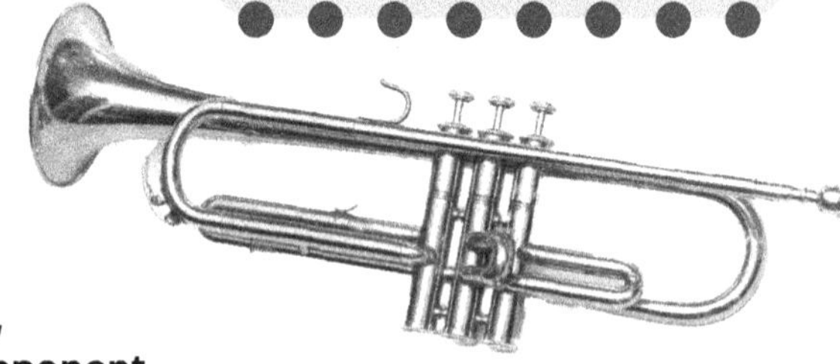

Was it the trumpets and the smashing of the jars that scared away the Midianites? (*Children respond.*) **No! Was it the size of Israelites army?** (*Children respond.*) **No! On their own, 300 men armed with jars and trumpets wouldn't be much of an opponent. But it wasn't the Israelite army that the Midianites feared or their crazy choice in weapons. It was God. Just like God promised, he delivered Israel from their enemies.**

God was with Gideon, just as he promised, and God will be with you wherever you go!

Additional Activity Options

What Time Is It, Mr. Fox?

Materials

- Masking tape or rope

Do: Use masking tape or rope to make two lines on opposite ends of the playing area. Select one child to be Mr. Fox. Mr. Fox stands behind one line with their back to other players behind the opposite line.

Players ask Mr. Fox, "What time is it?" Mr. Fox replies with a time (2 o'clock). Players take that many steps towards Mr. Fox to try to touch them. After a few turns, Mr. Fox calls out, "Midnight!" and turns around to tag players before they run to safety behind their starting line. Any player tagged joins Mr. Fox in tagging players. When there is only one player left, that player becomes the new Mr. Fox.

Say: **Whenever Mr. Fox yelled "Midnight!" you had to turn around and run to safety. When the Midianites heard the trumpets' sounds, they tried to run away to safety, too. What happened instead?** (*Children respond.*) **Because God was with Gideon, God helped him lead Israel to victory, just like he promised. God promises us he will be with us (believers), too! And if God promises it, God will be with you!**

Shout It Out Shakers

Materials

- Dark colored permanent markers
- Clear plastic cups, two for each child
- Glitter
- Pony beads
- Clear packing tape

Do: Children print "God is with me" on their cups with a permanent marker. In the bottom cup, children place pony beads (to make noise) and glitter. Set the second cup on top upside-down with the rims touching. Seal the cups together using the packing tape.

Say: **God was with Gideon, helping Israel to defeat the Midianites. As they marched into battle, the men shouted, "For the Lord." Let's make some noise with our shakers, today! Tell each other, "God will be with you!"**

Optional: Put on some upbeat praise music. Children sing and praise God using their shakers.

Fact Face-Off Bible Review

Do: Form two teams. Team members face off against each other, one at a time, answering the questions and earning points for their team.

1. **Who were God's people—the Israelites or the Midianites?** (The Israelites)
2. **Why did God allow Israel to be under attack from Midian?** (They were disobeying God and worshiping false gods.)
3. **God appeared and gave a big job to whom?** (Gideon)
4. **What promise did God make to Gideon?** (That he would be with him)
5. **How did Gideon ask God to prove that he would provide victory for Israel?** (First by making there be dew on the ground but not the fleece, and then by making the fleece wet but the ground dry)
6. **How many men did Gideon start out with to defeat the Midianites?** (32,000)
7. **Why was the army of 32,000 soldiers too many?** (Israel would think it was because of their strength when they were victorious, not by God's strength.)
8. **Why were 22,000 men sent away?** (They were scared.)
9. **How many men went into battle?** (300 men)
10. **What did the Israelites carry into battle?** (Trumpets and torches)

Enrichment Idea: Purchase buzzers for children to use to buzz in with the correct answer.

Discussion Questions

1. **Why did Gideon ask God to prove to him that he would lead Israel into victory?**
2. **God remained with Gideon, just as he promised. He promises to be with us as well. Will he keep that promise? How do you know?**
3. **Have you ever done something and relied on God's strength and power instead of your own?**

God Is With You Word Search: Photocopy page 46, making one copy for each child plus extras. Kids complete in class or take home.

God Is with You Word Search

Fill in the missing words from the memory verse. Then, find the words in the word search.

Do _ _ _ *be* _ _ _ _ _ _ *or* _ _ _ _ _ _ _ _ _ _ _, *for the*
_ _ _ _ *will* _ _ _ _ _ _ _ _ _ _ _ _ _ _ _ _ _ *of*
_ _ _ _. *He* _ _ _ _ *be* _ _ _ _ *you; he will* _ _ _ _ _ _ _
_ _ _ _ *you nor* _ _ _ _ _ _ _ *you.* _ _ _ _ _ _ _ _ _ _ _ **31:8**

X V Q U F Q X N O T X V U L V
L G S R L F A I L M S L F S Y
J R F L R W E M T V W D D R G
G Q O P E R S O N A L L Y W Y
O E T U A B A N D O N J P I D
I V D E U T E R O N O M Y L Z
Y L E Q L O R P A Y W B L L D
T L Z S F U P L E B Y M Y Y I
A B R G K Q G J L O R D T U A
F N E I T H E R W J T W Y O U
R W Q B M Q K A G A H E A D I
A I H Y D E P C W Y C Z D K F
I T U D N R V S X Q M K B T Y
D H Q D I S C O U R A G E D O
Z V Y R L C X I J G Y J L W A

Chapter 9: Martha

Luke 10:38–42

Seek [God's] *will in all you do, and he will show you which path to take.* **PROVERBS 3:6**

Overview

Say: **Life is busy. Even for kids! Think about all of the things that you have to do in a single day: get dressed, eat breakfast, make your bed, do your chores, go to school, practice sports or music, do your homework, eat dinner, get ready for bed, and pack your bag for school the next day. Phew!**

Then there's all of the things that you want to do—spend time with friends, play video games, read books, or watch TV. Life is busy! So busy that some days you run out of time to get everything done!

The Bible tells us that a woman named Martha was a busy lady. She was preparing a meal for Jesus, her family, and the disciples. We don't know the exact number of people, but if all the disciples were there, it would have been at least fifteen people for dinner. If you've ever helped get things ready for a big dinner, you'll know that there is a lot of work to be done! While Martha was busy getting things ready—and stressing out about it—Jesus reminded her of what was important.

If we take the time to listen, **God shows us what is important**, too!

Materials

- Large sheets of paper
- Markers or crayons

Opening Activity

Party Planning

Say: **Imagine that you are hosting a dinner party. Now, this isn't any regular dinner party like parties you've hosted for your friends before. This dinner party has a very special guest—more special than the president or a king. Jesus himself is going to be at your dinner party!**

Obviously, you can't serve him last week's leftover pizza and let him see your room with dirty socks all over your floor. You have to get ready for his arrival!

Do: In groups or individually, children plan their party for Jesus. Encourage them to think through all of the things their party needs (decorations, menu, entertainment) and all of the things that need to be done (cleaning, food prep, etc.). After a few minutes of planning, children share their party ideas with the rest of the group.

Younger Child Option: Younger children draw pictures for party decorations. On walls, post pictures along with party streamers. Children sit under the party décor to hear the Bible story.

Say: **Those sound like some great party ideas! Wouldn't it be awesome if Jesus was actually coming to your house to eat dinner? It would be stressful, though, to get everything ready. At least, that's how a woman named Martha felt when Jesus came to her house for dinner.**

Bible Story

Choose volunteers to play Mary, Martha, and Jesus and act out the Bible story as you read it. Volunteers put on Bible-times costumes. Have volunteers begin with Mary sitting at Jesus' feet, while Martha sweeps the floor.

Say: **When Jesus was here on Earth, he traveled from town to town, telling people about God's love. He made many friends in the different towns he visited. In the town of Bethany, Jesus made friends with a man named Lazarus, who lived with his two sisters, Martha and Mary. Lazarus, Martha, and Mary all loved Jesus very much. Whenever Jesus was going to be near Bethany, they looked forward to visiting with Jesus.**

Read: Luke 10:38–42

Say: **Martha was rushing around doing all of those dinner preparation things that had to be done. But what was her sister Mary doing?** *(Children respond.)* **Mary wasn't helping Martha. She wasn't doing any of the cooking or the cleaning. She was just sitting at Jesus' feet, listening while he talked.**

Now, if you were Martha and your sister wasn't helping you AT ALL, how would you feel? *(Children respond.)* **You'd probably feel pretty upset! Martha did. She complained to Jesus about it. "Lord, it's unfair!" she said.**

But Jesus' response wasn't what Martha was hoping for or expecting. Martha wanted Jesus to tell Mary to help out. But Jesus didn't. He told Martha that Mary was doing what was important.

What was Mary doing that was more important than getting dinner ready? *(Allow children time to reflect. Consider going straight into small group discussion time from here, to allow children time to discuss.)*

Martha wasn't doing anything wrong. Working hard and wanting to make a nice meal for her guests wasn't a bad thing. It was a good thing! But Martha had forgotten that the BEST thing was being able to spend time with Jesus and learn from him. She'd gotten caught up with things that weren't really important, and even worse, was getting upset and angry over it!

That's why Jesus said that Mary had chosen the only thing worth being concerned about. Jesus showed Mary what was important and God shows us what's important, too.

Pray: Give children time to talk with God and encourage them to ask God to help them make him the most important thing in their lives.

Object Lesson

Everything Fits

Materials

- 2 clear same-sized jars or vases
- Ball small enough to fit in the jars or vases
- Sand, enough to fill a jar or vase

Say: **This jar represents all the time we have in a day. We all have a lot of things to fit in to our day.** *(Begin pouring sand in a jar or vase.)* **There's the time we spend getting ready, doing our chores, going to school, eating, traveling, talking to our friends, practicing sports or instruments, maybe watching some TV or playing games. And before you know it, your day is filled.** *(Jar or vase should be full.)*

Before you know it, it's time for bed, and suddenly you remember you haven't

read your Bible or prayed to God. *(Try to shove the ball in the sand-filled jar.)* **So you try to cram in a little time with God—because you know you are supposed to. But it doesn't fit! Maybe you're so tired you fall asleep while praying. You didn't leave any room for God, any room for spending real time with him.**

And that's not good. You made time for good things, but not the BEST thing.

But wait a minute . . . What if, like Mary, you did what was truly important first? *(Place the ball into the empty jar, and then fill it with sand.)* **When you make God your first priority, when you do the most important thing first, everything fits!**

That's why Jesus responded to Martha's complaining like he did. Yes, getting dinner ready is important—we have to eat. But more important than dinner, more important than brushing your teeth and playing with friends, is spending time listening to God and allowing him to lead and guide your life.

That's what Martha learned that day. God showed her what was important—that he was important. God shows us what is important, too!

Additional Activity Options

Messy Mess Game

Materials
- Masking tape, rope, or clothesline
- Sheets of paper, four or five for each player
- Laundry baskets or trash cans

Preparation: Use masking tape, rope, or clothesline to make a line down the center of the playing area.

Do: Players divide into two teams and stand on opposite sides of the masking-tape line. Give each group half of the sheets of paper. Players crumple all the paper into balls.

Staying on their own side of the masking-tape line, players try to toss the paper balls onto the other team's side. After a few minutes, signal play to stop. Teams count the paper balls. The team with the fewest paper balls on their side of the line recites the memory verse, answers a discussion question from page 50, or tells a sentence about the Bible story.

Say: **What a mess! On the count of three, I want everyone to work together to help clean up this mess. 1, 2, 3!** *(Children race to put all of the paper balls into the baskets or trash cans.)*

Great job! Working together, you all got that mess cleaned up super quick! Martha felt that her work would have gone quicker if she and Mary worked together. But Jesus reminded her that spending time with him was what was more important. God shows us what's important, too!

Prayer Journal

Materials
- Small notebooks
- Decorating materials (markers, crayons, stickers, rhinestones, glitter glue, etc.)

Do: Children to decorate the cover of their prayer notebook.

Say: **By spending time with Jesus, Mary did what was important. Writing down your prayers is a great way to spend time with Jesus. Use your new notebooks as you spend time with the Father!**

Optional: Encourage older children to write Bible verses throughout the pages of the notebook, on the bottom of pages. Younger children can place stickers throughout.

Multiple Choice Bible Review

Preparation: Use masking tape to make two lines, dividing the playing area into three sections. Use masking tape to label the sections, *A*, *B*, and *C*.

Say: **For each question, stand next to the letter of the answer you think is correct.**

1. What were the two sisters' names?
   a. Michelle and Miranda
   b. Meredith and Mary
   c. Martha and Mary
2. Who was coming to dinner?
   a. Lazarus
   b. John the Baptist
   c. Jesus
3. Which sister was doing the bulk of the work preparing dinner?
   a. Mary
   b. Martha
   c. Neither. They ordered takeout.
4. What was Mary doing?
   a. Cleaning
   b. Listening to Jesus
   c. Baking a cake
5. What was Martha's reaction to Mary not helping?
   a. She complained to Jesus.
   b. She stormed off in anger.
   c. She didn't mind because Mary can't cook.
6. Was Jesus upset with Mary for not helping?
   a. He was super angry.
   b. He felt that Mary lied to him.
   c. He told Martha that Mary didn't do anything wrong.
7. Which was most important?
   a. Listening to Jesus
   b. Doing the work
   c. Both
8. Is it important for us to listen to and learn from Jesus as well?
   a. Yes
   b. No
   c. Maybe
9. How can we sit with Jesus like Mary did?
   a. Read the Bible
   b. Pray
   c. Go to church
10. What's the Big Idea of today's lesson?
   a. God will show us what's important!
   b. God will show us how to bake a cake!
   c. God will show us that dessert is important!

Discussion Questions

1. What was Mary doing that was more important than getting dinner ready?
2. Why was listening to Jesus more important?
3. Is spending time listening to the Father (Reading his Word, and spending time in prayer) the most important thing in your life?

All in My Day

Do: Give children time to fill out their daily calendars with all of the things they normally do in a day.

Materials

- Daily Planner (p. 51)
- Pencils

Say: **When you look at your calendar, at all of the things you do in a day, how many of you have a scheduled time to do what is most important?** (*Children respond or time to reflect.*)

Take some time, right now, to make a commitment to do what is truly important every day this week. Write in your calendar when you will spend time with God, reading your Bible and praying. Then make sure to do it!

Daily Planner

Schedule

Top Goals

To Do List

Notes

Chapter 10: Thomas

John 20:1–29

Jesus told him, "You believe because you have seen me. Blessed are those who believe without seeing me." **JOHN 20:29**

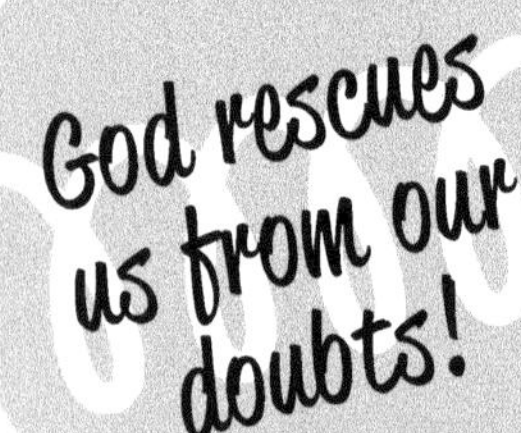

Overview

Say: **Imagine that aliens came to Earth in their flying saucer and gave everyone ice cream cones. You weren't there, but your friends were. Would you believe your friends when they told you the impossible just happened?**

It's human nature to want to see things before we believe them. You and I are probably this way. Thomas, one of Jesus' disciples, was this way, too. He wasn't there when Jesus first appeared after his resurrection, and he had trouble believing it until he had proof.

Today we're going to hear about how God gave Thomas the proof he needed. Just like he did with Thomas, God rescues us from our doubts!

Opening Activity

Materials

- Masking tape, rope, or clothesline

Believe It or Not

Preparation: Use masking tape, rope, or clothesline to make a line down the center of the playing area.

Do: Assign one side of the room "Believe It" and the other "Not." Read each statement below aloud. Children decide if they believe that it's true or not, and then move to the corresponding side.

1. **Koalas' fingerprints are so similar to humans, that they are mistaken at crime scenes for the culprit.** (Believe It)
2. **Polar bears have black skin.** (Believe It)
3. **A man in Australia actually has the ability to teleport.** (Not)
4. **The mantis shrimp's punch is faster than the speed of a bullet.** (Believe It)
5. **If you swallow a watermelon seed, it will grow inside your stomach into a plant.** (Not)
6. **Ketchup was originally created and sold as a medicine.** (Believe It)
7. **Squirrels cause most power outages in the United States.** (Believe It)
8. **The Leaning Tower of Pisa was built at an angle.** (Not; it's actually sinking!)
9. **You can hear a blue whale's heartbeat from two miles away.** (Believe It)
10. **The world's largest pyramid isn't in Egypt.** (Believe It; it's in Mexico!)

Say: What if something unbelievable happened for the very first time? Would you have trouble believing it if you didn't see it for yourself? (*Children respond.*)

Today we're talking about something that anyone would find hard to believe. Even if they'd heard it would happen. Even if people they knew said it had happened!

Younger Child Option: Since younger children might not enjoy a fact-based game, create an activity for them where a leader or helper does something difficult. State what is going to be done (like juggling or doing a backflip, whatever your leader or helper chooses). Then ask the children whether they believe it can be done or not, before doing the task.

Bible Story

Doubting Thomas

Say: Jesus traveled around preaching, teaching, and performing miracles for about three years. But he wasn't alone during this time. Who traveled around with Jesus? (*Children respond.*) Jesus' friends, the twelve disciples, traveled around with him, learning from Jesus, and helping him help and teach others.

Let's see if we can name all twelve of Jesus' apostles! (*Children respond.*) Jesus' twelve friends were: Peter, Andrew, James, John, Philip, Bartholomew, Matthew, Thomas, James (son of Alphaeus), Simon the Zealot, Judas (son of James), and Judas Iscariot.

Enrichment Idea: Play a learning game to learn the names of each disciple, such as doing a chanting and clapping call and response. (For example: LEADER: *clap, clap* "Matthew;" CHILDREN: *clap, clap*, "Matthew.")

In their time together, Jesus turned water into wine, walked on water, healed the sick, raised the dead, and multiplied bread and fish to feed thousands of people, just to name a few of the amazing things he did. And all the while, Jesus had been teaching his disciples about who he was. Jesus is the one and only Son of God, the Messiah, one with God himself. Jesus also told them what he was going to do as the Savior.

Read: Luke 9:21–22

Say: The disciples knew who Jesus was and what he planned on doing. Over and over, Jesus had told them that he would die and then rise from the dead. They'd even seen him raise other people from the dead.

Since Jesus had been telling them this for the last three years, it shouldn't have been surprising that everything Jesus told them happened exactly as he said. Jesus was killed and laid in a tomb, but he rose again on the third day. After he rose, Jesus stayed on Earth for 40 days and appeared to lots and lots of people, including his disciples. But Thomas wasn't there when Jesus appeared.

If you were Thomas and hadn't seen Jesus after he rose from the tomb, and all of your friends told you they had seen the risen Christ, would you believe their story? (*Children respond.*)

Read: John 20:24–29

Say: **Thomas needed to see in order to believe that Jesus was risen. We can't put our hands in Jesus' scars, but we can trust him to do exactly what he said he would do. We can have faith in Jesus!**

Evangelical Moment: **Jesus told Thomas, "Blessed are those who believe without seeing me." We don't have to see Jesus with our eyes to believe in him. When we choose to believe, we become members of God's family. And one day, we will see Jesus when we go to live with him forever in heaven. If you would like to know more about becoming a member of God's family, see me when our lesson is over.**

Pray: Children talk to God about any doubts they might be having regarding who he is or their relationship with him.

Object Lesson

Materials

- Sheet of paper
- Pencil
- Penny
- Scissors
- Quarter

It's Impossible

Preparation: Use pencil to trace penny in the center of the sheet of paper. Poke a hole in the center of the circle you drew and cut out the circle, leaving the rest of the paper intact.

Say: **What if I told you I could make this quarter go through this hole without tearing the paper. Notice that the hole is smaller than the quarter. Do you think it's possible?** (*Children respond.*) **Even though I've told you I can do it, some of you probably want to see it before you believe it. Right?**

Do: Fold paper in half over the middle of the hole. Place quarter inside the fold so that part of the quarter shows through the hole. Now grasp the folds on either side of the hole and pull up and at an angle (see image at right). The hole's circumference will expand and the quarter will slip through without tearing the paper.

Say: **Now that you've seen it, you believe it can be done. Right? This is how Thomas was. He knew what Jesus had said would happen. He knew the miracles Jesus was capable of doing. But still, he doubted.**

Jesus loved Thomas even though he doubted, and rescued him from his doubt. Thomas was just an ordinary man, but God used him as part of his extraordinary plan. Because of Thomas's story, we know that God loves us when we have doubts, just like he loved Thomas. And just like Thomas was rescued from his doubts, God rescues us from our doubts.

Additional Activity Options

Rescue Tag

Do: Depending on the size of your group, select one to three children to be Rescuers and one to three children to be Taggers. Taggers will tag other players. Once tagged, players sit down and raise their arms in the air. Rescuers will tag seated players to "rescue" them.

After a few moments, signal players to freeze. All seated players recite the memory verse. Resume play after choosing new Rescuers and Taggers from the seated players.

Say: **Our Big Idea today is God rescues us from our doubts. God wants us to be rescued from our doubt just like Thomas was. What are some things we can do when we have doubts about who God is, what he has done, or what he can do?** (Read the Bible. Pray. Talk to teachers or family members who are members of God's family.)

Stained Glass Cross

Materials

- Stained Glass Cross (p. 56)
- White card stock
- Decorative materials (paints and brushes, markers or crayons, stickers, adhesive gems, glitter glue, etc.)

Preparation: On card stock, photocopy Stained Glass Cross, making one for each child.

Do: Children use decorative materials to decorate crosses.

Say: **Whenever you have doubts, read the verse under the cross and remember that God rescues us from our doubts.**

Thumbs Up Thumbs Down Bible Review

Say: **Give a thumbs up if the answer to the question is true. Give a thumbs down if it is false. If the answer is false, explain what makes it false.**

1. **Jesus traveled alone.** (False)
2. **Jesus had twelve disciples.** (True)
3. **The disciples knew who Jesus was.** (True)
4. **Jesus predicted his death to the disciples.** (True)
5. **Jesus never performed a miracle or displayed any power in front of his disciples.** (False)
6. **Jesus died and rose again, just like he promised.** (True)
7. **Thomas said he needed an angel from God to tell him Jesus was alive in order to believe.** (False)
8. **Thomas saw Jesus and still didn't believe.** (False)
9. **Jesus rescued Thomas from his doubt by appearing to him.** (True)
10. **Jesus wants us to believe in him, even without physically seeing him.** (True)

Discussion Questions

1. **If you had heard what Jesus promised and had seen his power, would you doubt that he rose again, like Thomas?**
2. **Is there anything in the Bible you doubt?**
3. **What can we do when we doubt God?**

Crazy But True

Materials

- Poster board or large sheets of paper
- Markers or crayons

Do: Groups work together to make a big list of crazy but true things God did through the Bible—either God the Father, Jesus, or God working through ordinary people. For example, God rained down frogs, made a donkey talk, and Jesus turned water into wine. After several minutes, groups share their ideas with the rest of the class.

Say: **One word to describe God is *omnipotent* which means all powerful. God can do anything, even come back to life after being dead for three days. We don't need to doubt like Thomas. We can believe without seeing. But when we do have doubts, we can remember that God wants to rescue us from our doubts.**

Stained Glass Cross

Jesus loves us and cares for us so much that he died to take the punishment we deserve for our sins. When we ask him, Jesus will forgive our sins.

To see where Jesus died, color the dotted sections red. Then, color the rest of the sections other colors.

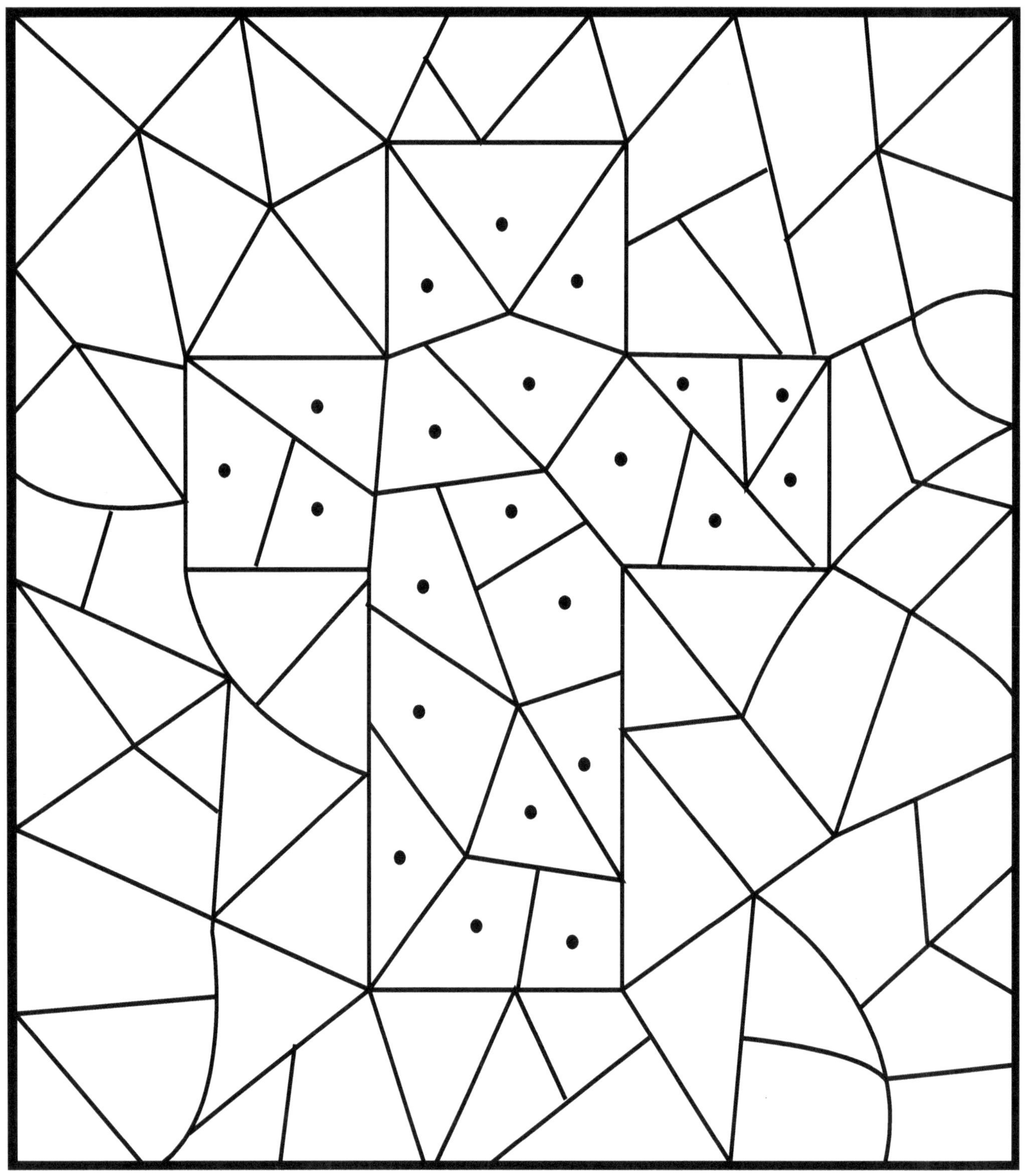

Jesus told him, "You believe because you have seen me. Blessed are those who believe without seeing me." **JOHN 20:29**

Chapter 11: Sarah

Genesis 18; 21

Jesus looked at them intently and said, "Humanly speaking, it is impossible. But with God everything is possible." **MATTHEW 19:26**

Overview

Say: **Do you like to wait on good things to happen?** (*Children respond.*) **Of course not! When we know that something good is supposed to be happening, we want it right away. And when we have to wait, sometimes we feel like it might not happen.**

This is what happened to Sarah in the Bible. Something amazing was promised to her, but it was taking so long, she thought it would never happen.

Through Sarah's story, we see that God keeps his promises, even if we don't believe.

Opening Activity

Don't Make Me Laugh

Do: Choose one or two children to be the museum guards. The museum guards suspect that the statues in the museum come alive, so it is their job to try and make the statues laugh. Guards may not touch the statues.

The rest of the children spread out through the playing area and freeze as statues. When the guards aren't looking, the statues can move around, but they must not get caught moving. And no matter what, they must not laugh!

Say: **We laugh when things are silly. We sometimes laugh when something crazy happens. And every once in a while, we laugh when we can't believe something. Today's Bible story is about a woman named Sarah who laughed when she heard a promise from God. She couldn't believe it was true!**

Younger Child Option: Change the object of the game to having the statues race to tag the museum guards without getting tagged themselves. Have a leader be the museum guard, constantly turning their back to the children. This game is sure to end in giggles from the children in no time!

Bible Story

The Birth of Isaac

Preparation: Use paper to make a paper chain of people. Fold a sheet of paper widthwise, accordion style. Draw a person in the middle of the rectangle, with hands and feet extending to the folds on either side. Carefully cut through all layers, making sure not to cut through the folds at the hands and feet. Keep the chain folded until prompted to open it during the story.

Materials

- Paper

Say: **God made a big promise to a man named Abraham. God told Abraham that he would bless him with as many descendants as there are stars in the sky. He would give him a new land and his descendants would be a great and mighty nation. Talk about an amazing promise from God!**

There was a small problem with this promise though. Abraham and his wife Sarah didn't have any children. In order to have all these descendants, they needed to have kids. And not only did they not have kids, they were old. REALLY old. At the time God gave his promise to Abraham, Abraham was seventy-five years old and Sarah was sixty-five. Both were well past the age of having children.

Even then, they didn't have children right away. Year after year went by with no baby. Finally, when Abraham was one-hundred years old and Sarah was ninety, some visitors arrived at their tents.

Read: Genesis 18:1–11

Say: **When she heard that in a year's time she would have a son, she laughed! Sarah couldn't believe that at ninety years old she would have a son. She couldn't believe it, even though God promised!**

Sarah laughed when the Lord appeared to Abraham and said that she would have a son in a year's time. But listen to what the Bible says in Genesis 21:1, "The LORD kept his word and did for Sarah exactly what he had promised."

What do you think that means? What happened to Sarah? (*Children respond.*) **Sarah gave birth to a son, just like God promised, and they named the baby Isaac.**

But wait! God promised Abraham that his descendants would be more numerous than the stars. Isaac is just one child. (*Begin unfolding the paper chain.*)

Abraham and Sarah were the parents of Isaac. Isaac was the father of Jacob. Jacob had twelve sons. These twelve sons had lots of sons and daughters. Their family grew and grew . . . until they were the nation of Israel. And there were too many people to count!

God kept his promise to Sarah! Sarah was just an ordinary woman, but she was important in God's extraordinary plan. Not only was she the mother of the nation of Israel, but her story teaches us that God keeps his promises, even if we don't believe.

Pray: Challenge children to talk to God about any of his promises they may be struggling to believe.

Object Lesson

Waiting

Materials

- Stopwatch

Do: Children practice waiting like Sarah and Abraham did. Since Sarah was ninety before she saw God's promise fulfilled, challenge children to wait silently, for 90 seconds.

Enrichment Idea: Children stand up before starting the stopwatch. When they think 90 seconds is up, children sit down. The last child to sit before the stopwatch hits 90 seconds chooses two or three volunteers to recite the memory verse with them.

Say: **Waiting is hard. Even just waiting silently for 90 seconds was super hard. Imagine how Sarah felt, waiting years and years and years for God's promise to her to come true.**

After all of that waiting, she stopped believing that it would come true. But, God's promise to Sarah came true. Sarah gave birth to a son, Isaac, just like God said. Even though Sarah grew tired of waiting, and even stopped believing, God kept his promise to her and fulfilled his plan for her.

God keeps his promises, even if we don't believe.

Additional Activity Options

Impossibly Small Pictures

Materials

- Colored pencils or markers
- Shrinky Dinks, one sheet for each child
- Permanent markers
- Aluminum foil
- Oven or toaster oven
- Potholders
- Scissors

Do: Preheat over to 325°F. Using colored pencils or markers, children draw a large image on a Shrinky Dinks sheet. Children color the drawing, and then cut it out. After writing their name on a piece of aluminum foil, children place their Shrinky Dinks sheet on foil. Leader places foils in oven or toaster oven for 1–3 minutes.

Tips:

- Use as much color as possible on your pictures. Remember, once baked, colors will become darker and more vibrant.
- Shrinky Dinks will curl as they shrink to one-third of their original size. When it has flattened, the shrinking has finished.

Say: **Did you believe that your creation could get that small? It's almost impossibly small!**

Sarah had trouble believing. She thought it was impossible for her to have a child at her age. But with God, all things are possible! You can believe that God keeps his promises!

Slow-Motion Race

Do: Children compete in a slow-motion race. The last child to reach the finish line wins!

Say: **Waiting is hard! When things are going slow, we want to hurry them along. Do you think Sarah wanted to hurry along God's promise? Why?** (*Children respond.*)

Enrichment Idea: For more Bible learning, tell about the birth of Ishmael (Genesis 16:1–16).

Beanbag Bible Review

Materials

- 2 or 3 beanbags

Do: Children stand together. Choose a volunteer to stand with their back to the group a few feet away. Volunteer then tosses beanbags, one at a time, to the group. Children who catch the beanbags work together to answer one of the questions beginning below.

1. **Who was Sarah's husband?** (Abraham)
2. **What did God promise to Abraham?** (That he would have as many descendants as stars in the sky; to become a great nation)
3. **What was the big problem with God's promise to Abraham?** (They didn't have kids.)
4. **When the Lord appeared to Abraham (in Genesis 18) where was Sarah?** (In the tent)
5. **What was Sarah's reaction when the Lord told Abraham that in a year Sarah would have a son?** (She laughed.)
6. **Did God keep his promise?** (Yes!)
7. **How old was Sarah when she had her son?** (90 years old)
8. **What was Sarah's son's name?** (Isaac)
9. **How many years did it take for God's promise to Sarah and Abraham to come true?** (25 years)
10. **What does our memory verse, Matthew 19:26, say?** (With God, all things are possible.)

God Promised Sarah a Baby: Photocopy the coloring page on page 61, making one copy for each child plus extras. Kids complete in class or take home.

Discussion Questions

1. **Why did Sarah have such a hard time believing God's promise would come true?**
2. **Do you ever have a hard time believing God's promises?**
3. **What examples in your own life, or in the Bible, do you have of God keeping his promise (even if it took a while)?**

Promise Pass

Materials

- Beach ball

Do: Kids will toss a beach ball to each other, saying a promise of God each time they catch it.

Say: Isn't it great that **God keeps his promises, even when we don't believe!** He is a promise keeper.

God Promised Sarah a Baby

Chapter 12: Zacchaeus

Luke 19:1–10

But the LORD said to Samuel, "Don't judge by his appearance or height, for I have rejected him. The Lord doesn't see things the way you see them. People judge by outward appearance, but the LORD looks at the heart." **1 SAMUEL 16:7**

Overview

Say: **Have you ever felt left out? Or felt like no one liked you?** *(Children respond.)* **Maybe the way you look or speak or dress, even, causes people to leave you out. Or perhaps your actions make people not want to be around you.**

This happened to a man in the Bible. Something important was happening, but he was being left out. He wasn't even a nice guy, really. The man's name was Zacchaeus. He took money he didn't deserve from others. So it wasn't too surprising that Zacchaeus wasn't popular with the other people in town.

But despite the fact that he made bad choices and wasn't popular, Jesus saw him. Jesus cared about him. If God could care about someone like that, you can know for sure that God cares about you, no matter what.

Opening Activity

Musical Clumps

Materials

- Children's worship music and player

Do: Play the music while children walk around the playing area. Randomly pause the music and call out a number. Children race to get into groups of that number. Any children not in a clump of the correct number sit down. Continue play until there is only one clump left. Repeat if time and interest allow.

Say: **How did it feel when you were left out in our game?** *(Children respond.)* **No one likes to feel left out. Why do people get left out sometimes? Have you ever been left out?** *(Children respond as time allows.)*

Now, imagine that Jesus is coming through town. You want to see him! But a lot of people want to see him, too. Now imagine you don't have friends to save you a place in front, so you try to get a glimpse of Jesus from the back of the crowd. But you're too short to see! You'd probably feel left out. That's exactly how a man name Zacchaeus felt when Jesus came to his town.

Younger Child Option: Younger children do not handle sitting out of a game well. Instead, place hula hoops on the floor. Call out a statement such as "Get in a hoop if you have a dog" or "Run into a hoop if you have a dress on today." Children to run into a hoop if the statement called out is true. This type of play allows all the children to participate all through the game.

Bible Story

Jesus Visits Zacchaeus

Materials

- Toy figures, puppets, or even popsicle stick puppets to represent Jesus, Zacchaeus, and other people
- Small potted tree (real or artificial) or picture of a tree

Say: **Today's Bible story is about Zacchaeus, a tax collector. Tax collectors were not popular during Jesus' day. It wasn't just because they worked for the Roman government collecting taxes. Tax collectors were often dishonest, charging people more than they actually owed. And what do you think they did with that extra money?** (*Children respond.*) **They kept it! No wonder tax collectors were not very popular or well liked.**

As we listen to today's story, remember that Zacchaeus was a tax collector (and not an honest one, either).

Do: Visually illustrate this lesson using toy figures, puppets, or even craft-stick puppets to represent Jesus, Zacchaeus, and other people. Also, use a small potted tree (real or artificial) or a picture of a tree.

Optional: Act out the Bible story, using props and costumes, climbing on a chair or ladder for the tree.

Read: Luke 19:1–10

Say: **Jesus had been traveling around, preaching, healing, and performing miracles. One day, a man named Zacchaeus heard that this amazing man, Jesus, was coming to his town! What do you think Zacchaeus thought about Jesus coming to his town?** (*Children respond.*) **I'm sure everyone in town wanted to see Jesus. Jesus was very popular. Everywhere he went, he drew in crowds of people.**

Zacchaeus wanted to see Jesus, too, but when he got to the place where people were gathering around to see Jesus, Zacchaeus was too short to see over the crowd. He couldn't get a glimpse of Jesus from where he stood. Zacchaeus didn't let that stop him, though. He looked around and saw the answer: a tree!

Zacchaeus climbed up a sycamore tree so that he could see Jesus. But Jesus didn't just walk on past Zacchaeus sitting up in that tree. He stopped at the tree, looked up at Zacchaeus, and then did something that amazed Zacchaeus and everyone else. Jesus told Zacchaeus that he was going to visit him at his house.

Why do you think Zacchaeus and everyone else was amazed that Jesus would go to his house? What was unusual about Jesus going to Zacchaeus's house? (*Children respond.*) **Zacchaeus was a tax collector. The Jewish people, especially the religious leaders, did not consider tax collectors to be good people. They believed a teacher of the law like Jesus shouldn't associate with tax collectors—and he definitely shouldn't be going to his house.**

But Jesus went to the house of Zacchaeus—a sinner. Why do you think Jesus did that? (*Children respond.*) **Jesus cared about Zacchaeus, even though he was a tax collector and a sinner. How does it make you feel to know that Jesus cared about Zacchaeus, even though others didn't like him?** (*Children respond.*)

Just like Jesus cared for Zacchaeus, God cares about you, no matter what!

Object Lesson

What's in Your Heart?

Materials

- Commercial donut box (such as from a donut shop)
- Rocks
- Plain paper bag, crumpled
- Donuts, one for each child

Preparation: Fill the commercial donut box with rocks. Place donuts in the crumpled paper bag. Before class, place the donut box and paper bag on a counter or table in your room.

Do: Before revealing what is in the containers, invite the group of children to vote on which container they want their snack from. Then, ask a volunteer to reveal what is in the donut box first, and then what is in the crumpled bag.

Say: **What made you choose the box? The bag?** *(Children respond.)* **Did you think the nice, expensive donut box would have the best snack? Or did you think the crumpled bag would hold the tasty snack?** *(Children respond.)* **Lots of times, we might think that the better something looks, the more we'll like it. That somehow things that look nice are automatically better. That's not how God thinks.**

Read: 1 Samuel 16:7

Say: **We are told in 1 Samuel that God doesn't look at a person's outward appearance, but rather what is in their heart. Jesus didn't care that Zacchaeus was short. He didn't care that he was a tax collector. He didn't care that Zacchaeus was a thief. Jesus looked at Zacchaeus and saw a sinner in need of a Savior.**

When God looks at your heart, what does he see? *(Pause and allow children time to reflect and respond.)* **No matter what you look like, how you act, or what you've done, when God looks at you, he sees one of his special creations. He loves you and wants you to follow him. God cares about you, no matter what!**

Pray: Allow silent time for children to examine their hearts and pray. Close prayer time with a quick prayer. **If you would like to know more about becoming a member of God's family, please see me or one of the other adult helpers.**

Additional Activity Options

Coin Search Game

Materials

- 100 plastic gold coins
- Easter basket grass or crinkle gift wrap filler
- Inflatable wading pool

Preparation: Place the coins and the Easter basket grass or crinkle gift wrap filler in the inflatable wading pool.

Do: Divide into up to four teams. Teams line up for a relay race to find the most gold coins. On your signal, the first player on each team races to the pool, searches for a coin, returns to team, and tags the next player to take a turn. After five minutes, signal play to stop. Teams count their coins. The team with the most coins answers one of the questions below or recites the memory verse.

Say: **Luke 19:10 says,"For the Son of Man came to seek and save those who are lost." Zacchaeus was lost. He was a sinner**

in need of the Savior. That's why Jesus went to his house—to tell him how to be saved from the punishment for his sin. That's why Jesus came to Earth, to seek and save lost sinners like you and me. He did this because **God cares about you, no matter what!**

Optional: Read the parable of the lost coin in Luke 15:8–10.

Materials

- Heart Patterns (p. 66)
- White card stock
- Scissors
- Masking tape
- 4-inch white square ceramic tiles, mini-canvases, or pieces of card stock
- Paint
- Premoistened towelettes

Heartprints Craft

Preparation: On white card stock, photocopy Heart Patterns, making one heart for each child. Cut out hearts and place them on a table in the activity area.

Do: Children use a loop of masking tape to stick a heart to a ceramic tile, mini-canvas, or piece of card stock. Then, they make fingerprints and thumb prints around the card-stock heart. Children clean their fingers before changing colors. When done, remove the card-stock heart and set aside to dry.

Say: **These heartprints will remind you that God cares about you, no matter what! He sees you and he loves you.**

Tic-Tac-Trivia Bible Review

Materials

- Large sheet of paper
- Marker

Do: Draw a Tic-Tac-Toe grid on a large sheet of paper. Children divide into two teams, the *X*s and *O*s. Teams take turns answering one of the questions below. If they answer correctly, they write their *X*s or *O*s in a space on the grid. If they don't answer correctly, the other team has a chance to answer. Draw additional grids as needed.

1. **What did Zacchaeus do for a living?** (He was a tax collector.)
2. **Why didn't people like tax collectors?** (They charged people more for taxes and kept the money.)
3. **Why couldn't Zacchaeus see Jesus?** (He was too short.)
4. **Why was a crowd gathered?** (Jesus was coming through/Jesus was popular.)
5. **What type of tree did Zacchaeus climb?** (Sycamore)
6. **What did Jesus do that shocked (and displeased) people?** (He went to Zacchaeus's house.)
7. **What did Zacchaeus promise Jesus he would do?** (Zacchaeus said he would repay any money he took wrongly.)
8. **What happened to Zacchaeus at his house with Jesus?** (He was saved.)
9. **What did Jesus say was his purpose?** (To seek and save the lost)
10. **Does God care more about your appearance or your heart?** (Heart)

Discussion Questions

1. **Why did some people think Jesus visiting Zacchaeus was a bad thing?**
2. **Think about the people that Jesus hung out with while he was here on Earth. Was it just the godly people or the sinners? Why do you think he did that?**
3. **Does Jesus want everyone to be saved, no matter who they are, how they act, or what they have done?**

Alternate Idea: Challenge children to see themselves how God sees them. Then, on a sticky note, children write words they think God would use to describe them. Have children place sticky notes on a wall.

Heart Patterns

Chapter 13: Eli

1 Samuel 2

All he does is just and good, and all his commandments are trustworthy. They are forever true, to be obeyed faithfully and with integrity. **PSALM 111:7–8**

Overview

Say: **God wants us to follow him. He's given us rules and commands to follow, but it's not always easy to faithfully follow God's rules and commands. The word *faithful* means to be loyal and steady. So when we talk about being faithful to God, we mean that we try hard to always follow God's commands.**

But because we are human, sometimes we mess up. The Bible word for messing up and not following God is *sin*. Romans 6:23 tells us that the punishment for the sins that we all commit is death. Sin is a big deal to God. He loves us and wants us to live the very best life. That's why God gives us commands and why God warns us to be faithful to what he teaches us.

Opening Activity

Do What I Say

Do: Lead the children in playing a game similar to Simon Says. In this version, the leader does the opposite motion of every command given. For example: If the leader says, "Step right," the leader then steps left.

Children must be careful to do what the leader says, not what they do.
If a child moves in the wrong direction, they are out.

Say: **Was it easy to follow what the leader said and not what they did?** (*Children respond.*) **It was easy to get mixed up and do the wrong movement, especially if you were seeing the leader do the opposite of what they said.**

Some rules are easy to follow, like wearing your seatbelt all the time. Others are hard to follow one hundred percent of the time. Even people who love and follow Jesus sometimes have trouble following God's commands. Even pastors and church leaders sin. But through his Word, God warns us to be faithful. God knows it is the only way to live the very best life.

Younger Child Option: Stick to the same six simple motions for younger kids: step forward and step back, sit and stand, hands up and hands down.

Bible Story

Hannah Is Faithful; Eli's Sons Are Not

Say: Today we can read about how God wants us to live in the Bible. But what about in Bible times? (*Children respond.*) It sounds funny to say, but in Bible times, the people didn't have Bibles like ours! There were, however, priests who were in charge of leading God's people and giving them messages from God. God gave the prophets his Word to tell the people. And the priests would offer the people's sacrifices to God as a way to say they were sorry for their sins. It was a big responsibility and a big honor to be a priest.

The Old Testament tells of a man named Eli who was the high priest of Israel. He wasn't even just the high priest. He was also a judge of Israel. Being a judge meant Eli was chosen by God to lead God's people. It was an important responsibility.

One day, in the temple, Eli saw a woman named Hannah acting in a strange way. Eli thought Hannah was drunk because she was crying out to God without making a sound. Hannah prayed and prayed for God to bless her with a child. She promised God that if he blessed her with a child, she would give that child back to God.

God did bless Hannah with a son. Hannah named him Samuel. When Samuel was old enough, Hannah sent him to live with Eli and be trained by Eli to serve God. Samuel became a very important priest, judge, and prophet. And it all started because Hannah was faithful to the promise she had made God. Good things happened because of her faithfulness.

Samuel faithfully followed God, but Eli's own sons had a little more trouble. Eli's two sons, Hophni and Phinehas, were priests. But they weren't following the Lord like they were supposed to. They were sinning in their actions. Eli warned his sons to return to following God. God even sent other men to warn Eli that what his sons were doing was wrong. God even spoke to Samuel to warn Eli!

Read: 1 Samuel 2:23–25

Say: After Eli warned them, did Hophni and Phinehas listen and return to following the Lord? (*Children respond.*) No! Over and over, God warned Eli that his sons weren't following the Lord and that God would soon punish Eli's household unless they stopped their evil ways.

God wants us to be faithful and follow him. **God warns us to be faithful.** Eli's sons didn't listen, and they were punished for this disobedience.

Object Lesson

Materials

- 2 drinking straws
- Scissors
- Coin
- Baseball bat
- Deck of cards
- Number cube

Taking Turns

Preparation: Cut one of the drinking straws to be shorter than the other.

Say: (*Hold up the two drinking straws, coin, baseball bat, cards, and number cube.*) What do all of these objects have in common? (*Children respond.*) If I told you that all of these items could be used to help you decide who gets to take the first turn, how would you do that

with these two straws? *(Continue, asking children to identify the ways each object can be used to decide first turns: short straw loses, coin flips, hands placed one over the other and top hand wins, highest card drawn, highest number tossed on number cube.)*

There may be many ways to choose who gets a first turn at a game, and there are many times each day when you have a choice whether to be faithful and obedient to God, or choose to do things your own way instead. God warns us to be faithful, because he knows that being faithful to him and his Word is how we make the best choices.

Pray: Children talk to God about whether or not they have been obedient and faithfully follow him. Allow a moment for silent prayer, and then close by thanking God that he has given us his Word, the Bible that tells us how to follow him.

Additional Activity Options

Blindfolded Obstacle Course

Preparation: Set up an obstacle course.

Do: Children pair up and take turns leading one another through the obstacle course. The partner that is not blindfolded should warn the other of dangers they must avoid.

Say: **How did your partner warn you of dangers?** *(Children respond.)* **Did you always listen to the warnings? Why?** *(Children respond.)*

God warns us to be faithful and follow him as well. We have the Bible, with examples like Hannah and Eli's sons to warn us of what might happen when we choose to follow or not to follow the Lord.

Materials

- Objects for obstacle course (safety cones, ropes, chairs, etc.)
- Blindfolds, one for every two children

Obedience Beads Craft

Preparation: Cut cording into 10-inch lengths, making one for each child plus extras.

Do: Children create bracelets as reminders to obey the Lord by using alphabet beads to spell out the word *OBEY*, a cross bead, and other beads to fill in. Tie a pony bead to one end of the cording. String on the other beads, and then tie the ends together in a knot. Add a drop of glue or clear fingernail polish to the knot and set aside to dry

Say: **God didn't punish Eli and his sons the first time they stepped out of line. God warned Eli, over and over again. God warns us to be faithful. He wants us to follow him! Our bracelets can serve as a reminder for us to obey and follow the Lord. Every time we see them, we can be reminded that God warns us to be faithful.**

Materials

- Elastic cording
- Scissors
- Pony beads in a variety of colors
- Alphabet beads, one each of *O*, *B*, *E*, and *Y* for each child
- Cross bead, one for each child
- Glue or clear fingernail polish

Younger Child Option: Instead of elastic cording, younger children use pipe cleaners.

Ridiculous Rules

Materials

- Index cards
- Markers

Preparation: On separate index cards, print each of the following real-but-ridiculous rules.

- In Washington it is illegal to kill Bigfoot. The penalty is five years in prison.
- It is illegal to hunt and kill animals on Sunday in Virginia . . . unless it's a raccoon.
- In Texas, you don't have to show up to your own wedding. You can have someone stand in your place (A proxy wedding).
- If you bit off someone's arm in Rhode Island, you could earn twenty years in prison.
- You are guilty of a misdemeanor in Oklahoma if you are caught eavesdropping (listening to others' conversations).
- In North Carolina, it's illegal to hold meetings where members wear costumes.
- If you are murdering someone in New Jersey, you'll get in trouble if you're wearing a bulletproof vest while you do it.
- No lying down on sidewalks in Nevada. It's against the law.

Do: Distribute the cards to children to read aloud, one at a time:

Say: **Some of these rules seem a little ridiculous! Some of them, even though they might be a bit weird, are there for a reason. Not lying down on the sidewalk seems like a weird law, but it's practical. People walking might get hurt if they were to trip on someone just lying down.**

God warns us to be faithful. He has given us good rules to follow. Why does God give us rules? (*Children respond.*) **God gives us rules to follow so that we live the best life! God wants us to be holy like he is holy, but sin gets in the way. When we follow God's rules, we are being faithful.**

Seat Switch Bible Review

Children sit in a circle. Leader or volunteer closes their eyes as children switch seats. When everyone is seated, without opening their eyes, leader or volunteer names a child. That child, plus the children seated on either side of them, answers one of the questions below. Repeat seat switching until each question is answered.

1. **Who was Eli?** (The high priest of Israel)
2. **What was it Hannah wanted so badly?** (A baby)
3. **What were Eli's sons' names?** (Hophni and Phinehas)
4. **What did Eli's sons do for a living?** (They were priests.)
5. **How did Samuel know Eli?** (Samuel was raised by Eli.)
6. **What are some of the things you know God wants you to do?** (Love others. Obey him. Go to church. Don't lie or steal. Etc.)
7. **What did God do about Hophni and Phinehas's disobedience?** (God warned Eli he would punish them.)
8. **Did God just give one warning before he punished them?** (No, he gave several warnings.)
9. **Why does God want us to obey his commands?** (So we can be like him. So we can life the very best life.)
10. **What does our verse, Psalm 111:7–8, say about God's commands?** ("They are forever true, to be obeyed faithfully and with integrity.")

Discussion Questions

1. **What does following God's commands look like?**
2. **Which of God's commands do you think kids your age might have trouble following?**
3. **Why do you think people sometimes struggle to follow God's commands?**

Psalm 111:7–8 Word Search

Find and circle the words of Psalm 111:7–8 in the word search below. Some words appear more than once in the verse, but they are only in the word-search puzzle once.

All he does is just and good, and all his commandments are trustworthy. They are forever true, to be obeyed faithfully and with integrity. **PSALM 111:7–8**

H	Z	J	R	D	D	Q	O	Y	T	A	R	E	G	S
L	T	O	O	P	O	B	O	H	E	L	K	C	O	I
P	R	S	G	G	E	Z	C	I	F	B	P	O	L	S
S	U	T	T	F	S	O	D	S	F	F	S	M	O	K
A	S	H	C	A	B	Y	Q	N	K	O	A	M	J	C
L	T	E	R	I	E	V	K	M	T	R	L	A	D	F
L	W	Y	A	T	U	A	L	B	O	E	M	N	G	Q
F	O	P	N	H	X	L	J	E	B	V	S	D	O	Z
J	R	L	D	F	W	B	U	H	E	E	R	M	O	E
G	T	G	M	U	R	R	S	X	Y	R	W	E	D	I
Y	H	O	T	L	T	Y	T	J	E	C	I	N	Q	N
J	Y	S	R	L	U	G	E	G	D	H	T	T	X	H
P	O	C	U	Y	T	R	Y	Q	Y	A	H	S	K	F
I	N	T	E	G	R	I	T	Y	V	X	R	D	B	P
W	A	C	P	D	V	Q	U	K	R	D	L	C	Y	H

Chapter 14: Abraham

Genesis 12; Genesis 21

Understand, therefore, that the LORD your God is indeed God. He is the faithful God who keeps his covenant for a thousand generations and lavishes his unfailing love on those who love him and obey his commands. **DEUTERONOMY 7:9**

Overview

Say: **Has a parent or guardian ever asked you to do something, like take out the trash, but instead of doing it right away, you said you'd do it later?** *(Children respond.)* **Did you remember to do what you were asked to do, or did you forget?** *(Children respond.)*

Sometimes, when things aren't happening right away, we forget about them. It can even feel like we are forgotten when things take a long time to happen. Imagine being promised something but having to wait for twenty-five years until it came true! By that point, you'd be thinking you were forgotten.

God made a promise to a man named Abraham. It took years and years before Abraham saw God fulfill his promise, but God did exactly what he said he would do. Even if it takes longer than we want, it's important to remember, God doesn't forget his promises.

Opening Activity

Going on a Trip Game

Preparation: Use masking tape or rope to make start and finish lines at opposite sides of the activity area.

Do: Children divide into teams of four to six players. At the start line, place the swim ring and beach hat for each team.

Teams line up behind start line. The first player on each team puts on the hat and the swim ring, hurries to cross the finish line, and then returns to team and tags the next player. Play continues until each team member completes the relay. The first team to finish recites the memory verse. Continue as time and interest allow.

Materials

- Masking tape or rope
- Inflatable swim rings, one for each team of four to six players
- Oversized beach hats, one for each team of four to six players

Say: **When we go on a trip, like a trip to the beach, we pack the things that we need. Today we're going to hear a story about a man named Abraham. One day, God told Abraham to move his family and everything he owned to a whole new place.**

Younger Child Option: Instead of having younger children putting on the same pieces each time, have a pile of accessories at the start line. On their turn, younger children grab one and put it on to take their turn.

Bible Story

The Birth of Isaac

Say: In a land called Ur, there lived a man named Abraham. Abraham was a righteous man that followed the Lord. One day, God made a really big promise to Abraham.

Read: Genesis 12:1–3

Say: What a promise from God! God told Abraham that he would give him a new land and bless him with lots of descendants—as many as there are stars in the sky. Descendants are a person's children and the children of those children and so on and on. These descendants would make Abraham the father of a great nation.

What would you do if God came to you with a big promise like that? Would you be ready to move or would you have trouble trusting and believing God? *(Children respond.)*

Well, Abraham started packing right away! Imagine how much Abraham and his wife Sarah had to pack! And Abraham had a lot of stuff to pack! He was very wealthy and had lots of cattle, livestock, and servants. Even though it was a lot of work, when God told him to go to the land he was giving to him, Abraham didn't hesitate.

What did God promise to Abraham? *(Children respond.)* He promised to bless him with a new land and lots of descendants. Abraham eventually got to the land that God promised him, but there was a small problem with the other promise God made. In order to have lots of descendants, he needed to have at least one child to start with. But Abraham and Sarah didn't have any kids! How could the promise God made to them, to have more descendants than there are stars in the sky, come true if they didn't have ANY kids?

Oh, and there's another small problem. Abraham and Sarah were old . . . really old. Abraham was around seventy years old when God promised that he would have a son! And his wife Sarah was about sixty!

But Abraham didn't have a son at seventy. Or at seventy-five. He didn't have a son by the time he was eighty, either, or ninety, or even at ninety-five. By the time Abraham was 100 years old, he had been waiting for God's promise to come true for a really long time, and it still hadn't happened.

How do you think Abraham was feeling? Do you think he was still waiting patiently on God's promise or do you think he felt like God had forgotten him? *(Children respond.)*

It took a long time until God's promise to Abraham came true, but **God doesn't forget his promises.**

Listen to what Genesis 21:1–2, 5 says: *"The Lord kept his word and did for Sarah exactly what he had promised. She became pregnant, and she gave birth to a son for Abraham in his old age. This happened at just the time God had said it would . . . Abraham was 100 years old when Isaac was born."*

God's promise to Abraham happened, just like he said it would!

Object Lesson

Jars of Sand

Preparation: Count the number of individual candies and the number of bouncy balls as you put them in the jars.

Do: Challenge the children to guess the number of items in the jar of candy and the jar of bouncy balls. Show the jar of sand last.

Optional: Have children write down their guesses on scrap paper. Announce the names of children who guess the correct number of items in the first two jars.

Materials

- 3 jars
- Individually wrapped candies, at least one for each child
- Bouncy balls, at least one for each child
- Sand

Optional

- Scrap paper
- Pencils or markers

Say: **Some of you had great guesses about how many grains of sand were in the jar, but you know what? I don't even know how many grains of sand there are! There are too many to count!**

If we can't count the amount of sand just in this jar, how much sand do you think there is on the beach? Or in the world? God promised Abraham (Genesis 22:17) **that he would be blessed with more descendants than there are stars in the sky and sand on the seashore!**

God doesn't forget his promises. Abraham and Sarah only had the one child, their son Isaac. But Isaac had twin sons, Esau and Jacob. Jacob had twelve sons and each son had a lot more sons! These sons of Jacob became the nation of Israel, that new nation God promised to Abraham. And just like God promised, there were more descendants than anyone could count! God's promise to Abraham didn't happen right away, but it happened just like he said it would. God doesn't forget his promises.

Pray: **Thank you, God, for always keeping your promises. We know your promises might not happen right away or when we want them, but we trust that your timing is always the best. Thank you for never forgetting your promises.**

Additional Activity Options

Waiting Races

Materials

- Masking tape or rope

Preparation: Use masking tape or rope to make start and finish lines at either end of the activity area.

Do: Children divide into two teams and line up behind the start line. Explain that unlike other relay races, they can only move after you say "Go" and if you say "Stop," they must immediately freeze and wait for you to say "Go" again. Each player then takes a turn to run to the finish line, back to the start line, and tag the next player to take a turn. Be sure as the race is run, that you stop each player at least once.

Optional: Before you say "Go," instruct children to move in a different way: hopping, skipping, baby steps, side run, backwards run, army crawl, etc.

Say: **What did you think of our race? Was it easy to stop, freeze, and wait for the instruction to go? Waiting is hard. When are some other times you might have trouble**

waiting? (To open presents on Christmas morning, to have dessert until everyone has cleared their plates, etc.) **Imagine waiting like Abraham did—over twenty-five years to have the son God promised.**

Even though it took a long time, God didn't forget his promise to Abraham. God was just waiting until the time was right. Whenever you're having a hard time waiting for God, remember that God doesn't forget his promises.

Glow in the Dark Stars

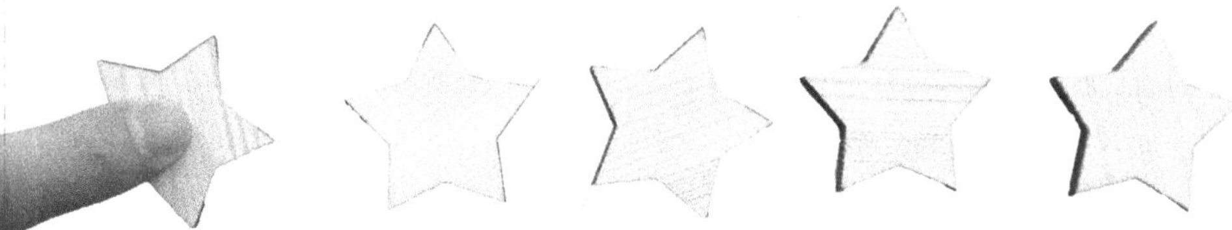

Materials

- Wooden stars
- Glow in the dark paint
- Paintbrushes
- Wipes or paper towels for clean-up

Do: Children paint a wooden star with glow in the dark paint.

Say: **Whenever you look at your stars, night or day, you can remember God's promise to Abraham and be reminded that God doesn't forget his promises!**

Stand Up If It's True Bible Review

Say: **Stand up if the answer to the question is true, but sit down if it is false. If the answer is false, explain what makes it false.**

1. **Abraham lived in the land of Canaan.** (False)
2. **Abraham was a priest.** (False)
3. **God told Abraham that he would give him a new land.** (True)
4. **Abraham's wife was named Sarah.** (True)
5. **Abraham was really poor, so his move to Canaan was quick.** (False)
6. **Abraham and Sarah already had two sons when God made his promise.** (False)
7. **Abraham was around seventy years old when God made a promise to him.** (True)
8. **God's promise to Abraham happened within one year of it being made.** (False)
9. **Abraham was one hundred years old when his son Isaac was born.** (True)
10. **After Isaac, Abraham and Sarah had many more children.** (False)

Discussion Questions

1. **What other Bible promises from God took a long time to happen?** (***Hint:*** Think about the most important story in the Bible.)
2. **We know that God doesn't forget his promises. So why does it sometimes take a while before the promise comes true?**
3. Before asking children to respond to this last question, give an age-appropriate example from your own life. **When was a time it felt like God had forgotten about you?**

Optional Activity

Faithful God Verse Search

On card stock, photocopy page 76, cut out verse stars, and hide them around the room. Children find the stars, look up the Bible verses on the stars, and discuss how God is faithful to those promises.

Faithful God Verse Stars

Deuteronomy 7:9

Isaiah 26:3

Isaiah 41:10

Isaiah 41:13

Jeremiah 29:11

Matthew 11:28–29

Chapter 15: Aaron

Exodus 4–13

Don't look out only for your own interests, but take an interest in others, too. **PHILIPPIANS 2:4**

Overview

Say: Helping people is important. When we help people, it's not just doing something nice for them, though. It's actually doing something for God—like giving him a gift. Our actions to help can even tell people about him!

Here are some quick questions to help you decide if you're a happy helper or a grudging helper.

- **When your mom is unloading groceries from the car and asks you to help, are you a happy helper? Or do you complain?**
- **If your teacher drops his stack of papers, do you help him pick them up? Or do you look around to see if anyone else is helping so you don't have to?**
- **Do you help your friend clean up his room after you two have been playing? Or do you play and make a mess right up to the minute you have to go home and then leave your friend to do all the work?**

God chose Aaron to be a helper to Moses, to speak for him, and to lead the people. Aaron's actions (as a helper) not only helped Moses, but also led people to follow God. Just like God chose Aaron to be a helper, God can use us to help others!

Opening Activity

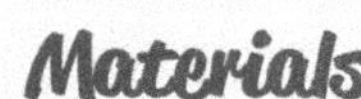

Materials

- Masking tape

Helping Hand Relay

Preparation: Create start and finish lines at opposite sides of the activity area.

Do: Children divide into two evenly numbered teams and line up behind the start line. The first player on each team races to the finish line, lies down behind the line, and then crosses their arms across their chest. Until standing again, player is not allowed to use their hands.

The next player races to the first one, helps player to their feet, and then lies down and crosses their arms across their chest. First player returns to team and the next player races to the aid of the player lying down.

Play continues until the first player helps the last player to their feet and both players return to the start line. The team that finishes first answers one of the questions beginning on page 83 or recites the memory verse.

Say: **Great job! This game sure would have been hard without helping hands to help you up! There are times in all of our lives when we will need someone to help us.**

Prior to today's Bible story, Moses was standing by a burning bush (that didn't burn up!), talking to God. God had a very big job for Moses to do. But Moses was a bit scared and unsure he could do this job. He asked God for a helper. So God chose Moses' brother Aaron to be that helper. Just like Aaron helped Moses, God can use us to help others!

Younger Child Option: Have younger children work together in pairs to carry hula hoops or balloons one at a time to the finish line. Both children have at least one hand on the hula hoop or balloon.

Bible Story

Aaron Helps Lead God's People

Since Aaron helped speak for Moses, use a puppet to help you tell today's Bible story. Use a hand puppet, enlist another volunteer to help you with the puppet, or use a puppet stage.

Say: **God chose Aaron to help Moses speak to Pharaoh. Since Aaron was helping to speak, I brought someone to help me speak today.** (*Introduce the puppet that will help you tell the Bible story.*)

The Israelites were living as slaves in the land of Egypt . . . and there were a lot of them. The people cried out to God to save them, to free them from their terrible situation in Egypt. God heard their cries and sent Moses and Aaron to speak to Pharaoh.

After this presentation to Israel's leaders, Moses and Aaron went and spoke to Pharaoh. They told him, "This is what the Lord, the God of Israel, says: Let my people go so they may hold a festival in my honor in the wilderness."

But Pharaoh didn't let the Israelites go. In fact, he made things even harder for them.

Read: Exodus 5:6–9.

God sent Moses and Aaron back to Pharaoh.

Read: Exodus 7:8–13.

But God wasn't done with Pharaoh. Through Aaron and Moses, God sent plagues—terrible plagues, one after another until Pharaoh would let God's people go.

First the Nile River turned to blood.

Then God sent a plague of frogs. The frogs were everywhere. You couldn't escape them. Then God sent gnats.

Next was the plague of flies. Pharaoh still wouldn't let God's people go, so God sent a plague that killed all of the livestock.

Next the people had painful boils pop up all over their skin. And still Pharaoh wouldn't let God's people go.

Next came a plague of hail, and then locust. Locusts are like grasshoppers. After the locust, God sent a plague of darkness to cover the land. The darkness was so thick that you couldn't see your hand stretched out in front of you.

Nine terrible plagues, but Pharaoh still refused to let God's people go.

So, God sent one last, terrible plague—the death of the firstborn. God protected his people by having Aaron and Moses instruct them to put the blood of a lamb on their door frames. That night, every firstborn male in every house without the lamb's blood on the doorframe was killed by the angel of the Lord.

After this last plague, Moses and Aaron led God's people out of slavery and out of Egypt. God had freed them!

Pray: Children pray, asking God to show them opportunities to help others.

Object Lesson

Helping Box

Materials

- Cardboard box or other container
- Items used to help others (clothes or toys to donate to those in need, garden gloves to help pull weeds, spatula for cooking, etc.)

Preparation: Place items gathered in the cardboard box or other container.

Do: Show children the contents of your helping box while reading the following:

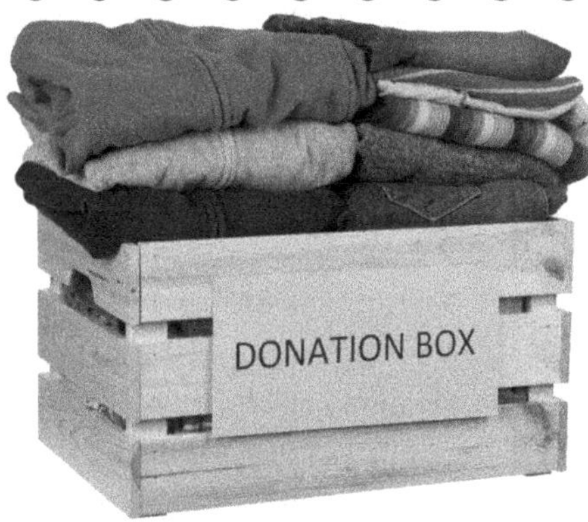

Say: **There are lots of different ways we can help people. We can donate clothes, toys, or food to those in need. We can pull weeds for an elderly neighbor. We can help our parents bake cookies or make a meal for a sick friend.**

It might not seem like a lot, but when we help someone, Jesus tells us it's like we are doing it for him (Matthew 25:35–40). **When we give clothes to the needy, it's like we are clothing Jesus. When we feed the hungry, it's like we are feeding Jesus. When we help someone in need, it's as if we are helping God!**

Aaron helped Moses to lead God's people. After speaking for Moses to Pharaoh, Aaron helped Moses lead the people—and there were a lot of people! Even though he wasn't perfect, in addition to helping Moses lead, Aaron became the high priest. Just like God used Aaron to help, God can use you to help others!

Additional Activity Options

Helping Hands Craft

Materials

- 12x18-inch large sheets of construction paper
- Crayons or markers

Do: With their fingers slightly spread out, children trace both of their hands on their sheet of paper.

On the palms, children write HELPING HANDS.

On each finger, children write ways they can help others this week, such as picking up trash, holding the door open, doing the dishes, etc.

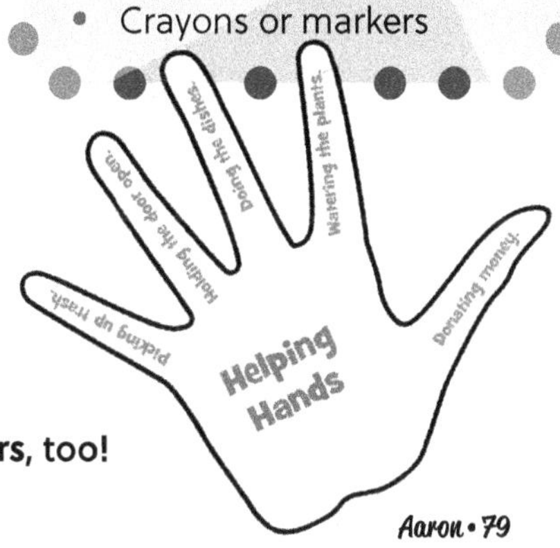

Say: **Just like God used Aaron to help Moses, God can use us to help others, too!**

The Ten Plagues

Materials

- Ten Plagues Cards (p. 81)
- Card stock
- Scissors

Preparation: On card stock, photocopy The 10 Plagues, making one copy for each team of four or five players. Cut out the lists and circles. Hide circles in the classroom.

Do: Players divide into teams of four or five players. Hand a list of plagues to each team. On your signal, players search room to find one of each of the plagues.

Once teams have found a circle for each plague, they place plagues in the order in which they occurred. The first team to finish recites plagues in order and then answers one of the questions below or recites the memory verse.

Multiple Choice Bible Review

Materials

- Masking tape

Preparation: Use masking tape to make two lines, dividing the playing area into three sections. Use masking tape to label the sections, *A*, *B*, and *C*.

Say: **For each question, stand next to the letter of the answer you think is correct.**

1. What extra work did Pharaoh make the Israelites do in addition to building with bricks?
   a. Made them dig ditches.
   b. Made them gather the straw to make the bricks they built with.
   c. Made them polish his gold candlesticks.
2. Why did God appoint Aaron to help Moses?
   a. Moses didn't think he could do the job on his own.
   b. Moses wasn't a good leader.
   c. Aaron was Moses' boss.
3. What did Moses and Aaron ask Pharaoh to do for God's people?
   a. Let them have a longer lunch break.
   b. Let them go free.
   c. Pay them more money.
4. How did Pharaoh respond to Moses and Aaron?
   a. He immediately agreed.
   b. He said they could leave when they finished the building they were working on.
   c. He refused to let God's people go.
5. What did God turn Aaron's staff into when Aaron threw it down?
   a. A serpent
   b. A scorpion
   c. A spider
6. For the first plague, what was water from the Nile turned into?
   a. Ice
   b. Blood
   c. Tea
7. What was the last plague God sent?
   a. Frogs
   b. Death of Livestock
   c. Death of First-Born Males
8. How did God protect the Israelite people from the last plague?
   a. The angel of the Lord "passed over" them.
   b. Put a force field around their homes.
   c. Made their homes invisible.
9. What did the Israelite people do so that the angel of the Lord would know to pass over their houses?
   a. Painted lamb's blood on their doorframes.
   b. Posted a sign saying they were Israelites.
   c. Spent the night in another town.
10. What did Pharaoh do after the last plague?
   a. Pharaoh believed God.
   b. He told the Israelites to go!
   c. Both of the above.

Discussion Questions

1. How do you think Moses felt about having Aaron's help?
2. What sort of an attitude should we have when we help others?
3. Has anyone ever asked you for help? What kind of help was needed? What did you do?

Ten Plagues Cards

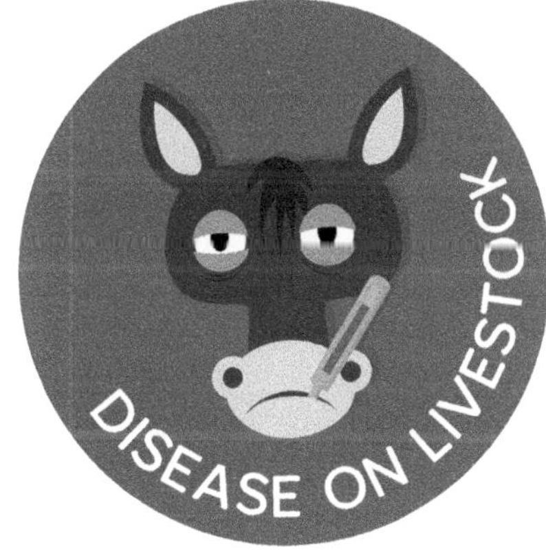

The Ten Plagues

1. Waters Turn to Blood
2. Frogs
3. Lice
4. Unhealable Boils
5. Hail
6. Locusts
7. Flies
8. Disease on Livestock
9. Darkness
10. Death of Firstborn

Chapter 16: Zechariah

Luke 1

So we are Christ's ambassadors; God is making his appeal through us. We speak for Christ when we plead, "Come back to God!" **2 CORINTHIANS 5:20**

Overview

Say: **There is an old saying: "Only a fool learns from his own mistakes. The wise man learns from the mistakes of others"** (Otto von Bismarck). **If you saw me put my hand on a hot stove and get burned, you'd know not to do that, because you learned from my mistake. You didn't need to try it out yourself to see if it was hot. You learned through watching me.**

But it's not just through mistakes that people learn. You can learn through the good things in people's lives as well. If you watched your older brother work really hard mowing lawns all summer to save up for a new video game console, you might learn that hard work pays off.

Something crazy was going to happen to Zechariah. But not only was this amazing thing going to happen to Zechariah, God was going to use Zechariah's story to teach others about him.

Just like God used Zechariah to teach others, God can teach others through us, too. And that includes you!

Opening Activity

Don't Speak Game

Do: Similar to charades, select a volunteer to act out a phrase (without speaking) while the rest of the children try to guess the phrase.

- I am hungry.
- What time is it?
- I am 10 years old.
- God created the world.
- Jesus loves you.
- Unicorns make me happy.
- Open the door.
- Where is the baby?

Say: **It sure is hard trying to communicate with others without being able to talk, isn't it? What would you do if you had something really important to say, but you couldn't speak?** *(Children respond.)* **After a visit from an angel of the Lord, the priest Zechariah found himself in a similar situation. But Zechariah learned that God can teach others through us**

Younger Child Option: Instead of having children try to guess what is being acted out, give the children something to pantomime together. Remember, no talking!

Show me being mad, happy, sad.
Tell me that you're hungry, sleepy, scared, etc.

Bible Story

The Birth of John the Baptist

Encourage group to pantomime actions along with you, while telling the Bible story. Suggested actions are in italic.

Materials

- Bible-times costumes (Zechariah, Elizabeth, Angel, two to three other people)
- Baby doll
- Notebook
- Pen

Say: **Zechariah was a Jewish priest.** (*Lead children to wave "Hi."*) **His wife was named Elizabeth.** (*Lead children to wave "Hi."*) **Zechariah and Elizabeth were older, but they had no children.** (*Lead children to shake head "No" and look sad.*)

One day, Zechariah was in the temple when something amazing happened. An angel of the Lord appeared to him! (*Shake heads "No" and look sad.*)

How would you feel if an angel suddenly appeared in front of you? (*Children respond.*) **Zechariah was shaking with fear. But the angel said, "Don't be afraid, Zechariah! God has heard your prayers. Your wife, Elizabeth, will give you a son, and you are to name him *John*. You will have great joy and gladness, and many will rejoice at his birth, for he will be great in the eyes of the Lord . . . He will be filled with the Holy Spirit, even before his birth. And he will turn many Israelites to the Lord their God"** (Luke 1:13–16).

Zechariah didn't really believe the angel. (*Lead children to shake head as if in disbelief.*) **He asked, "How can this happen when my wife and I are so old? How can we have a child?"**

The angel of the Lord didn't like Zechariah's answer. (*Lead children to place hands on hips and shake an index finger at Zechariah.*) **The angel said, "I am Gabriel! I stand in the very presence of God. It was he who sent me to bring you this good news! But now, since you didn't believe what I said, you will be silent and unable to speak until the child is born. For my words will certainly be fulfilled at the proper time"** (Luke 1:19–20).

Zechariah couldn't talk. (*Lead children to place hands on mouth and look surprised.*) **And when he came out of the temple, people knew that he had seen a vision from God, or something, because of the way he was acting.**

Elizabeth was thrilled that she would soon have a baby. And just like the angel said, Elizabeth gave birth to a baby boy. (*Hold up baby doll.*) **She said, "His name is John." But the people didn't like that name** (*Lead children to look unhappy.*)**, because no one in Zechariah and Elizabeth's family had the name of John.**

So, the people asked Zechariah what to name the baby. John still couldn't talk, so he gestured for his writing tablet. (*Pick up notebook and pen and write "His name is John."*) **Zechariah wrote "His name is John."** (*Show writing to audience.*) **Instantly Zechariah could speak again.** (*Look surprised.*) **And do you know what he did? Zechariah started praising God.** (*Lead children to say, "Hallelujah!"*)

Enrichment Option: Instead of acting out actions yourself, select volunteers to act out the story as you tell it. When a Bible person is speaking, the volunteer playing that person can move their mouth as if speaking.

Object Lesson

Actions Speak Louder

Materials

- Treats (cupcakes, doughnuts, cookies, etc.), one for each child plus two extra

Say: *(Begin eating the treat.)* **Oh. Ugh! This tastes terrible!** *(Take another couple of bites.)* **We were going to have a treat for class today, but I don't think I can give you something so terrible.** *(Reach for another treat and begin eating.)* **Yeah, I definitely can't give you something that tastes so bad!**

(Children should be pointing out that you are still eating, but saying it tastes bad.) **I guess I should let you try one for yourself, huh?** *(Give each child a treat to eat.)*

Why didn't you believe me when I said that the treats didn't taste good? *(Children respond.)* **I kept eating the treats even though I said they tasted bad. If I had spit it out when I took a bite, would you have believed me that they tasted bad?** *(Children respond.)* **Probably! Often, our actions speak louder than our words.**

The angel said to name the baby boy John. When Elizabeth told others what the name would be, others were confused. At that time, babies were often named for family members and no one in their family had that name. These people asked Zechariah what the baby's name would be. Zechariah could have picked any name he wanted. Instead, he asked for his writing tablet and wrote "His name is John," which was exactly what the angel told him to do!

Zechariah didn't just say—or in this case write—that he believed what the angel Gabriel said God promised. Zechariah backed it up with his actions.

As soon as he did, Zechariah could speak again! His actions proved that he believed God. He knew that his baby John would be exactly who God said he would be, someone filled with the Holy Spirit who would help others find their way to God. Zechariah even started praising God and telling other people about God's promise. Word of what happened spread, and because of Zechariah's actions, people were wondering about the important job God had for John.

Pray: Lead children in prayer, asking God to use each of them to teach others about him.

Additional Activity Options

The Name Game

Materials

- Pool noodle

Preparation: Cut pool noodle to 3 or 4 feet in length.

Do: Select a volunteer to be "It" and give them the pool noodle. The remaining players sit in a circle around "It." Review the names of all the players before play begins.

Leader calls out the name of a player in the circle. "It" tries to tag the named player with the pool noodle. To avoid getting tagged, player must quickly call out another player's name.

When "It" tags a player with the pool noodle, those players trade places. After a few moments of play, ask "It" to choose two additional players to answer a discussion question from page 85 or recite the memory verse. Play continues as time and interest allow.

Say: **The angel Gabriel told Zechariah exactly what he was to name his son. When the baby was born, even though he couldn't speak, Zechariah told everyone (by writing) that the baby's name would be John!**

By naming his son John, just like Gabriel told him, word spread and caused people to wonder what God had in store for John. God used Zechariah to teach others about him, and God can teach others through you, too!

Praise Prayers Paper

Read: Luke 1: 68–79

Materials

- Paper
- Crayons or markers
- Thin ribbon
- Scissors

Say: **After John was born and Zechariah could speak again, he began praising God. Let's create our own prayers of praise to God! When others hear or read our praise to God, they learn about him. It's one way God can teach others through us.**

Do: Children write or draw prayers of praise to God, and then roll them into scrolls, securing with a length of ribbon.

Optional: Instead of giving each child their own papers, use a large piece of butcher paper and make a praise mural to post in your classroom or in a hallway.

Write It! Bible Review

Materials

- Paper
- Crayons or markers

Play a team review game. All teams try and answer the question by writing their answers down. Any team that has the right answer written down receives a point. After the review, the team with the most points leads the group to recite the memory verse aloud in the manner of their choosing: loud, soft, fast, slow, silly, singsong, etc.

1. **What job did Zechariah have?** (Priest)
2. **Who surprised Zechariah with an unexpected visit?** (The angel Gabriel)
3. **What was the name of Zechariah's wife?** (Elizabeth)
4. **How many kids did Zechariah and Elizabeth have?** (None)
5. **What news did Gabriel give Zechariah about what would be happening?** (He would have a son.)
6. **Why did Zechariah have trouble believing the angel?** (He thought he was too old to have a son.)
7. **What punishment did Zechariah receive for not believing the angel's message from God?** (He lost his ability to speak.)
8. **How did the people outside the temple know that something had happened inside?** (Zechariah was in there so long; he couldn't talk when he came out.)
9. **Why did people not believe Elizabeth that the baby should be named John?** (No one in their family had the name *John*.)
10. **How did Zechariah show he believed God?** (He wrote down that the baby would be named John.)

Discussion Questions

1. **Why was Zechariah afraid of the angel at first?**
2. **If an angel appeared to you with a special job from God, how would you respond?**
3. **How can your life tell people about God?**

Family Tree Crossword: Photocopy the crossword puzzle on page 86, making one copy for each child plus extras. Kids complete in class or take home.

Family Tree Crossword

Zechariah's son John was Jesus' cousin. There's a "cousin" in the family tree below. Write each family member's relationship name in the appropriate place in the crossword puzzle. *Cousin* has been done for you!

Chapter 17: The Woman at the Well

John 4

Jesus replied, "Anyone who drinks this water will soon become thirsty again. But those who drink the water I give will never be thirsty again. It becomes a fresh, bubbling spring within them, giving them eternal life." JOHN 4:13–14

Overview

Say: **Can you imagine being an outcast? Imagine that you had no friends and no family. People in your town made fun of you. No one talked to you. The way you were treated was so bad, that you began to avoid going out when other people would be around.**

That doesn't sound like a fun way to go through life, does it? How would you feel if that's how you were being treated? (*Children respond.*) **You'd probably feel pretty rotten.**

Now imagine how great you'd feel if someone wanted to be your friend. And what if that someone was Jesus himself!

Today we're going to hear what happened when Jesus decided to speak to a Samaritan woman. To Jesus, it didn't matter who she was or what she had done. Jesus wanted to be her friend and Savior. This story shows us that no matter who you are or what you've done, God doesn't let your mistakes get in his way.

Opening Activity

Crayon Predictions Gospel Illusion

Materials

- 4 crayons of different colors (red, blue, yellow, green, etc.)

Do: Hand the four crayons to a volunteer and turn your back to them. Encourage volunteer to feel the crayons, and reassure the audience that there are no distinguishable marks on the crayons.

Ask volunteer to choose one crayon, show it to the audience, place the crayon into your outstretched hand (keeping your back to the volunteer), and hide the remaining crayons behind their back.

Holding the crayon with both hands behind your back, gently scratch the tip of the crayon with the fingernail of your dominant hand's thumb. Get some of the crayon wax under your fingernail to allow you to see the color. As you continue to hold the crayon behind your back, begin gesturing with your dominant hand in front of you as you talk. Glance at hand to see what color crayon was chosen.

Announce to children the color of the crayon and then show the crayon itself. If you perform the illusion two or three times to prove it wasn't a lucky guess, be sure to clean under your nail before each attempt!

Say: **That was pretty amazing! But it wasn't magic, it was just an illusion. I couldn't know what crayon your chose just by reading your mind or knowing your past actions.**

Let's hear about a time a woman in Samaria met someone who already knew all about her life.

Bible Story

The Woman at the Well

Do: Children use cardboard blocks or boxes to build a well in the area where the Bible story will be told.

Make this Bible story come to life by having children become living pictures to illustrate it as you read the Bible story (John 4:1–30) aloud.

Materials

- Cardboard blocks or boxes
- Bible-times costumes (bathrobes, headwraps or hand towels, and sashes or neckties to secure bathrobes and headwraps, etc.)
- Jar or bucket

Say: **Not only was this woman an outcast because of her life choices, but she was a Samaritan woman. The fact that Jesus spoke to her was a big deal. At that time, a man didn't talk to a woman unless she was a family member or his fiancé. But Jesus talked to this woman. He even started talking first!**

Then there was the fact that this woman was from Samaria. Jewish people like Jesus usually did not get along with Samaritans. A Jewish man would not be seen talking to a Samaritan woman. But Jesus did!

He didn't care what she had done in her past. He didn't care where she was from. Jesus wanted her to know that she could have living water, eternal life, with him!

Object Lesson

Living Water

Materials

- Paper
- Pen
- Tape
- Pitcher of water
- Can of soda
- Juice box
- Bottle of water

Preparation: Print "Living Water" on a piece of paper and tape to the pitcher of water. Hide the pitcher labeled "Living Water" near where you will be leading the object lesson. Place the can of soda, juice box, and bottle of water in plain sight in front of you.

Say: **If you were really thirsty, which drink would you want?** *(Children respond.)* **We love drinks that taste yummy! But think about this: Which drink would keep you from feeling thirsty again the longest?** *(Children respond.)*

(Hold up the different drinks as you mention them.) **As yummy as it might be, soda won't keep you from being thirsty for too long. It can actually make you even thirstier. Juice is good, but water is probably the best. But will water—as great as it is for your body—keep you from ever being thirsty again?** *(Children respond.)* **No! Of course not.**

But remember, Jesus told the woman at the well that he had a water that would keep her from ever being thirsty again. What kind of water was it? *(Children respond.)* **Jesus offered this woman**

living water. Does this mean he had a magical water for her to drink? *(Children respond. Pull out the pitcher of "Living Water.")* **No! If Jesus wasn't talking about regular water that she could drink, what was he talking about?** *(Children respond.)*

Jesus is called the Living Water. This means that he gives us eternal life. Just like the woman at the well, we can be forgiven of our sins, if we choose to follow Jesus. The woman at the well wanted his water. She wanted to follow Jesus.

It didn't matter who she was, where she was from, or what she had done. Jesus wanted her to follow him, to be his child. And even though she was an outcast with no friends, she was so excited about what Jesus offered her, that she ran and told the whole town. And many of them wanted living water as well. God doesn't let your mistakes stand in his way.

Are you interested in knowing more about following Jesus and becoming a member of God's family? If so, see me or one of the other adult helpers today before you go home.

Pray: Close activity in prayer, thanking Jesus for being Living Water.

Additional Activity Options

Materials

- Buckets, two for each team of five or six players
- Water
- Paper or plastic cups, one for each team

Cup of Water Relay

Preparation: Fill half the buckets halfway with water and place on one side of the playing area. Place the remaining buckets on the opposite side of the activity area.

Tip: This game is best played outside. If you play it inside, you might want to lay a tarp down and bring towels to clean up any spills.

Do: Children divide into teams of five or six players and line up behind the buckets containing water. Hand the first player on each team a paper or plastic cup. Teams will race to fill their bucket with water by pouring water from their cup to their teammate's cup.

The team to fill their bucket the fastest answers one of the questions, tells a sentence about the Bible story, or recites the memory verse!

Say: Jesus asked the woman at the well for a drink of water, but then he offered her something more, something greater than regular water—living water. He said, "Anyone who drinks this water will soon become thirsty again. But those who drink the water I give will never be thirsty again. It becomes a fresh, bubbling spring within them, giving them eternal life" (John 4:13–14).

Pick-a-Side Bible Review

Materials

- Masking tape, rope, or clothesline

Preparation: Use masking tape, rope, or clothesline to make a line down the center of the playing area.

Do: Play begins with children standing along the rope or clothesline.

Say: **Choose one of two ways to complete the following statements, *A* or *B*. If you choose *A*, jump to the right side of the line. If you choose *B*, jump to the left side.**

1. **Jesus was *A*—a Gentile or *B*—Jewish.** (*B*—Jewish)
2. **The woman at the well was from *A*—Samaria or *B*—Israel.** (*A*—Samaria)
3. **Jesus asked the woman for *A*—water or *B*—food.** (*A*—water)
4. **When Jesus spoke to her, the woman was *A*—angry or *B*—surprised.** (*B*—surprised)
5. **The woman was surprised Jesus spoke to her because *A*—men didn't talk to women or *B*—Samaritans and Jews didn't get along.** (Both are correct)
6. **Jesus then told the woman all about her *A*—past or *B*—future.** (*A*—past)
7. **Jesus offered the woman *A*—living water or *B*—eternal life.** (Both are correct)
8. **To receive salvation we must *A*—ask Jesus to forgive our sins or *B*—try to be the best person we can.** (*A*—ask Jesus to forgive our sins)
9. **After talking with Jesus, the woman *A*—ran away from her town or *B*—ran to her town to tell everyone about Jesus.** (*B*—ran to her town to tell everyone about Jesus)
10. **The woman referred to Jesus as *A*—the Messiah or *B*—a friend.** (*A*—the Messiah)

Discussion Questions

1. **How did Jesus know the woman's past?**
2. **How can Jesus give living water?**
3. **The woman called Jesus the Messiah. What does that name mean?**

Water Cups Craft

Materials

- Origami Cup (p. 91)
- Paper
- Scissors or papercutter
- Crayons or colored pencils
- Water

Preparation: Cut sheets of paper into an 8.5x8.5-inch square, preparing at least one square for each child.

Do: Children decorate a sheet of paper, and then follow the instructions to fold their paper to make a cup. Children drink from their cups.

Say: **To get water that quenches our thirst, we use a cup! But you can't get living water from a cup! Living water comes through Jesus alone. His death and resurrection give us forgiveness and eternal life. Jesus told the woman that he is the Messiah—the one sent to save people from their sins. He is the Living Water, the Savior of the World, and the Bread of Life. Jesus has many names we can use to praise him!**

Origami Cup

Follow the instructions below to make a paper cup from a paper square. You can actually drink from it!

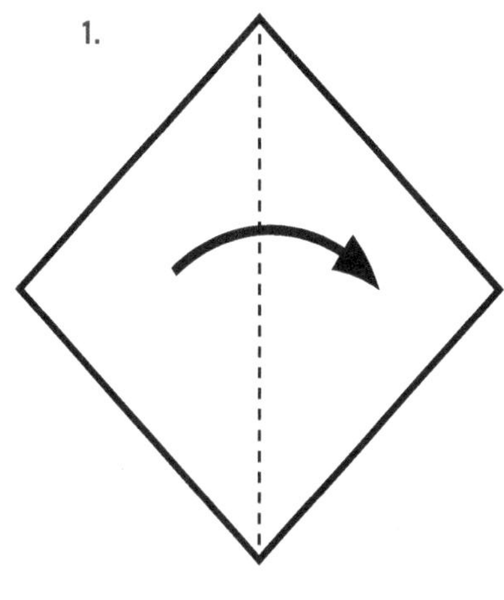

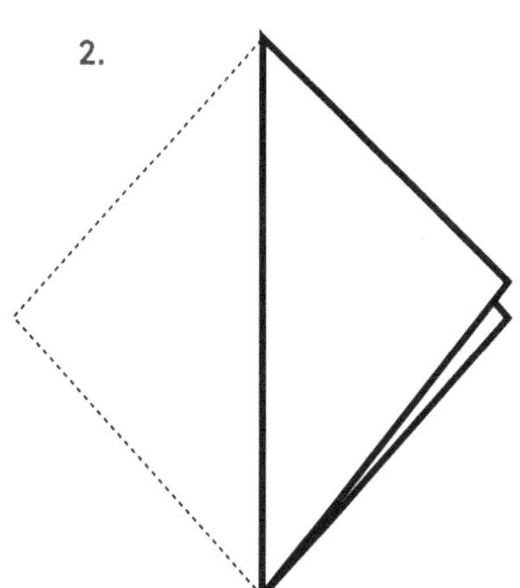

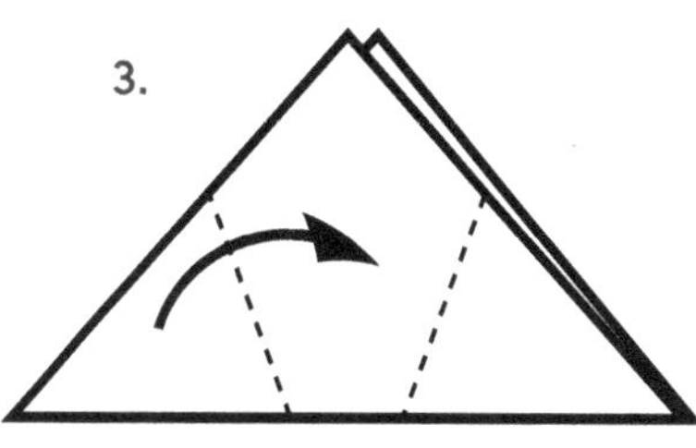

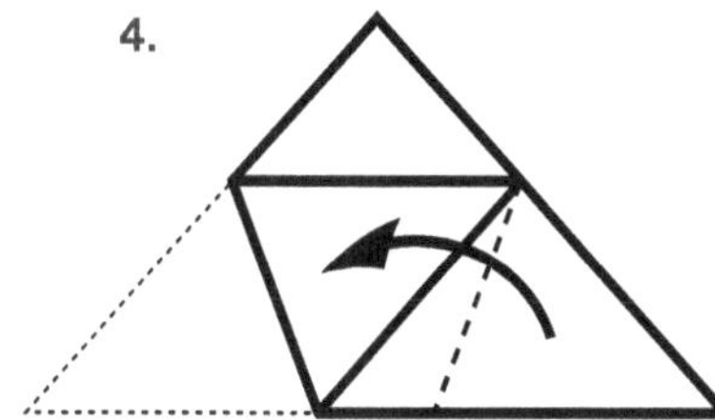

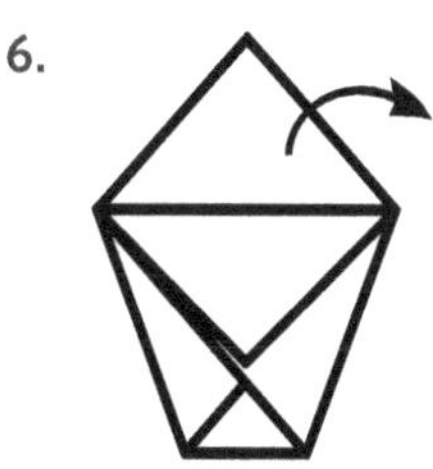

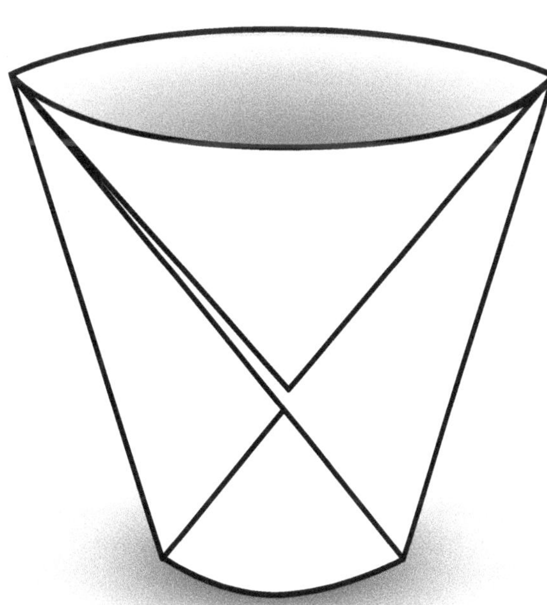

Chapter 18: Solomon

1 Kings 3:1–13; 11:1–13

Fear of the LORD is the foundation of true knowledge, but fools despise wisdom and discipline. **PROVERBS 1:7**

Overview

Say: **Do you think you are a wise person?** *(Children respond.)* **Wisdom and knowledge are actually different, though. You might know a lot of things, like 9x9 and the capital of Alabama, but that doesn't mean that you are wise. Knowledge is knowing facts and information, but wisdom is knowing how to use all of that knowledge.**

God is a wise God, and he wants his children to be wise, also. One man, King Solomon, was given the gift of wisdom from God. He became the wisest man ever! We can't be wise like King Solomon was, but God wants us to be wise, too!

Opening Activity

Temple Building

Do: Children divide into groups of five (or fewer) and spread the groups out throughout the room. Groups use plastic cups to design and build their best tower.

Materials

- 100 plastic cups for each group of five children

Say: **Great job building! Building is an important job. Do any of you know someone who builds for a living?** *(Children respond.)*

After God's people, the Israelites, escaped slavery in Egypt and formed their own country, God's presence—in the Ark of the Covenant—didn't have a permanent place. The only place the people had for the Ark was a portable, tent-like building which they called the *Tabernacle*. The Tabernacle was dedicated to God and the people worshiped him there. When the Israelite people traveled, the tabernacle moved with them. Imagine not having a building to worship God in! Or not even having a building to live in!

Even after the Israelites were settled in their new land, it wasn't until their second king, King David, reigned that plans were made to build a permanent temple for God. It was David's son, King Solomon, who actually built a temple for God.

God deserved a permanent structure where he could be worshiped, and because he loved the Lord like his father David did, Solomon built a temple for the Lord. He's kind of famous for building the temple, but that's not the only thing he was known for.

Younger Child Option: Allow each child to build their own tower out of cups or blocks.

Bible Story

Solomon Asks for Wisdom

Say: **If you were being given a gift, and you could ask for anything in the world, what would you ask for?** *(Children respond.)*

Optional: Children toss around a ball or pass a crown or scepter when answering questions during the Bible story.

Say: **Solomon was the king of the Israelite people, the third king of Israel, following after his father David. More important than Solomon being a king, he was a king that loved and followed the Lord.**

One night, God appeared to Solomon in a dream and asked him, ***"What do you want? Ask, and I will give it to you!"***

If you were a king, what are the sorts of things you think it would be important to ask for? *(Children respond.)* **Solomon could have asked for anything in the world—for riches, to live forever, or to be the most powerful king in the world.**

Solomon could have asked for any of these things. And God had promised to give him ANYTHING! Listen to what he asked for.

Read: 1 Kings 3:7–9

Say: **Solomon asked God for wisdom. Why would wisdom be something a king would need?** *(Children respond.)* **Solomon wanted wisdom so that he could lead God's people better. Instead of asking for power or wealth to force or pay for people to do his will, he asked for wisdom.**

God gave Solomon the wisdom he asked for. In fact, there was no one as wise as Solomon! Because God was so pleased that Solomon asked for wisdom, God also blessed him with riches and fame!

Just like God granted Solomon with wisdom, God wants us to be wise.

Object Lesson

The Fear of the Lord

Materials

- Plastic spider
- Toy snake
- Flashlight

Say: *(Hold up plastic spider.)* **Jump up and look scared if you have a fear of spiders.** *(Children respond.)* **You can sit down again. The fear of spiders is called** ***arachnophobia*****. Say that word with me.** *(Children respond.)*

(Hold up toy snake.) **Now, jump up and look scared if you have a fear of snakes!** *(Children respond.)* **You can sit down again. The fear of snakes is called** ***ophidiophobia*** (ow-fuh-day-ow-FOH-bee-uh)**. Let's say that word together.** *(Children respond.)*

(Turn on the flashlight.) **Run to me and look scared if you have a fear of the dark.** *(Children respond.)* **You can sit down again. Fear of the dark is called** ***nyctophobia*** (nihk-tuh-FOH-bee-uh)**. Let's say that word together.** *(Children respond.)*

There are lots of different things people are afraid of, even crazy things like *turophobia* (toor-uh-FOH-bee-uh). **What do you think that might be?** (*Children respond.*) **It's the fear of cheese!**

Proverbs 1:7 tells us that "Fear of the Lord is the foundation of true knowledge, but fools despise wisdom and discipline." If the foundation of knowledge is fear of God, does that mean that we are supposed to be afraid of God, like some people are afraid of snakes or spiders? (*Children respond.*) **No way! God loves us and wants us to think of him as a loving father. He doesn't want us to jump up and run away from him.**

What do you think the verse means when it talks about fearing the Lord? Fearing God doesn't mean that we are afraid of him. Fearing God is to have a healthy respect for who he is and what he can do! And when we fear God like that, we are wise!

Pray: Lead children in prayer, encouraging them to ask God to give them wisdom!

Additional Activity Options

Riches and Power Game

Materials

- Gold Coins (p. 96)
- Yellow card stock
- Hula hoops, one for each team

Preparation: On card stock, photocopy Gold Coins, making two or three copies for each team. Place the gold coins in the middle of the playing area. Place each hula hoop in a different place in the activity area.

Do: Children divide into teams, assigning each to a hula hoop. Explain to teams that each hula hoop is their "treasure chest."

Teams race to gather coins for their team's hula-hoop treasure chest. Players can only carry one coin at a time. When the coins in the center of the playing area are gone, the team with the most coins answers one of the questions beginning on page 95 or recites the memory verse.

Optional: Children try to take coins from other team's treasure chests. Each team assigns a Guard to protect their treasure. If a Guard tags someone trying to steal a coin, the tagged player has to put down any coins they picked up and give that team one of their own team's coins!

Say: **Even though in our game we were trying to gather the most coins, that's not something God wants us to focus on in our lives.**

Most kings—and people—want more riches and more power than anyone. Not Solomon, though. What did Solomon ask God for? (*Children respond.*) **Wisdom! Solomon wanted to be a wise king, able to lead God's people well.**

God gave Solomon wisdom. God will give us wisdom, too. We can be wise like Solomon by fearing the Lord. Understanding God's wisdom and respecting his power is the first step in becoming wise.

Simplification Ideas

- **Instead of cutting out coins by cutting around each one, use a paper cutter to cut them apart quickly and easily in squares.**
- **Instead of photocopying and cutting out coins, use toy coins. You'll want about 50 to 60 coins for each team.**

Wisdom Posters

Do: Children create a poster reminder of how to be wise—to fear God—by writing or drawing reminders of who God is and things he has done.

Materials

- Poster board sheets
- Markers or crayons

Optional: Children write Proverbs 1:7 on their posters.

Say: **Proverbs 1:7 tells us "Fear of the Lord is the foundation of true knowledge, but fools despise wisdom and discipline." Who does this verse say despises wisdom and discipline?** (*Children respond.*) **Fools! I'm sure none of us want to be fools, and neither does God. God wants us to be wise!**

Number Groups

Do: Lead children in discussing the difference between their fears and fearing God. Children walk randomly around the room. After a few moments, call out a number between two and five. Children gather into groups of the number called. Any child left without a group tells something they are afraid of.

After a few rounds, ask children what the difference is between things they fear and the fear of God.

Continue playing game, this time asking children left without a group to tell something they know about God or a way to show that they understand and respect God's wisdom and power.

Thumbs Up Thumbs Down Bible Review

Say: **Give a thumbs up if the answer to the question is true. Give a thumbs down if it is false. If the answer is false, explain what makes it false.**

1. **Solomon was never king, just a priest.** (False)
2. **Solomon was the first king of Israel.** (False)
3. **Solomon built the Temple.** (True)
4. **King David and King Solomon followed God.** (True)
5. **King Solomon was wise because he followed God and never sinned.** (False)
6. **God gave Solomon a gift through a dream.** (True)
7. **Solomon asked God for more wishes.** (False)
8. **Solomon asked God for more riches.** (False)
9. **Solomon asked God for wisdom.** (True)
10. **Because Solomon asked God for wisdom, God blessed Solomon with riches and fame, in addition to wisdom.** (True)

Discussion Questions

1. **Why is it good to be wise?**
2. **How can you show that you fear (understand and respect) God?**
3. **Our verse says fools despise wisdom and discipline. How does discipline show a person is wise?**

Gold Coins

Chapter 19: Elijah

1 Kings 18:16–45

Remember the things I have done in the past. For I alone am God! I am God, and there is none like me. ISAIAH 46:9

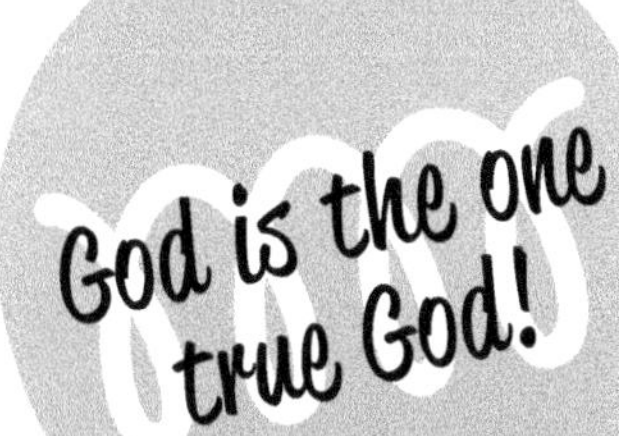

Overview

Say: The people of Israel saw God do some amazing things as he led them out of the land of Egypt where they were slaves. He sent the plagues to Egypt: water to blood, frogs, lice, flies, death of livestock, boils, hail, locust, darkness, and the death of the firstborn sons. God split the Red Sea in half, so the people could walk on dry land. He sent bread from heaven every day and brought water from a rock!

Over and over again, God showed his people, the Israelites, that he was God. But over and over again, the Israelites messed up. They started worshiping other gods. They kept forgetting something very important. **God is the one true God!**

Opening Activity

Invisible Messages

Materials

- UV ink pen with blacklight (available online)
- Paper

Say: What are some ways you have gotten a message before? (*Children respond.*) Maybe someone sent you a card in the mail, telling you "Happy Birthday!" Or maybe someone sent you an invitation to come to their birthday party. Or maybe someone has a message to tell you from someone else. "Your grandma wants me to tell you that she's proud of you."

Messages are a way to get across important information. God even had special message deliverers to help him—the prophets.

God would choose a man, a man who loved and followed God, to be his prophet. The job of the prophet was to tell God's messages to the people.

Sometimes it was a bad message, like when Jonah had to tell the people of Nineveh that God would destroy them if they didn't turn from their ways. Other times, God had good messages to give to his people. The prophet Isaiah told the Israelites messages about the coming Savior.

Today we're going to hear about the prophet Elijah who had a message for God's people.

Preparation: Use UV ink pen to print "God is the one true God" on separate sheets of paper. Prepare one message sheet for every group of two or three children.

Do: Children discover the secret message by revealing it using the black light on their pen. Children create their own messages using the UV pens writing ways they can know God is the one true God or other facts they know about God. After they've created their secret messages, children switch papers and reveal the messages using the UV light on the pens.

Alternate Idea: Create your own invisible ink by using lemon juice. Heat reveals the message.

Say: **This was the message that the prophet Elijah had for God's people. The Israelites had started to worship the false god Baal AND the one true God. They were trying to worship both! But God wants his people to worship him only. God is the one true God, and God was about to prove it!**

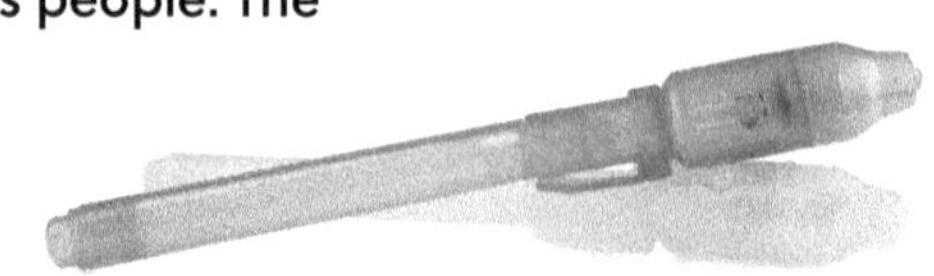

Bible Story

Elijah on Mount Carmel

Preparation (Optional): In a pan of sand, build an altar out of sticks or small pieces of wood. Use glue dots or hot glue to hold the altar together.

Make a moat around the blocks, and when the time is right in the story, show the children how Elijah poured water on the altar.

Create a fire prop (using tissue paper, cardboard, or cellophane) and replace the altar with the fire after God sends down fire.

Say: **Elijah challenged the prophets of Baal to a sacrifice competition. The prophets of Baal and Elijah (God's prophet) would set up their altars of sacrifice, but they would not light the fire. Instead, they would pray to their God. Whoever's god answered the prayers and lit the fire would be revealed as the true God.**

Read: 1 Kings 18:26–39

Say: **God answered Elijah's prayers. The fire he sent didn't just burn up the sacrifice, it burnt up the wood, the rocks, and even the water surrounding the altar!**

God is the one true God! **And everyone there that day on Mount Carmel knew it!**

Object Lesson

Phone Prayers

Materials

- Animal statue or piñata
- Phone

Do: Use the objects to illustrate prayer.

Say: *(Sit the animal statue or piñata in front of you.)* **If I prayed to this (piñata), would it hear me?** *(Children respond.)* **Would it be able to jump up and spin around if I asked it to?** *(Children respond.)*

No way! It's not real. It's just a thing. And praying to a thing seems ridiculous. But that's what some people in Elijah's day did. They prayed to statues and other things, which were supposed to represent their "supposed gods." But those gods weren't real.

Our God, though, IS real! When we pray, he answers. *(Hold phone up to your ear.)* **Prayer is kind of like a phone call. When you call your best friend on the phone, the call is not one-sided, right? If you ask your friend a question, they answer. Your friend is on the other end of the line.**

That's the same with God. When we pray to him, he answers. He's on the other end of our prayer line, because he is real. God is the one true God!

Pray: Pray, praising God for being the one true God!

Additional Activity Options

Real or Not Game

Materials

- Masking tape, rope, or clothesline

Preparation: Use masking tape, rope, or clothesline to make a line down the center of the playing area.

Do: Designate one side of the room "Real" and the other side "Not Real." Children decide if something is real or not by moving to that side of the room.

- **Zonkeys: half zebra, half donkey** (Real)
- **Unicorns** (Not Real)
- **Flying Cars** (Not Real)
- **Umbrella Shoes** (Real)
- **Donut Burgers: donuts instead of buns** (Real)
- **Vampires** (Not Real)
- **Talking Donkeys** (Real. Balaam's donkey from the Bible! Numbers 22:21–34)
- **Amphibocycles: bicycles for water** (Real)
- **Time Travel** (Not Real)
- **Dead People Rising from their Graves** (Real. Jesus did it!)

Say: **It is important to know what is real or not. Saving up all of your money to buy a sparkly pink unicorn isn't a great idea, since unicorns don't exist. Praying to a god that isn't real isn't a good idea either. But that's exactly what the Israelites were doing by worshiping Baal. Elijah showed the people that God was real. God is the one true God!**

Fiery Altar Snack Craft

Do: Children place a slice of yellow cheese onto a plastic or paper place and use a plastic knife to cut the slice into flame shapes. Children eat scrap bits of cheese. Next, children place a handful of stick pretzels to represent the altar and then place the flames on top or above the pretzels to represent the fire God sent from heaven.

Say: **Our snack reminds us of the altar God covered with flames of fire, proving he is the one true God!**

Materials

- Stick pretzels
- Plastic or paper plates
- Sliced yellow cheese
- Plastic knives
- Napkins

Younger Child Simplification: Instead of using plastic knives to cut flame shapes, younger children use small teardrop- or flame-shaped cookie cutters.

Fact Face-Off Bible Review

Do: Form two teams. Team members face off against each other, one at a time, answering the questions and earning points for their team.

1. **What was the job of a prophet?** (To tell God's messages)
2. **Who were the Israelites?** (God's chosen people)
3. **Before Mount Carmel, how should have the Israelites known that God was real?** (All of the amazing things he did while leading them out of Egypt)
4. **What false god were the Israelites also worshiping?** (Baal)
5. **What happened when the prophets of Baal prayed for him to send fire?** (Nothing/no answer)
6. **What did Elijah say about Baal?** (Maybe he was sleeping or couldn't hear them; he was on a trip.)
7. **What did Elijah put on the altar to the Lord?** (Jugs and jugs of water)
8. **Did God answer Elijah's prayer?** (Yes)
9. **What did the fire from God do?** (It burned up the sacrifice, the rocks, and even the water.)
10. **Which God is real, God or Baal?** (God)

Discussion Questions

1. In your own life, how have you seen that God is real?
2. Does God still answer prayers? Why do you think that?
3. Tell us about a time that God answered your prayer.

Teaching Tip: Before asking children to give an example of answered prayer, share an age-appropriate example from your own life.

Be Still

Do: **Part of prayer is being still and listening to God.** Allow time for silent prayer for children to go to God and be still in his presence.

Elijah Challenges Baal Coloring Page: Photocopy the Bible story art on page 101, making one copy for each child plus extras. Kids color art in class or take home.

Elijah Challenges Baal Coloring Page

Chapter 20: Judah

Genesis 49:8–12

"I know that you can do anything, and no one can stop you." **JOB 42:2**

Overview

Say: **If you have a sibling, put a finger on your nose.** *(Children respond.)* **If you think the oldest child gets the most attention, put your hand on your head.** *(Children respond.)* **If you think the youngest child gets the most attention, put a hand on your chest.** *(Children respond.)* **If you think it's someone else in the family, stand up and dance in a circle!** *(Children respond.)*

Sometimes it seems like if you are one of the children in the middle, you might get lost in the crowd. If you were living in Bible times, it would be even worse. Usually only the oldest son received the blessing and the birthright—the chance to lead the family. The oldest child would expect this as they were growing up. So, imagine the surprise when Jacob didn't give his oldest son the family blessing . . . it went to his son Judah who was in the middle of the family. And it was a big blessing.

We like to make plans for our lives, but today we will see that **God's plans are the best plans!**

Materials

- White board or large sheet of paper
- Dry-erase markers (if using a white board) or regular markers (if using large sheet of paper)

Opening Activity

Who Is Judah?

Say: **Raise your hand if you know who Judah is?** *(Children respond.)* **Judah is really important to God's plan, but he's not very well known. So, before we see what blessing Judah was given, let's figure out who Judah is.**

(While explaining the family tree, on a board or large sheet of paper, draw stick people and a family tree, for children to visualize who is who.)

God made a promise to a man named Abraham. He promised to bless him with as many descendants as there are stars in the sky and to make him into a great nation.

Abraham had a son named Isaac. God made the same promise to Isaac that he had made to Abraham.

Isaac had twin sons, Esau and Jacob. Esau was older and should have received the blessing and the birthright, but Jacob tricked his dad Isaac into giving him the blessing.

Jacob, whose name God changed to Israel, had twelve sons. These twelve sons would become the twelve nations of Israel and the beginning of the fulfillment of God's promise to Abraham. Jacob's sons were Reuben, Simeon, Levi, Judah, Dan, Naphtali, Gad, Asher, Issachar, Zebulun, Joseph, and Benjamin.

Bible Story

Judah's Blessing

Say: Twelve sons are a lot of sons! I imagine that there was a lot of fighting in their house! Do any of you fight with your siblings? Or maybe you feel like your parents treat your brother or sister differently than they treat you. *(Children respond.)*

This is exactly how Jacob's sons felt. But it was even worse for them. Their dad, Jacob, loved Joseph the most. Joseph was his favorite child, and because of that, he treated him differently. Joseph, even though he was child number eleven in the birth order, was given a special colorful coat that no one else received.

How do you think the brothers felt about Joseph and his special treatment? *(Children respond.)* Well at first, they were jealous. But then their jealousy moved into hatred. They wanted to kill Joseph. The brothers came up with a plan to throw him into a well and leave him to die! It was Judah who came up with the idea to sell Joseph as a slave instead.

Although Joseph's brothers didn't want good things to happen to him, **God's plans are the best plans!** Joseph would end up being sold again, and then imprisoned for something he didn't do. God was with Joseph, though, and he had a plan for him. Joseph ended up being second in command to the Pharaoh of Egypt! God gave him the ability to interpret dreams, and because Joseph listened to the Lord, he was able to help the Egyptians (and his family) survive a long, seven-year famine.

Now, remember the promise that God made to Abraham, to make him into a new nation? This promise was passed down through Abraham's son Isaac, and Isaac's son Jacob. *(Refer to the family tree you made in the Opening Activity.)* All twelve of Jacob's sons would be a part of this blessing. But God had another, special blessing to give out.

Which of those twelve sons would you choose to receive a blessing from God? Joseph that followed the Lord, or one of his brothers? Stand up if you would choose Joseph.

Let's read the Bible and find out who God chose to bless.

Read: Genesis 49:8–10

Say: Judah received a big blessing! Jacob wasn't saying that Judah would become king himself or that he would be getting a pet lion. Judah was receiving a "messianic prophecy"—this prophecy is what is going to happen with Jesus, the Messiah! That's a big promise!

Object Lesson

Pass the Scepter

Materials

- Toy scepter or wand
- Music

Do: Begin playing the game Hot Potato using a toy scepter or wand. Play several times, with the winner of each round being named King or Queen.

Say: **Would this be a good way to choose who would be king or queen of a nation?** (*Children respond.*) **No!**

Think back to the prophecy and promise that Jacob gave to Judah. Judah, the fourth son in line, the same son that hated his brother and sold him into slavery, would be in the family line of the King of kings, the Lion of Judah, the Messiah—Jesus. Jesus would come from the family line of Judah.

But why Judah?

Wouldn't Joseph, who followed God, have been a better choice? Or the first-born son of Jacob, Reuben. Why Judah?

Well . . . we don't know why. Judah wasn't perfect. Just like you and me, he was a sinner. We don't know why God chose Judah instead of Reuben or Joseph. But Judah is who God chose to be in the family line of Jesus, the King that will sit on the throne forever. While we don't know why God chose Judah, we can trust that God's plans are the best plans!

Pray: Thank God for being the King and Creator of the universe and for having the best plans for our life.

Additional Activity Options

Sleeping Lions Game

Materials

- Masking tape, rope, or clothesline

Preparation: Use masking tape, rope, or clothesline to make a line down the center of the playing area.

Do: Select one or two children to be Lions. The Lions lay asleep in their den, while the other players (at the opposite end of the playing area) try to sneak up and tag the Lions. If any of the Lions are tagged, they join the other players trying to tag Lions.

Whenever the Lions decide to wake up, they roar and begin chasing the children. Any children tagged will then become Lions.

Say: **The prophecy Jacob gave to Judah talked about a lion. Do you know that Jesus is referred to as the Lion of Judah?**

Revelation 5:5 says, "But one of the twenty-four elders said to me, 'Stop weeping! Look, the Lion of the tribe of Judah, the heir to David's throne, has won the victory. He is worthy to open the scroll and its seven seals.'"

The Lion of Judah is Jesus! The Lion from the tribe of Judah.

Lion of Judah Scepter Craft

Preparation: On card stock, photocopy Crown Patterns, making two for each child.

Do: Children decorate both crowns on their paper before cutting them out. Tape the end of a dowel to the back of one of the crowns. Then sandwich the dowel between both crowns, back to back, and glue together to form a scepter.

Say: **Our scepters remind us that God's plans are the best plans! Hundreds and hundreds of years before the birth of Jesus, God promised that Jesus would come from the family of Judah.**

Jesus would be the Savior of the world, the King of kings, and the Lion of Judah.

Materials

- Crown Patterns (p. 106)
- Card stock
- Decorating materials (markers or crayons, adhesive-backed craft-foam shapes or gems, ribbons, etc.)
- Scissors
- Dowel rod, one for each child
- Transparent tape
- Glue

Tic-Tac-Trivia Bible Review

Do: Draw a Tic-Tac-Toe grid on a large sheet of paper. Children divide into two teams, the *X*s and *O*s. Teams take turns answering one of the questions below. If they answer correctly, they write their *X*s or *O*s in a space on the grid. If they don't answer correctly, the other team has a chance to answer. Draw additional grids as needed.

Materials

- Large sheet of paper
- Marker

1. **What was the promise God made to Abraham?** (To bless him with lots of children and make him into a new nation)
2. **What was the name of Abraham's son?** (Isaac)
3. **How many sons did Isaac have?** (Two)
4. **Which son (of Isaac) did the blessing go to?** (Jacob)
5. **How many sons did Jacob have?** (Twelve)
6. **What did Jacob's name get changed to?** (Israel)
7. **Which son was most loved by Jacob?** (Joseph)
8. **What did Judah want to do to Joseph?** (Sell him into slavery)
9. **Where was Judah in the birth order?** (Fourth)
10. **What blessing did Judah receive?** (Jesus would be born from his family.)

Discussion Questions

1. **Why didn't God tell us his reasons for choosing Judah's family line for Jesus?** (God's plans are the best plans! He doesn't have to tell us why!)
2. **Read Jeremiah 29:11. Does God have a plan for your life and future?**
3. **What attributes of God tell us that his plans are the best?** (God is sovereign and omniscient.)

Jesus' Family Tree

Read: Matthew 1:1–16

Say: **What names in Jesus' family tree stick out to you? Did God's promise to Judah come true? Even if we don't understand it, God's plans are the best plans! And his plans always come true.**

Crown Patterns

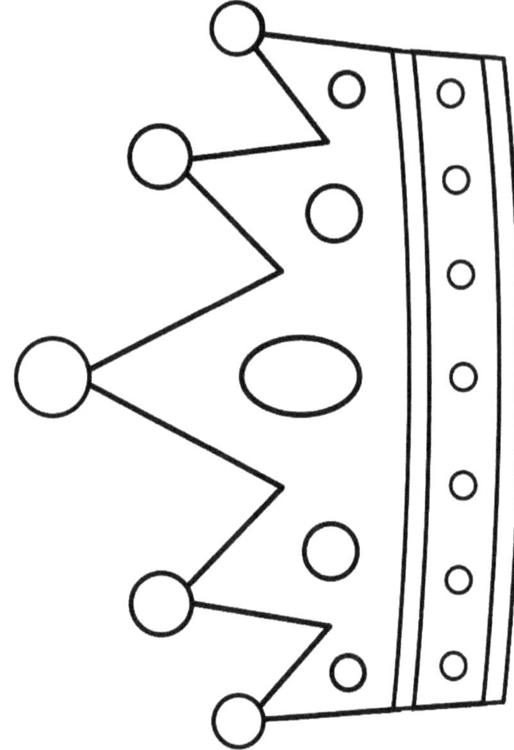

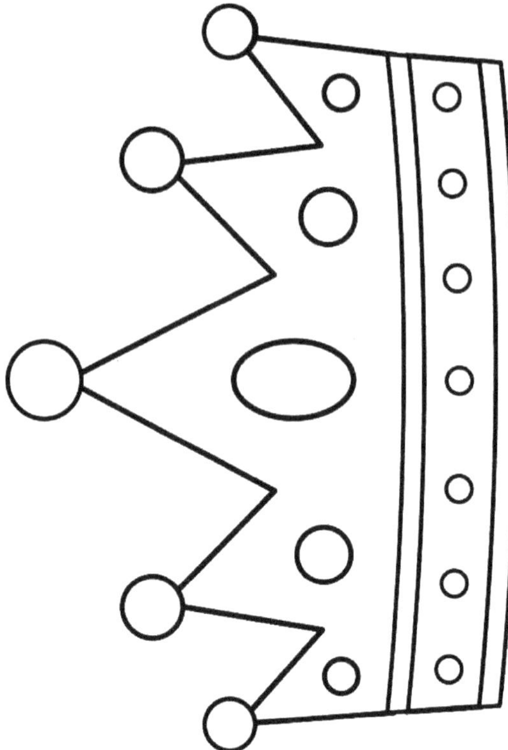

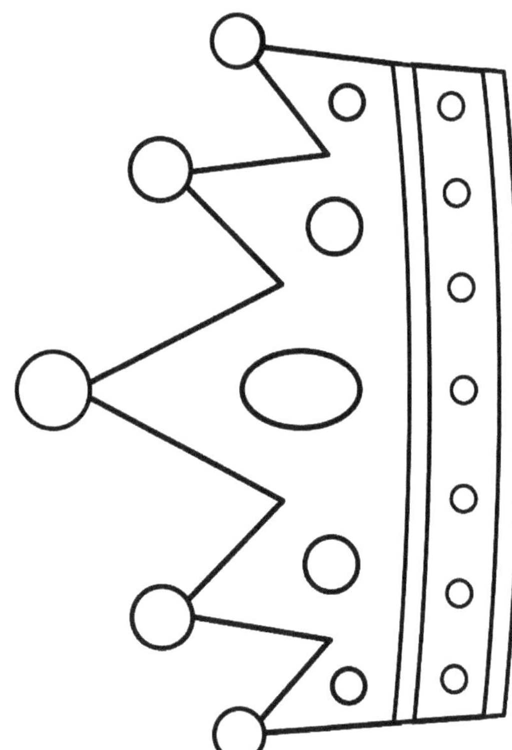

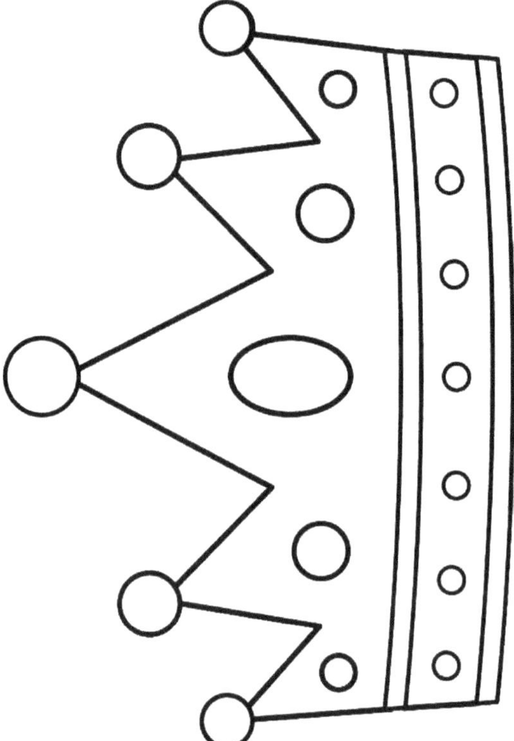

Chapter 21: Rahab

Joshua 2

Let the whole world fear the L*ORD, and let everyone stand in awe of him.* **PSALM 33:8**

Overview

Say: **Fearing God and being afraid of God are two different things. But the Bible tells us over and over to fear the Lord. What does that mean?**

We might be afraid of things like spiders or the dark. There are things that scare us. We aren't supposed to be afraid of God. God would never hurt or harm us.

We are supposed to fear him, though. This meaning of the word *fear* means that we are supposed to have a deep respect for God—respect for who he is and what he does, for his holiness and power.

Rahab feared God. She knew who God was and what he had done for the Israelite people. Because of this healthy kind of fear, she made an important decision. We're going to hear about it in our Bible story.

Opening Activity

Sneaky Spies

Materials

- Masking tape, rope, or clothesline
- Approximately 100 colored playground balls or inflated balloons

Preparation: Use masking tape, rope, or clothesline to make a line down the center of the playing area. Place half of the balls or balloons on either side of the line.

Do: Children divide into two teams. Each team is assigned a half of the playing area. Children try to sneak to the opposing team's side, grab a ball or balloon, and make it back to their side without being tagged. If they are tagged before they return to their side, they return the ball or balloon and then sit down on their team's side of the playing area.

The team with the most balls or balloons at the end of the game recites the memory verse together.

Younger Child Option: Instead of playing this game by tagging, place all of the balls or balloons in the middle and have younger children race to collect as many balls/balloons for their team as they can.

Say: **Do you think you would make a very good spy?** (*Children respond.*) **Imagine having to sneak into the enemy's territory, grab an item, and make it back home without getting caught! That's exactly what Moses told twelve Israelite spies to do in today's Bible story. All but two of the spies, Joshua and Caleb, thought that the land was too hard to take as their homeland. Joshua and Caleb didn't forget who God was, how powerful he is, and that he had promised they would be victorious. Joshua and Caleb had a very healthy fear of God!**

Bible Story

Rahab Hides the Spies

Materials

- Masking tape, rope, or clothesline
- Approximately 100 colored playground balls or inflated balloons

Say: **Under the leadership of Moses,** the Israelites were going to be invading the land of Jericho, the land God had promised them. First, they needed to scout out the land. They were supposed to see what the land was like, what defenses the people had, and even what kind of fruit grew there—and to bring some of that fruit back with them.

Unfortunately, the Israelite people listened to the ten men who didn't believe in God's promises. They were afraid and began to grumble that they would be better off if they'd stayed in Egypt as slaves! Because of their lack of faith, for forty years, the Israelites wandered in the desert not getting to go into the land that God promised.

After Moses passed away, Joshua became the leader of the Israelites. It was almost time to take possession of the land God had promised the people so long before. So Joshua sent two spies to look at the city of Jericho.

But they ran into a problem . . .

The land of Jericho had a really big wall around it—a really big wall. The wall was around thirteen feet high and six feet wide. And that was just the first wall, the retaining wall. There was a second wall on top of that one, around twenty-six feet high. And behind that, there was another even taller wall.

A woman named Rahab lived on the wall. That sounds a little funny, huh? We don't think of people living on a wall! But those big walls around Jericho were so big, there were houses built right into the wall!

The king of Jericho found out that there were Israelite spies in his land. Oh, no! The king knew that the people of Jericho wanted to take over the city. So he wanted to STOP those spies! The two spies went to Rahab's house. What would you do if spies came into your house—spies that plan on taking over your home? (*Children respond.*) Many people would probably turn them in, telling the soldiers or police that they are there. That would probably seem the safest thing to do.

But Rahab didn't turn in the men. Even when the king sent people to Rahab's house looking for the spies! Instead, she took the men up to the roof and covered them with stalks of flax.

Optional: Explain what stalks of flax look like and what they were used for. Flax is used to make linen fabric. Rahab probably had flax on her roof, because it was common to leave the stalks out in the dew, to continue separating the layers from the stem. If you can, show children stalks of flax or linen fabric.

Why do you think Rahab hid the spies? (*Children respond.*)

Read: Joshua 2:8–11

Say: Even though Rahab was not an Israelite, one of God's people, or even a follower of God, Rahab had heard of what God had done for his people. She knew that he is the one true God. She wisely feared God—respected who he was and what he had done.

Rahab wanted to help the spies because she knew God would give the land to them, because he alone is God. Rahab knew that **God is to be feared!**

Pray: Pray with children, asking God to teach them to fear him, like Psalm 33:8 says.

Object Lesson

Safety First!

Do: Show the safety object(s) or pictures of safety objects you gathered. Children identify each object and explain how it keeps you safe. Lastly, show the scarlet cord.

Materials

- One or more safety objects or pictures of safety objects (fire extinquisher, safety cones, street signs, face mask, traffic light, etc.)
- Scarlet cord (red scarf or sash, length of braided or crochet red yarn or fabric, etc.)

Say: **Because Rahab helped to keep the spies safe, they made her a promise. When Israel invaded Jericho, she and her family would be safe.**

Remember how Rahab's house was in the wall surrounding Jericho? Well, how do you think she could she be saved when God would destroy that wall?

When it was time for Israel to invade, Rahab was to tie a scarlet cord and hang it out the window. This was a sign to the Israelites that Rahab (and her family) feared the Lord. They were on God's side.

Rahab told the spies, *"the Lord your God is the supreme God of the heavens above and the earth below"* (Joshua 2:11). **She knew who God was. She respected his power. And the scarlet cord was a sign that she and her family were to be kept safe. Rahab understood that God is to be feared!**

Additional Activity Options

Doggy, Doggy, Where Is My Bone? Game

Do: Players sit in a circle. Choose one volunteer to be "It." "It" stands in the middle of the circle with their eyes closed. When you start the music, the remaining players pass around the small object. After a few moments, stop the music. Whoever has the small object quickly hides it.

On the leader's signal, "It" opens their eyes and has three chances to guess which player is hiding the small object. If "It" guesses correctly, player hiding the small object becomes the new "It."

If "It" doesn't guess correctly, they remain "It" for up to two more rounds. If after three guesses, "It" hasn't guess correctly, "It" chooses a player who has not yet had a turn to be the new "It." Continue play as time and interest allow.

Materials

- Small object (dog toy, small ball, etc.)
- Children's worship music and player

Say: **Rahab didn't have to hide the two spies that came to her house. She didn't have to help them. They were there spying out the area before the Israelite army came and took over her land. She could have considered them her enemy.**

But Rahab hid them. In hiding the men, she risked getting caught and punished, like some of you were caught hiding the ball in our game.

The risk of getting caught didn't matter to Rahab. She feared God more—she respected God more. She knew that the God of the Israelites is the one true God. And God is to be feared!

Scarlet Cord Hearts Craft

Preparation: Before class, photocopy Heart Patterns, making one copy for every four children. Cut to separate hearts, making one for each child plus extras. Cut cardboard into 4x4-inch squares, making one for each child plus extras. Cut yarn into lengths about 2 yards long, making five or six for each child.

Do: Children cut out a heart pattern and then trace it onto a 4x4-inch cardboard square. Children cut out hearts.

Children tape one end of a length of red yard to the center of a cardboard heart and then wrap yarn around the heart. When they reach the end of the length of yarn, they attach another length and continue wrapping until the heart is completed wrapped. Then, they tie a knot in the yarn and trim it. Thread extra length of yarn at the top of the heart so it can be hung up at home.

Materials

- Heart Patterns, page 111
- Cardboard
- Ruler
- Pencils
- Scissors
- Red yarn
- Transparent tape

Say: **How did Joshua and the Israelites know that Rahab was not their enemy, that she was a friend and shouldn't be harmed?** (*Children respond.*) **She hung the same scarlet cord out her window that she used to sneak the spies out to safety. It was a sign that Rahab knew that God is to be feared!**

Our yarn hearts can be a sign that you fear the Lord. Hang your scarlet cord hearts in a place you'll see it every day: by your bed, on your bathroom mirror, etc. These hearts are a great reminder to have respect for who God is and what he does.

Younger Child Simplification: Trace and cut out hearts ahead of time, or ask older children to prepare the hearts for the younger ones.

Beanbag Bible Review

Materials

- 2 or 3 beanbags

Do: Children stand together. Choose a volunteer to stand with their back to the group a few feet away. Volunteer then tosses beanbags, one at a time, to the group. Children who catch the beanbags work together to answer one of the questions below.

1. **How many spies did Moses send the first time?** (Twelve)
2. **Were the spies scared or did they trust in God?** (All but two were scared)
3. **What was their punishment for not trusting God to deliver the land he promised to them?** (They wandered the desert for 40 years.)
4. **Who replaced Moses as leader?** (Joshua)
5. **How many spies did Joshua send in?** (Two)
6. **Whose house did the spies enter?** (Rahab)
7. **Who was looking for the spies?** (The King)
8. **How did Rahab keep the spies hidden?** (By hiding them on the roof under flax)
9. **Why did Rahab hide the spies?** (She feared God.)
10. **What did Rahab use to tell the Israelites that she was not to be harmed?** (A scarlet cord out her window)

Discussion Questions

1. **What does fearing the Lord mean?**
2. **How did Rahab fear the Lord?**
3. **How do you show your fear of the Lord?**

Heart Patterns

Chapter 22: Adam & Eve

Genesis 1–3

So God created human beings in his own image. In the image of God he created them; male and female he created them. **Genesis 1:27**

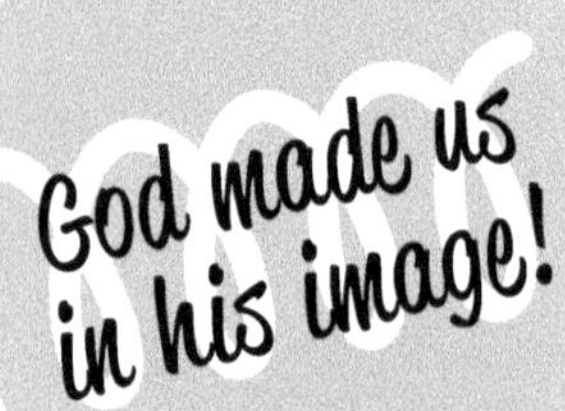

Overview

Say: **Close your eyes and imagine if you lived in the Garden of Eden. It was paradise! This beautiful garden was full of colorful plants and amazing animals. Can you see them? There were lots of fruits and vegetables to eat.**

Now imagine that you were in charge of taking care of the animals in the garden. And that all of the animals got along. Taking care of the animals would be easy, right? Sin hadn't entered the world yet, so there was no fighting or death. There wouldn't have even been any weeds in the garden. And the best part of all—you would have walked and talked with God there!

This is the world that God created for Adam and Eve, the first two people. But out of everything that God made, all of the animals and plants, people were different; they were special. Even though sin separates us from God, we are still God's special creations because God made us in his image!

Opening Activity

Creation Week Creations

Materials

- 1 fist-sized lump of play dough for each child

Do: Children use play dough to "recreate" something that God made. When children finish, volunteers show their creations and the rest of the children try to guess what it is.

Say: **Creating things can be difficult. Some of you did a great job creating things out of your play dough. Think about how much harder it would be to make something if you didn't have the play dough. Imagine having to create things from nothing—no ingredients. Just . . . nothing!**

That's what God did. He created the whole world and everything in it from . . . nothing. The phrase *ex nihilo* (EHKS nee-HEE-loh) is Latin for "from nothing." That's exactly how God made the universe. There was nothing anywhere until God spoke it into existence.

He spoke the universe and all that is inside of it—planets, stars, whole galaxies—into existence. All of our plants and trees, as well as the animals and birds were all spoken into being. And they were amazing! But after God had finished creating the world, the plants, the birds, the fish, and the animals, he spoke into existence his most special creation—man. **God made us in his image!**

Younger Child Option: Suggest simple objects for younger children: snake, apple, flower, etc.

Bible Story

Materials

- Sheets of paper
- Markers or crayons.

God Created Adam & Eve

Preparation: Place sheets of paper and markers or crayons on a table where children will be working.

Before reading the Bible story, instruct children to fold the paper in half vertically and then letter style, making three sections. Label the top section "Day 1." Continue labeling sections until there is one for each of the six days of God's creation.

Read: Genesis 1:1–31

Do: While the creation account from Genesis 1 is read aloud, children write or draw the things God created in the appropriate sections.

Pray: Praise God for all of the wonderful things he made, especially humans!

Object Lesson

The Image of God

Say: (*Look into the mirror.*) **We are made in the image of God. That means that God has brown hair like me, a few freckles, and green eyes. That's what being made in the image of God means, right? That we look like him?** (*Children respond.*)

Being made in the image of God doesn't mean that we look like him. It means that we, unlike anything else he created, can have the characteristics of God.

- **We can be creative like God the Creator.**
- **We can be kind and compassionate, like our loving Father.**
- **We can even be just and fair, just like God.**

But more than just having the characteristics of God, there is something even more important that makes us different than anything else. We have souls.

God gave humans, starting with Adam and Eve, the ability to choose whether or not to follow him. We can choose to obey God or not. He gave Adam and Eve the choice, but they disobeyed and ate from the tree God told them not to. That's when sin entered the world.

But it's more than just choosing right from wrong. Dogs know it's wrong to chew on shoes. Because we are made in the image of God, we can choose to follow him with our lives. We can accept him, and the gift of grace and forgiveness Jesus offered by dying on the cross, and we can live with him forever in heaven!

What a gift God has given us! God made man, Adam and Eve, in his image. God made us in his image! And that makes us unique in all of God's creation!

Additional Activity Options

Animal Races

Materials

- None

Do: Children divide into even teams and line up for relay races. If you have a larger group, divide into multiple teams of six or eight players.

Teams compete in relay races, moving like animals God created. The first team to have all of their children reach the finish line answers one of the questions on page 115, recites the memory verse, or tells a sentence about the Bible story.

- Jump like a kangaroo (Jump with both feet.)
- Run like an ostrich (Take wide steps while flapping arms like wings.)
- Slither like a snake (Wiggle on their bellies.)
- Run like a dog (Move quickly on both hands and feet.)
- Duckwalk (Squat-walk and flap arms like wings.)
- Waddle like a penguin (Keeping legs together, shuffle feet forward.)
- T-Rex stomp (Take big, giant footsteps.)
- Crabwalk (Walk on hands and feet, with bellies up and moving sideways.)
- Sloth run (Run in super slow motion.)

Say: **God was so creative when he made the world. Think of all of the different animals he made. Tropical birds are all so colorful and bright. Giraffes have crazy long necks and a beautiful, unique skin pattern. Chameleons can change color.**

There are so many different animals, all with unique features and cool designs. What is your favorite animal that God made? *(Children respond.)*

As amazing as the animals God made are, he made something else even more amazing. People! Everything God made was good. It was a perfect, sinless creation. But people are even more unique than the plants and the animals. God made us in his image! Nothing else in all of creation is made in his image! Only us, his special creation.

God Made Me! Craft

Materials

- Paper Person, page 116
- Markers or crayons

Preparation: Photocopy Paper Person, making one for each child plus extras.

Do: Children decorate their paper person cutout to represent themselves. Children write "I'm made in the image of God!" on their paper and take them home to place on a wall or mirror as a reminder that **God made us in his image!**

Say: **Whenever you look at your paper person, or whenever you look in the mirror, remember that God made you special. You are more special than all of the animals. As descendants of Adam, the first man God made, you too are made in the image of God! And that is pretty special!**

Enrichment Ideas:

Use yarn and fabric scraps to make hair and clothes on your paper people!
Cut out Paper Person and glue to a sheet of colored construction paper or scrapbook paper.

Creation Call-Out Bible Review

Say: **God made some amazing things in our world. Let's play a game to go over the things that God made.**

Do: Leader calls out something God made. Players hold up the correct number of fingers and call out on which day of creation God made that thing.

- Sunflowers—Day 3
- Ducks—Day 5
- The Ocean—Day 2
- Jupiter—Day 4
- Cheetahs—Day 6
- Light—Day 1
- Apple Trees—Day 3
- The Moon—Day 4
- Gorillas—Day 6
- Flamingos—Day 5

Continue with your own examples as time and interest allow.

Say: **Great job! I've got one last question for you. On what day did God make his most special creation?** *(Children respond.)*

Day 6! On day 6 of creation, after God had made all of the animals, he created people.

After everything that God made, he looked at it and saw that it was very good. There was no sin in the world yet, so there were no bad things. Everything was good!

But there was something different about how he created the first human. People were created in the image of God. Nothing else in all of creation is created in God's image.

Discussion Questions

1. **What does it mean to be created in God's image?**
2. **How are we all related to Adam?**
3. **Why did God make us in his image?**

Mirror Game

Do: Children pair up, facing each other. Select one child from each pair to be the Leader and their partner will be the Follower. Leader begins moving, while Follower mirrors their movements exactly. Play again with players switching roles.

Say: **Was it easy or hard to mirror your partner?** *(Children respond.)*

A mirror image is a reflection—a perfect copy. God made us in his image. We are supposed to be reflections of him. That means we should be treating people with love, like he does. We should have kind words, like God tells us to. We should be peaceful, fair, and generous. We should be mirroring God, trying to be a reflection of who he is!

Paper Person

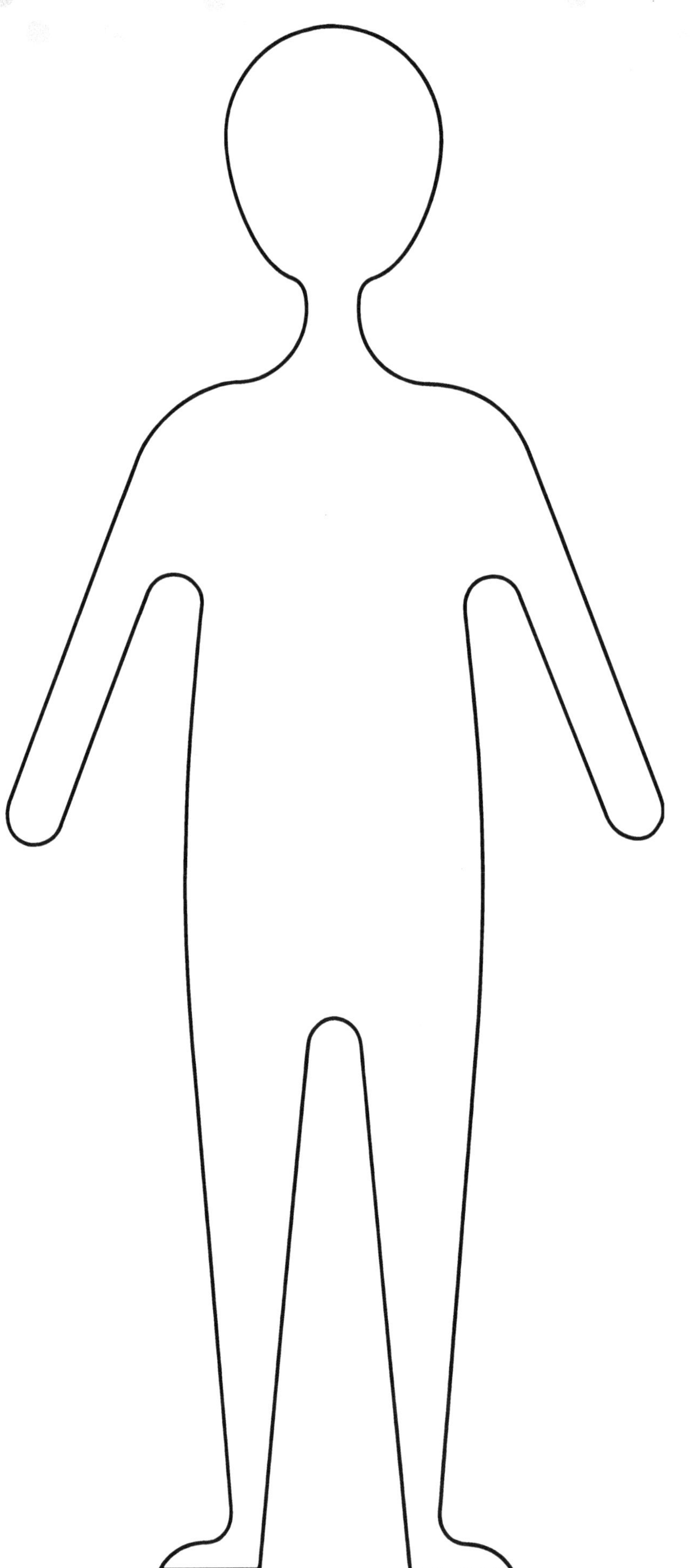

Chapter 23: The Thief on the Cross

Luke 23:26–43

God saved you by his grace when you believed. And you can't take credit for this; it is a gift from God. **EPHESIANS 2:8**

Overview

Say: **How well do you know Jesus?** (*Encourage responses.*)

When Jesus was here on Earth, many people thought Jesus was just a teacher or a prophet, some people understood who he is. Peter, one of Jesus' disciples, understood who he is and what his purpose was in coming to Earth. Even the thief on the cross, a man whose name we don't know, understood. We're going to hear that story today. Just like Peter and the thief on the cross, we know Jesus is the Messiah!

Opening Activity

Twenty Answers Game

Do: As the leader reads the clues, one-by-one, children stand up when they think they know the answer. Remind children not to shout out the answers!

Who Am I?

1. I am a male.
2. You can read about me in the Bible.
3. I lived in Egypt for a while.
4. My parents were Jewish.
5. I am related to Abraham, King David, and Ruth.
6. The Romans were in power when I was alive.
7. I had siblings, but their names were not mentioned in the Bible.
8. My mother was young.
9. My best friends were James and John.
10. I know how to catch fish.
11. I know the Old Testament Scriptures very well.
12. I spent lots of time in prayer, talking to God the Father.
13. You can't read much about my childhood—only one story.
14. I was popular.

15. But I was also hated.
16. I love little children.
17. I hung out with sinners.
18. I have more than one name.
19. When my friend died, I cried.
20. I was arrested even though I had done nothing wrong.

Younger Child Option: Use fewer and more obvious clues for younger children.

Say: **On the count of three, shout out the name of this person. 1 . . . 2 . . . 3!** (*Children respond.*)

It's Jesus! How quickly did you guess that's who I was talking about? Some of you guessed it pretty quickly. But the more and more clues I gave, the more you knew about the person, and the more confident you were in knowing who I was talking about.

All of those clues were about Jesus. It would have been super easy to guess Jesus if the clue was "I died on the cross to save you from your sins," wouldn't it? But to know that Jesus was popular and that his mother was young, you would need to know what the Bible says about him.

Believers today can know Jesus because we can read the Bible. The Bible tells us all about who he is and what he has done. But the people living while Jesus was alive and ministering didn't have the Bible to read! (It was being lived out!)

They could still learn about Jesus, though. Jesus, when he was here on Earth, revealed who he is to those who would accept him. We're going to hear about one of those people in today's Bible story. And, even more importantly, we know Jesus is the Messiah today!

Optional Activity: Whenever you need a time-filler, come up with your own statements about any Bible person and play Bible Person Twenty Answers! Or, and this requires less preparation, lead the kids in a traditional game of Twenty Questions telling them from the beginning that the answer is a person from the Bible.

Bible Story

The Thief on the Cross

Materials

- Handheld cross or picture of the crucifixion

While reading the Bible story, hold up or place the cross or picture you brought where children can see it.

Say: **Jesus' ministry is almost through. For three years, he has been traveling around teaching, preaching, and performing miracles. He healed the sick. He raised the dead. He spoke to Jews and sinners and told them how their sins could be forgiven. He told people how they could be saved.**

It made him very popular! Some people followed him around because of the miracles he performed. It also made him very hated. The religious leaders, the Scribes and Pharisees, hated Jesus. They liked their rules and their laws. They thought righteousness was something you earned by your actions. They didn't like what Jesus said. They hated him because of it.

Jesus was arrested and sentenced to die, even though he didn't do anything wrong. The soldiers mocked him. The people scoffed at him. But some still believed.

Read: Luke 23:26–43

Say: There were two men being crucified on crosses next to Jesus' cross. One man made fun of Jesus, saying, "So you're the Messiah, are you? Prove it by saving yourself—and us, too, while you're at it!"

But the other man stopped him. What did that man say about Jesus? *(Children respond.)* **He said that Jesus was being killed, though he didn't do anything wrong. He also asked Jesus to remember him when he went to his kingdom.**

The second thief on the cross knew who Jesus was—not just facts about Jesus. He knew in his heart that Jesus was the Savior of the world that God had promised to send.

Pray: Thank Jesus for being the Messiah and for the forgiveness and eternal life we can have through his death and resurrection. After you pray, offer an opportunity for anyone who would like to know more about becoming a member of God's family to talk with you or any of the adult volunteers.

Object Lesson

Materials

- 2 8½x11-inch sheets of white card stock
- Ruler
- Pencil
- Scissors
- Tape
- 1 transparency sheet
- Permanent markers

The Great Reveal

Preparation: Follow the instructions below to create an illusion in which children see words appear inside a cross.

1. Fold a sheet of card stock in half horizontally to make a 5½x8½-inch card.
2. Measure, trace, and cut a window out of the front of the card, leaving half an inch around the sides.
3. Cut the second piece of card stock in half. Cut one of the halves a bit smaller, about five-by-eight inches. Place inside the card and tape the bottom to the bottom of the card. (See image a.)
4. Leaving the top open, tape the bottom and sides of the card together.
5. Cut the remaining card-stock half and the transparency sheet to fit inside the pocket. Each should be about 5¼x¼ inches in size.
6. On the cut piece of card stock, print *MESSIAH* vertically and *JESUS* with a shared *S* in the middle. (See image b.)
7. Tape the transparency sheet and the card stock piece together at the top.
8. Place the transparency sheet over the word cross you just created and draw the outline of a cross around the words. (See image c.)
9. Carefully place the taped pieces inside the pocket, sandwiching the copy paper in the middle. Through the window in the pocket, you should be able to see the cross, but not the words.

a.

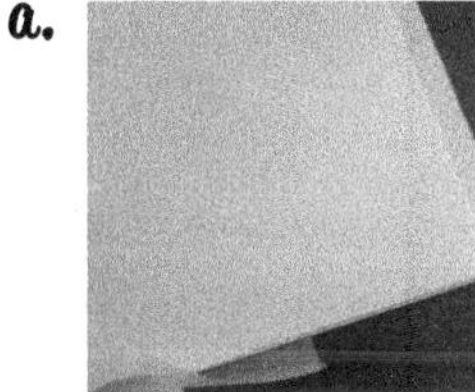

b.

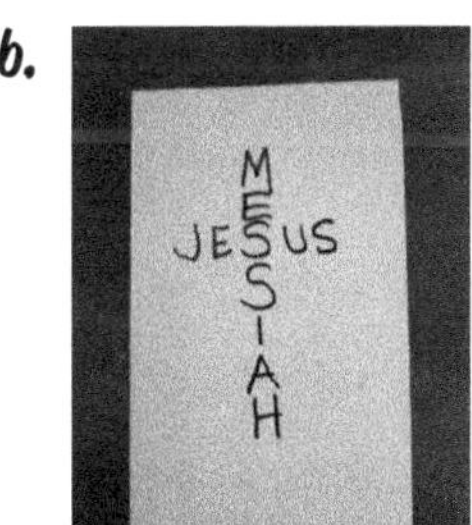

c.

Do: As you read the following, hold the pocket facing the children. At the time indicated, reach inside and slowly pull the taped transparency pieces out. As you do, the message JESUS MESSIAH will be revealed inside the cross.

Say: The truth about who Jesus is was revealed to everyone when Jesus was on a cross. *(Hold up cross pocket you prepared.)* **But unlike others who died on crosses, Jesus came back to life.** *(Pull out the taped transparency pieces.)* **Jesus' resurrection proved that he is the Messiah, the Savior of the world. There is no doubt. We know Jesus is the Messiah!**

Additional Activity Options

High Five, Jesus Is Alive Game

Materials
- None

Do: Play a version of Tag, where players unfreeze others by tagging them and saying, "Jesus is alive."

Say: **The thief on the cross knew who Jesus is. We know Jesus is the Messiah! And we can share this good news with others!**

Cross Biblemarks

Materials
- Biblemark Patterns, page 121
- Card stock
- Scissors
- Decorating materials (paint and paintbrushes, markers, crayons, stickers, glitter glue, etc.)

Preparation: On card stock, photocopy Biblemark Patterns, making one copy for every two children. Cut to separate patterns.

Do: Children cut out and decorate Biblemarks.

Say: **How can we learn more about who Jesus is?** (*Children respond.*) **By reading our Bibles! Our Biblemarks can remind us of Jesus and help us keep our place in our Bibles. We know Jesus is the Messiah because God's Word tells us!**

Stand Up If It's True Bible Review

Say: **Stand up if the answer to the question is true but sit down if it is false. If the answer is false, explain what makes it false.**

1. **Jesus was a regular human.** (False)
2. **No one understood who Jesus was.** (False)
3. **Jesus revealed who he was and what his purpose was.** (True)
4. **Everyone loved Jesus.** (False)
5. **Crowds followed Jesus.** (True)
6. **The Jewish religious leaders hated Jesus.** (True)
7. **Jesus was arrested for breaking laws.** (False)
8. **Jesus was crucified on a cross.** (True)
9. **One thief mocked Jesus.** (True)
10. **The other thief believed in Jesus.** (True)

Discussion Questions

1. **Read Matthew 16:13–20. Who did Peter say Jesus was?**
2. **Who would you say that Jesus is?**
3. **How does God reveal himself to us today?**

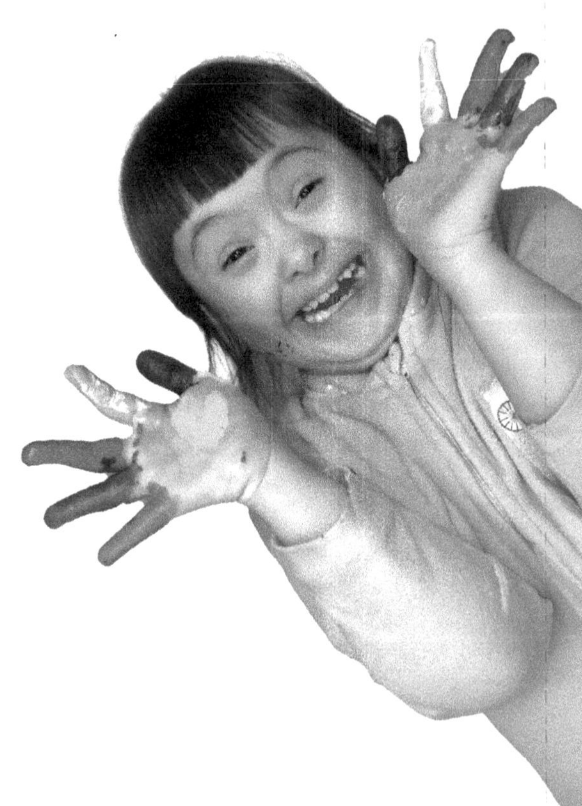

Biblemark Patterns

God saved you by his grace when you believed. And you can't take credit for this; it is a gift from God. **Ephesians 2:8**

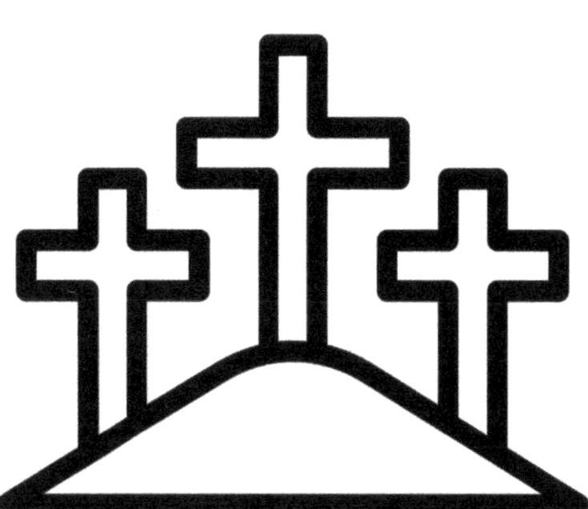

God saved you by his grace when you believed. And you can't take credit for this; it is a gift from God. **Ephesians 2:8**

Chapter 24: Esther

Esther

"If you keep quiet at a time like this, deliverance and relief for the Jewish people will arise from some other place, but you and your relatives will die. Who knows if perhaps you were made queen for just such a time as this?" **ESTHER 4:14**

Overview

Say: **Think about the five people you spend the most time with. It might be your parents, your siblings, or your friends. Do these people that you spend the most time with help you to follow God better? Or do they influence you to make bad choices?**

The people we are closest to influence our thoughts and actions. If you spend time with someone who is always kind and encouraging, you'll start to become kind and encouraging as well. But the opposite is true as well. If you spend time with someone who uses bad language, guess what will start coming out of you? Bad language.

We can listen to people who follow God! He wants us to spend time with (and be influenced by) people who love and follow him. Esther, a woman in the Old Testament, was a great example of how having the right influences in your life matters.

Opening Activity

Good Guy, Bad Guy Game

Do: One at a time, call out the name of a person from the Bible. (See suggestions below.) If players think the person is a good guy (a person that followed the Lord), they smile and cheer. If players think the person is a bad guy (a person that did not follow the Lord), they make a sad face and shake their heads.

- Abraham (Good)
- King Ahab (Bad)
- Moses (Good)
- King Herod (Bad)
- Goliath (Bad)
- David (Good)
- Delilah (Bad)
- Elijah (Good)
- Methuselah (Good)
- Ananias (Bad)
- Paul (Good)
- King Xerxes (Good)

Say: **King Xerxes was the king of Persia, not Israel. King Xerxes was a good guy who almost wasn't. He almost made a terrible, terrible choice that would have hurt a lot of God's people. Thankfully, King Xerxes's wife, Queen Esther, was there to stop him!**

We're going to hear all about it in our Bible story today.

Optional: Use a happy and a sad emoji face during this game for the good and bad guys. You could print them out, attach a handle, and ask volunteers to hold up the correct face for each person.

Bible Story

Esther Saves God's People

As you retell the story, say Haman's name faster and more frequently.

Interactive Storytelling Options:

- Tell the story the way it's told during Purim Festivals. Every time children hear Haman's name, they shout "BOO" and blow into a noisemaker to keep Haman's name from reaching God's ears, since he's the villain in the story.
- Follow instructions under Purim Puppets activity beginning on page 126. Volunteers use the puppets to act out the action as you tell the story.

Say: **King Xerxes was looking for a new wife. Out of all the women brought before him, he chose a young woman named Esther to be his new queen.**

Esther, though, had a secret. The new Queen of Persia was Jewish.

Her cousin Mordecai, who helped raise Esther, told Esther to keep it a secret that she is a Jew. At that time in history, the Jewish people didn't live in their own land anymore. As a punishment from God, their enemies had defeated them, and many Jews were displaced and living as slaves in foreign lands.

So, Esther kept her heritage a secret, even from the king.

The king had an adviser named Haman. Haman did not like the Jewish people. Hungry for power, he became very jealous when Esther's cousin Mordecai received special recognition from the king.

When Mordecai refused to bow down to Haman, his jealousy moved into hatred of the Jewish people. So, he devised a terrible plan.

Haman planned for the Jewish people living in Persia to be killed. He planned to have Mordecai hung on gallows that Haman had built in his yard. Haman convinced the king to agree to his plan, and King Xerxes signed it into law with his signet ring.

The Jewish people, God's chosen people, were about to be killed! The queen herself, if she were discovered to be a Jew, would be killed.

Read: Esther 4:13–14

Say: **Mordecai told Esther that perhaps she was made queen at this specific time so that she could help the Jewish people. She prayed and she fasted—she asked God what to do.**

She invited the king and Haman to a banquet. It's important to note that it was not acceptable for Esther, even though she was queen, to approach the king without permission. If it angered the king, he could put Esther to death just for approaching him. Esther must have been terrified!

But the king accepted her invitation. He offered Esther anything she wanted and said he would grant her request. But Esther just invited the king and Haman to another banquet the next day.

Read: Esther 7:1–6

Say: **Haman was a bad influence on the king. His suggestion to kill all of the Jewish people was a terrible one, but the king didn't realize it until Esther pointed it out.**

Because Esther was queen, King Xerxes stopped the execution of the Jewish people. He made a new law that allowed the Jewish people to defend themselves, and Haman was executed on the very gallows that he had built for Mordecai.

Haman wasn't a good influence on King Xerxes. But Esther was. And Mordecai was a good influence on Esther. God often speaks to us through the people who love and follow him. We can listen to people who follow God!

Fun Fact: The book of Esther in the Bible is the only book not to mention God by name.

Pray: Pray for godly influences in the lives of the children. Allow time for silent prayer so that children can thank God for the godly people in their lives.

Materials

- Water-based marker
- Coffee filter
- 2 clear glasses, 1 partially filled with water

Object Lesson

What Goes In

Preparation: Use water-based marker to color the bottom couple of inches of the coffee filter.

Say: **What does it mean to have an influence on another person?** *(Children respond.)* **Whenever we spend time with other people, a little of who they are rubs off on us. We might start talking like them, acting like them, playing the same games and reading the same books, and so on. That's what being an influence on someone means.**

(Hold up the glass of water.) **Let's pretend the water in this glass is like us.** *(Place the filter in the empty glass.)* **The filter is the influence other people can have on us.** *(Pour water from glass through the filter into the other glass.)* **You can see that the water is no longer clear. It's (blue). The water is different now.**

If you spend your time with people who aren't good influences, they will begin to influence you. Maybe your school friends lie or use bad language. As you hang out with them more and more, those things begin to come out of your life—bad language and lies.

But if you fill your life with godly influences, people that encourage you and help you follow God, that is what will start to come out of your life.

Haman was a bad influence on King Xerxes. But Mordecai was a good influence on Esther, and she was a good influence on King Xerxes. We can listen to people who follow God. We need to be influenced by people like Mordecai and Esther, people who follow God and help us to follow him, too.

Additional Activity Options

Purim Puppets

Preparation: On white card stock, photocopy Purim Puppets, making one copy for each child plus extras.

Do: Children color and cut out puppet shapes. Then, tape a craft stick to the back of each. Encourage children to take puppets home to retell the story of King Xerxes and Queen Esther to their families.

Say: Did you know that Jewish people still celebrate the Bible story of King Xerxes and Queen Esther? There's actually a holiday for it! It's called *Purim*. One of the traditional activities done during the Purim festival is the retelling of the story of Esther.

Materials

- Purim Puppet Patterns, page 126
- White card stock
- Watercolor markers
- Scissors
- Craft sticks, 4 per child
- Tape

Seat Switch Bible Review

Children sit in a circle. Leader or volunteer closes their eyes as children switch seats. When everyone is seated, without opening their eyes, leader or volunteer names a child. That child, plus the children seated on either side of them, answers one of the questions below. Repeat seat switching until each question is answered.

1. **What country was Xerxes king of?** (Persia)
2. **How did Esther become queen?** (The king picked her out of beautiful women.)
3. **Who was Esther's cousin?** (Mordecai)
4. **What was the secret Mordecai told Esther to keep?** (She was Jewish.)
5. **Who hated the Jewish people?** (Haman)
6. **Why are the Jewish people important?** (They are God's chosen people.)
7. **What law did Haman get the king to sign?** (To kill all of the Jewish people)
8. **What did Mordecai encourage Esther to do when she found out about the law?** (She fasted and prayed.)
9. **What did Esther invite the king and Haman to?** (A banquet)
10. **How were the Jewish people saved?** (The king made a new law saying they could defend themselves.)

Discussion Questions

1. **Did King Xerxes make good choices?**
2. **What kind of influences do you have—influences like Mordecai and Esther? Or like Haman?**
3. **What kind of an influence are you to others?**

Pray About It

Do: Children write a list of the things they are worried about or items that they want to pray about.

Say: Esther received bad, scary news. The Jewish people were going to be killed. She could be killed! But what did Esther do first? (*Children respond.*) **She prayed!**

Whenever we are faced with bad news or things that worry us, we should pray about them, just like Esther. And we can ask people who love God to give us good advice. We can also ask these godly influences to pray for us, just like Esther did!

Materials

- Sheets of paper, one for each child
- Markers, pens, or pencils

Purim Puppet Patterns

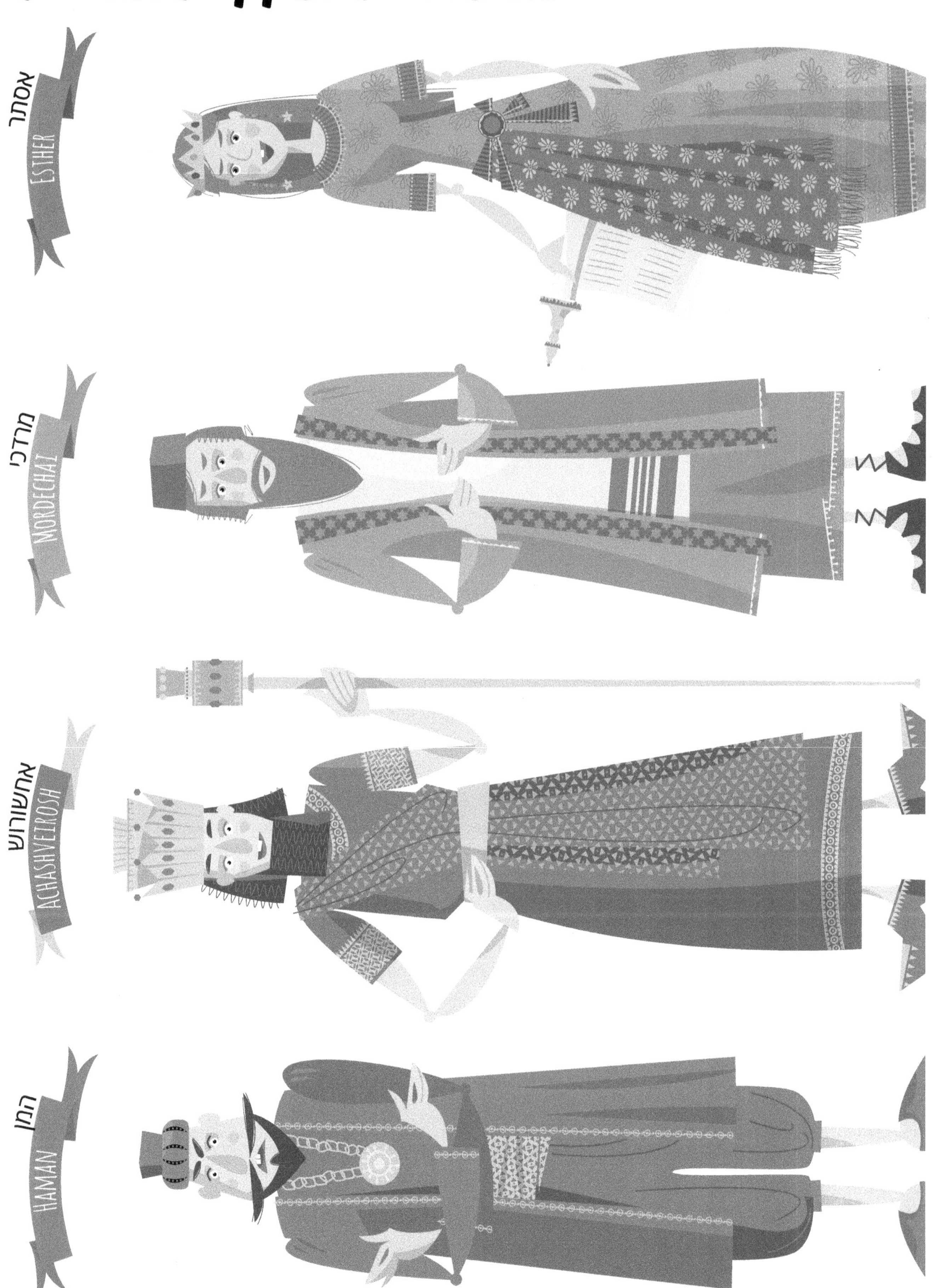

Chapter 25: Joseph

Genesis 37—50

We know that God causes everything to work together for the good of those who love God and are called according to his purpose for them. **ROMANS 8:28**

Overview

Say: **Have you ever been jealous?** (*Children share about a time they were jealous, as time allows.*)

If your sibling got all of the attention and special presents from mom and dad, you'd probably not like your sibling very much, would you? Imagine that out of their twelve children, if your parents had just one favorite—and it showed. All of the other kids would feel pretty jealous.

But would your jealousy make you want to kill someone?

Through the Old Testament story of Joseph, we will see how God can make bad things good.

Opening Activity

A Colorful Coat

Materials

- 4 differently colored rolls of crepe paper, one set of 4 rolls for each team of 6 to 8 players

Do: Divide kids into groups of six to eight players. Select one child from each team to be Joseph.

Teams race to use all four rolls of their crepe paper, creating a colorful coat their Joseph.

Say: **Those colorful coats look great! If you weren't Joseph, were you kind of sad that you weren't picked to be Joseph?** (*Children respond.*) **You might have been a little bummed, but I doubt any of you were so mad that you wanted to kill someone!**

This is kind of what happened with Jacob's twelve sons.

A man named Jacob lived in Old Testament times. Jacob already had ten sons when his wife Rachel gave birth to a son they named Joseph. And Jacob loved Joseph more than his other sons. It was obvious to the other sons that Joseph was the favorite. Jacob had even given Joseph a special gift that no one else received, a beautifully colorful coat.

The brothers didn't just have a little bit of jealousy. They had a lot of jealousy. Their jealousy was so bad that they hated Joseph and planned to kill him!

Younger Child Option: Choose only one Joseph. Precut lengths of crepe paper for children to tape onto Joseph to make his colorful coat.

Bible Story

Joseph's Tough Times

Say: Joseph's brothers hated him because their father loved him more. It didn't help that God gave Joseph dreams that all of the brothers—and even their parents—would one day bow down before him.

Their jealousy moved to hatred. Their hatred almost became murder. Jacob sent Joseph to check on his ten older brothers, who were out caring for the family sheep.

Read: Genesis 37:18–22

Say: Later, some traders came traveling by. The brothers decided that it would be an even better idea if they profited from this instead. So, they sold their brother to the traders as a slave. He eventually became a slave in the house of a man named Potiphar.

But Potiphar's wife told a lie about Joseph, and though he didn't do anything wrong, he ended up being thrown in prison. He sat there for two years. Eventually, because God gave Joseph the ability to interpret dreams, Joseph made it out of prison.

Read: Genesis 41:14–40

Say: Pharaoh made Joseph the second in command, ruling Egypt. When Joseph's family ran out of food, the brothers came to Egypt to buy grain. They didn't recognize their brother. But Joseph recognized them. Joseph was able to move his entire family to Egypt, feed them, and keep them safe from the famine.

Joseph went from almost being murdered, to being sold as a slave, to being in prison even though he was innocent, to being the second in command of all of Egypt. Because of the bad things that happened to Joseph, he was in the right place to save lots of people during the famine. He was able to save his brothers!

Joseph and his brothers are the twelve tribes of Israel, which are God's chosen people, the Israelites. If Joseph wasn't treated badly, he wouldn't have been where God needed him to be to save his people.

Read: Genesis 50:19–21

Say: Joseph's brothers meant to harm him, but God turned it into good. **God can make bad things good!**

Interactive Storytelling Option: Choose volunteers to act out the story as you read it.

Pray: Pray that God will take any bad situations and use them for his good!

Object Lesson

Lemons into Lemonade

Materials

- Lemon
- Sharp knife (adult use only)
- Lemonade
- Plastic cups

Preparation: Cut lemon into slices and place them into a resealable plastic bag.

Say: **When Joseph's brothers threw him into a pit and sold him, do you think they wanted good things to happen to him?** *(Children respond.)* **No way! But good things did happen to him.**

There's an old saying about making lemonade out of lemons. *(Hold up lemon slices. Allow volunteers to taste lemon slices. Ask them to describe the taste of the lemon.)* **Lemons taste very sour. Raise your hand if you'd like to drink a glass full of lemon juice.** *(Children respond.)*

But when you add sugar and water, the not-so-good lemon juice becomes delicious lemonade. *(Pour and pass out cups of lemonade to kids.)*

Additional Activity Options

Gathering Grain Game

Materials

- Styrofoam packing peanuts
- Stopwatch or timer

Preparation: Place Styrofoam packing peanuts in the center of the playing area.

Do: Children divide into teams of four to six players.

Round 1: Feast—Teams race to collect as many Styrofoam packing peanuts, or "wheat," as they can in three minutes. They can only grab one peanut at a time.

Round 2: Famine—Before playing, remove half the Styrofoam packing peanuts. Scatter the rest around the room. Teams race to collect "wheat" for their team, but relay race. Only one player per team can collect "wheat" at a time.

Say: **In Egypt and the surrounding areas, the famine happened just like Pharaoh's dreams had said. Joseph, through God, warned Pharaoh that a seven-year famine would be coming. Seven years without food growing is a long time. But, because of God's warning and Joseph's being in charge, Egypt was able to store and save enough grain during the seven good years of harvest to keep the people fed during the seven years of famine.**

Joseph's brothers had no idea that their hateful actions would lead to Joseph becoming Pharaoh's second in command and saving many people from the famine—including them! They meant their actions for bad, but God used them for good. God can make bad things good!

Joseph's Coat Craft

Preparation: On sheets of card stock, photocopy Joseph's Coat Pattern, making one copy for each child plus extras.

Do: Children cut out coat pattern and then glue it to a sheet of construction paper. Children then glue textile scraps to the pattern, making a coat of many colors.

Say: Reuben, Judah, and the rest of Joseph's brothers tried to harm him with their hateful actions. But Joseph's story has a happy ending because God can make bad things good!

Materials

- Joseph's Coat Pattern, page 131
- Card stock
- Textile scraps (fabric, felt, ribbon, trim, etc.)
- Scissors
- Glue
- Construction paper

Thumbs Up Thumbs Down Bible Review

Say: Give a thumbs up if the answer to the question is true. Give a thumbs down if it is false. If the answer is false, explain what makes it false.

1. **Jacob loved all of his sons the same.** (False)
2. **Jacob had twelve sons.** (True)
3. **Jacob loved his wife Rachel the most.** (True)
4. **Joseph was the oldest child.** (False)
5. **The brothers didn't mind that Joseph was the favorite.** (False)
6. **Reuben talked the other brothers out of killing Joseph.** (True)
7. **Joseph was sold as a slave.** (True)
8. **Because he committed a crime, Joseph was thrown in prison.** (False)
9. **Joseph saved lots of people during the famine.** (True)
10. **God used Joseph's bad situations for his (God's) good.** (True)

Discussion Questions

1. **How did God use Joseph's situation for his good?**
2. **Are there any bad situations you are facing right now?**
3. **How can God use the bad situations you are in right now for his good?**

Romans 8:28 Toss

Materials

- Large sheet of paper on which you have printed Romans 8:28
- Soft ball

Do: Players sit in a circle. Toss the soft ball to one of the players and say the first word of Romans 8:28, "We." Player who catches the ball says the next word, "know." That player tosses the ball to another player who says the next word and so on until the verse has been completed. The last player to catch the ball leads the group to repeat the entire verse in a style of their choosing: singsong, slowly, in a high voice, in a low voice, etc. Continue play as time and interest allow.

Joseph's Coat Pattern

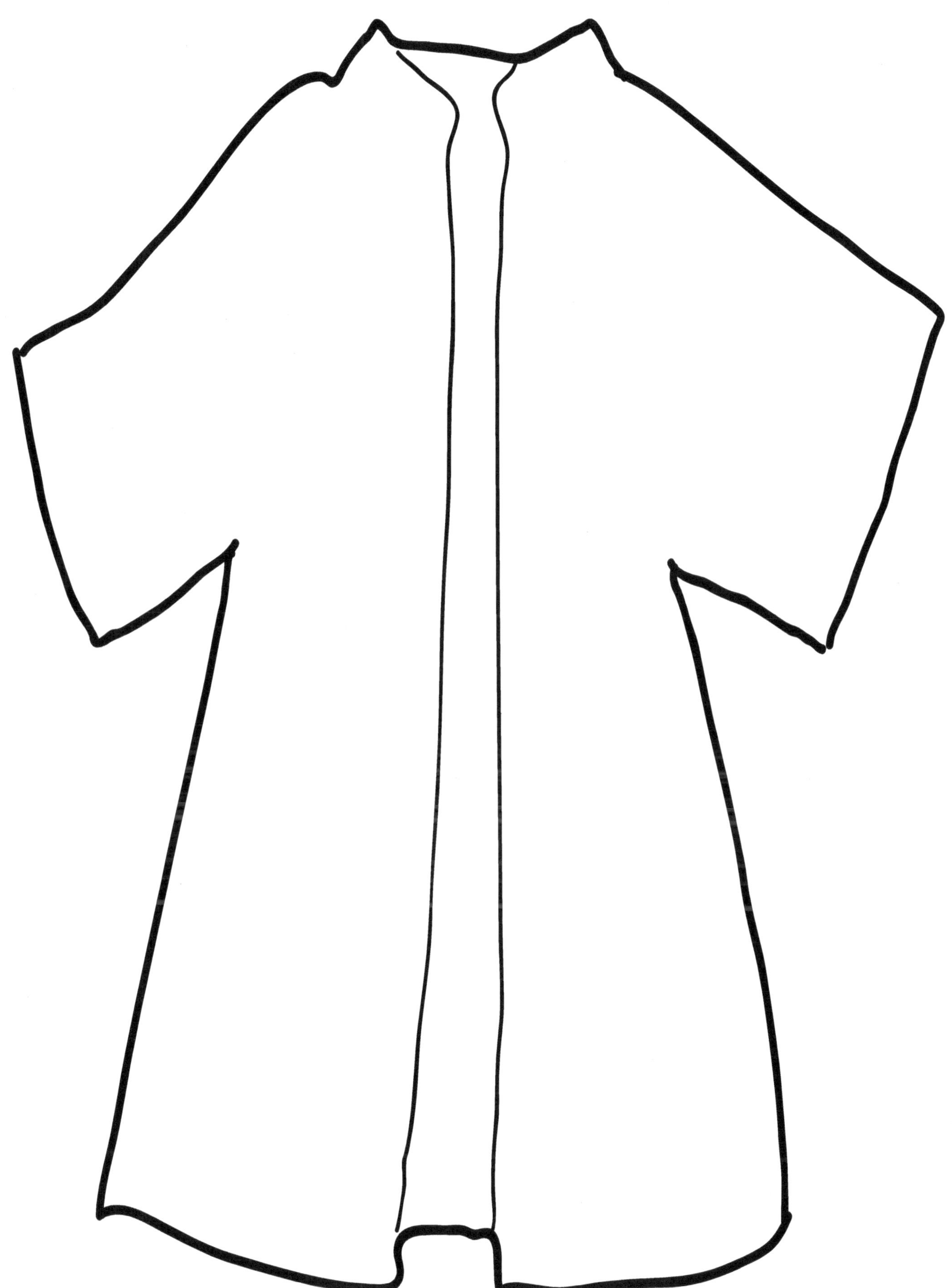

Chapter 26: Rebekah

Genesis 24

Be kind to each other, tenderhearted, forgiving one another, just as God through Christ has forgiven you. **EPHESIANS 4:32**

Overview

Say: **When we heard about Abraham, we learned about God's promise that Abraham would have more descendants than there were stars in the sky. Abraham was one hundred years old before his son Isaac was born. God then made the same promise to Isaac—that he would bless him with children as well.**

Before Isaac could have any children, he would need to have a wife. What are some of the things you would look for in someone to marry? *(Children respond.)* **I think everyone would agree that it would be good to marry someone who is kind. Kindness isn't always easy, but God helps us be kind.**

Opening Activity

Upside Down and Right-Side Up Cups

Do: Children divide into two teams. Give each team half of the cups. Tell one team their goal is to place all of the cups sitting up right. Tell the other team that their goal is to have all of the cups upside down.

After a few minutes, tell teams to freeze. Count the number of cups facing up and the number facing down. The team with the most cups facing their direction answers one of the questions beginning on page 135, recites the memory verse, or tells a sentence about the Bible story. Play additional rounds as time and interest allow.

Say: **We had fun playing our game with cups. But what do we usually do with cups?** *(Children respond.)* **We use cups to drink water and other beverages. Raise your hand if you can think of a time when you were really thirsty.** *(Children respond.)*

Today's Bible story is about a time when someone showed kindness to a man who was very thirsty. And it wasn't just a man who was thirsty!

Bible Story

Rebekah Is Kind

Say: Who remembers how old Abraham was when Isaac was born? (*Children respond.*) Abraham was one hundred years old when Isaac was born. He was even older when Isaac was old enough to get married. Abraham must have felt very anxious for Isaac to get married and have children. Abraham must have felt anxious to meet Isaac's children.

As anxious as Abraham may have been to have grandchildren, he wanted Isaac to marry the right young lady. Abraham asked his most trusted servant, a man name Eliezer, to do a very important job.

Read: Genesis 24:3–4

Say: The Canaanite people worship many gods instead of the one true God we worship. Abraham knew how important it is to have a spouse who believes in the one true God.

Eliezer was worried about something, "What if I can't find a young woman who's willing to come here? Should I bring Isaac there to live?"

Abraham quickly said no. "God promised to give this land to my children and my children's children. God will provide the right woman for Isaac. Whatever happens, my son is not to leave here to go there." Eliezer promised to obey everything Abraham had told him.

Eliezer prepared for his journey. He packed expensive gifts on to ten camels. In Bible times, it was customary for the family of the groom to give gifts to the family of the woman he was going to marry. Eliezer was prepared to find just the right woman who would be a good wife for Isaac.

Eliezer traveled to a town where Abraham's brother Nahor lived. He settled down near the town well. He must have been very thirsty after his long trip through the desert. But he had something even more important on his mind.

Eliezer must have been worried about choosing the right woman for Isaac. How could he know for sure which woman was the right woman? What would you do if you were Eliezer? (*Children respond.*) Eliezer did the right thing any time we have a decision to make. He prayed.

Read: Genesis 24:12–14

Say: Even before he had finished praying, a beautiful young woman came to the well. She had a jug with her to collect water from the well. Eliezer ran up to her, "Please, miss, may I have some water?" What do you think she said? (*Children respond.*)

The young woman's name was Rebekah, and she not only agreed to give Eliezer some water, but she then offered to give water to all ten of the camels! Wow! It was exactly what Eliezer had asked of God!

It must have been a big, hard job to give water to all those camels. It was Rebekah's kindness that convinced Eliezer that she was the woman to marry Isaac.

Read: Genesis 24:24–26

Say: When they got to Rebekah's family home, Eliezer explained who he was and the reason he had come all that way. He explained that Abraham's son Isaac needed a wife from a good family that believed in the one true God. He told them how he had asked God to send the right woman to him. He then explained that it was Rebekah's kindness that convinced him Rebekah was the right wife for Isaac. Then, he asked if they were willing to let Rebekah leave home and come with him. What do you think Rebekah's family said to all of that? *(Children respond.)*

Say: **Rebekah's family trusted that God would take care of Rebekah. They agreed Rebekah could go, but they asked Rebekah first. Rebekah must have trusted God with her whole heart. She agreed to go with Eliezer and marry Isaac. Eliezer gave Rebekah's family the presents he had brought with him.**

Just like Rebekah, every day we will have opportunities to be kind to others. When we are kind, it might require we do something very difficult. But if it's something God wants us to do, God helps us be kind.

Pray: Thank God for helping us to be kind to others and for the best gift of all, salvation through Jesus. Ask children interested in learning more about how to become a member of God's family to speak with you or another adult leader or helper.

Object Lesson

Gift Giving

Materials

- Wrapped gift box with enough treats inside for each child to have one

Say: **When Eliezer left to find a wife for Isaac, he took gifts with him. He gave these gifts to Rebekah and her family. It was his way of saying thanks for Rebekah's kindness and obedience to God in agreeing to become Isaac's wife.**

I have a gift here. (Hold up box.) **When are some times people have given you a gift?** *(Children respond.)*

Sometimes, like with Eliezer's gifts, someone might give us a gift in response to something kind we have done. But was Rebekah kind because she wanted a gift? *(Children respond.)* **No! Rebekah didn't even know about the gifts! It wouldn't really be kindness if Rebekah did it to get something in return. Then, she'd just be getting paid for the job she did.**

When someone gives us a gift at our birthday or Christmas, what did we do to deserve the gift? *(Children respond.)* **Nothing, right? Kindness is something we do when we don't expect anything in return. For that reason, it sometimes might be difficult to show kindness. But all the time, every day, God helps us be kind.** (Open up the gift box and give each child a treat.)

Additional Activity Options

Bouncing Ball

Materials

- Rubber ball or tennis ball

Do: Players stand in a circle, bouncing the ball to each other. At your signal, players stop. The player holding the ball chooses two volunteers to join them in answering one of the questions beginning on page 135, reciting the memory verse, or telling a sentence from the Bible story.

Say: **What are some ways you have shown kindness this week?** *(Children respond.)* **Kindness isn't always about doing nice things for people. It also is about an attitude we can show to others. By helping us have the right attitudes, God helps us be kind.**

Thank You Cards

Do: Children fold a sheet of paper in half to make a card. On the inside of the card, children write a thank you note to God, thanking him for all of the blessings he gives them. Children decorate the front of the card.

Say: **God helps us be kind! Jacob was blessed with the big promise that God had made to Isaac and Abraham. Maybe God hasn't given you a big blessing like he gave Jacob, but he blesses you every day—because he loves you. Even if life seems rough or not-so-great, there's always something that you can thank God for!**

Materials

- Sheets of colored paper
- Markers or crayons
- Decorative materials (stickers, glitter, ribbon, etc.)

Pick-a-Side Bible Review

Preparation: Use masking tape, rope, or clothesline to make a line down the center of the playing area.

Do: Play begins with children standing along the rope or clothesline.

Materials

- Masking tape, rope, or clothesline

Say: **As I read each statement, if you believe the statement is true, jump to the right side of the line. If you believe the statement is false, jump to the left side.**

1. **God promised Abraham to bless him with many descendants.** (True)
2. **Abraham's son was Jacob.** (False)
3. **Isaac and his wife Rebekah had twin sons.** (True)
4. **Isaac's twin sons were identical.** (False)
5. **Jacob was older.** (False)
6. **God told Rebekah that the two sons would always be against each other.** (True)
7. **Jacob sold Esau a bowl of stew for his birthright.** (True)
8. **Rebekah didn't realize that she was helping Jacob trick his father.** (False)
9. **Jacob wore goat skin to help him be hairy like Esau.** (True)
10. **Isaac blessed Esau.** (False)

Discussion Questions

1. **Did Abraham live to see God's big promise to him fulfilled?**
2. **Why did God bless Jacob and not Esau?**
3. **Does God's blessings mean that nothing bad will ever happen to you?**

- Camel Patterns, p. 136
- White card stock
- Markers or crayons
- Scissors
- Hole punches
- Paper fasteners, 2 per child
- Spring-type clothespins, 2 per child

Camel Craft

Say: **Let's make a camel craft to remind us of our Bible story and that God helps us be kind!**

Preparation: On card stock, photocopy Camel Patterns, making one copy for every two children. Cut to separate the sets of patterns.

Do: Children color patterns, cut out, and punch holes on the Xs. Using paper fasteners, the head and tail are connected to the camel's body. Clip spring-type clothespins to the body to form legs.

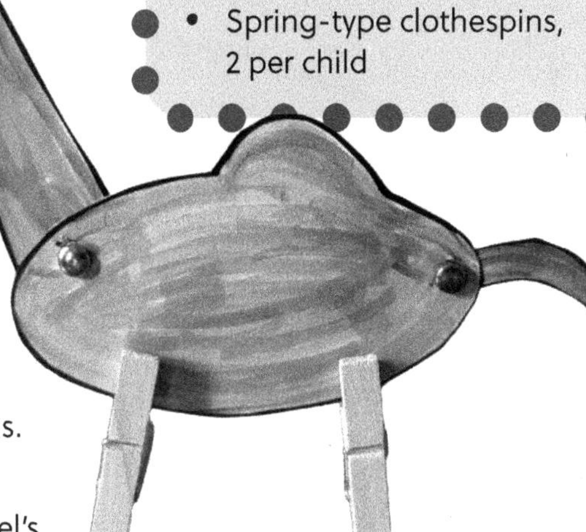

Camel Craft Patterns

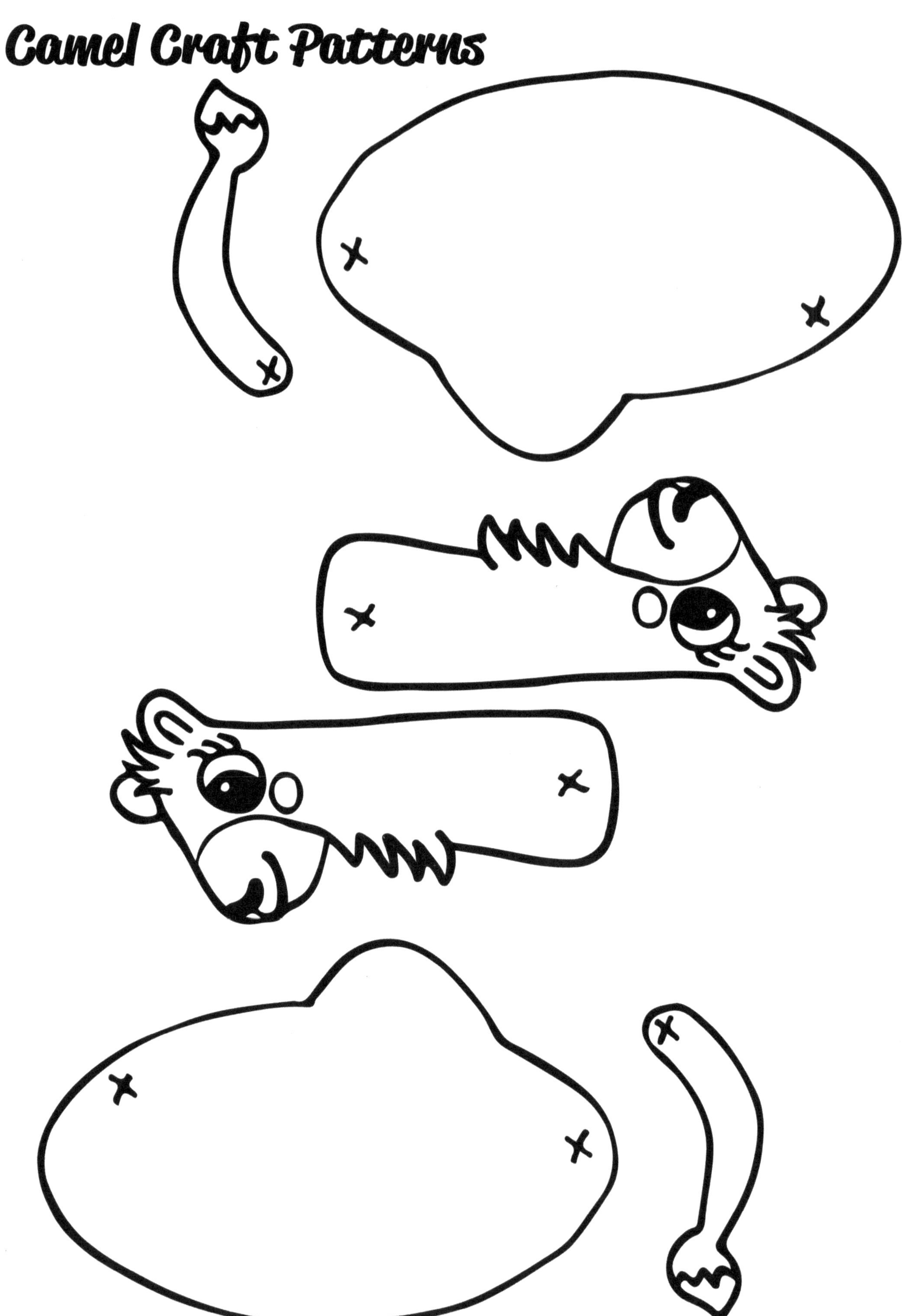

Chapter 27: Pharaoh

Genesis 41

Listen carefully to the voice of the LORD your God and do what is right in his sight. **EXODUS 15:26**

Overview

Say: **God had made a promise to Abraham to make him into a mighty nation, but it hadn't happened yet. God never told Abraham that his promise would be fulfilled right away. God hadn't forgotten though; he was busy getting everything ready and setting things into motion.**

Abraham's grandson Jacob had twelve sons, and their families would become the twelve nations of Israel. But before this nation—God's chosen people—could be in the new land God promised for them, God had to free them from slavery in Egypt.

Egypt wasn't a land that followed God. The Egyptians worshiped many false gods, such as Ra the sun god. Even though Pharaoh didn't follow him, God was about to use Pharaoh to help his chosen people.

With the help of Joseph, Pharaoh would be a part of God's plan. As we learn from today's lesson, we can see how it's important to listen to God's Word.

Opening Activity

Are You Listening?

Materials

- 2 distinctly different sounding objects (cowbell, squeaky toy, whistle, tambourine, rhythm sticks, etc.)

Do: Demonstrate the sounds for the children and lead them to practice the following motions:

- Every time they hear the (cowbell), they clap their hands one time.
- Every time they hear the (squeaky toy), they must stomp their feet.

Play the sounds several times, quickly, and in different orders. Children listen carefully to each sound and make the correct motion.

Say: **Was it easy or hard to make the correct motion? What did you do to know which motion to make?** (Listen carefully.)

Well, the same is true about everyday things. If we are listening, we can hear God telling us how to live the very best life. We live in a time where we can open up our Bibles and read God's Word for ourselves. In the Bible, he tells us what he wants us to do. These are things like putting God first and obeying our parents and others who care for us. Sadly, the people living in Bible times didn't have God's written Word to read. God spoke to them in different ways—God still speaks to us in these other ways, too!

For instance, God spoke to the pharaoh of Egypt through a dream. At first, Pharaoh didn't realize it was a message from God, and he had no idea what the dream meant. But God sent someone to help him. **It's important to listen to God's Word.**

Younger Child Option: Give younger children extra time between sounds. If possible, have a leader guide them, showing the appropriate response.

Bible Story

Pharaoh's Dreams

Preparation: Photocopy Pharaoh's Dreams and cut pictures apart.

Materials

- Pharaoh's Dreams Pictures, page 141
- Scissors
- Objects showing ways we get food (fast-food containers, grocery bag, toy refrigerator or picture of a refrigerator, take-out restaurant menu, etc.)

Say: **The Pharaoh of Egypt had some weird dreams one night.**

Lesson Illustrations Ask a volunteer to represent each of the four pictures. Hand each volunteer one of the pictures. Volunteers act out the actions of the dream as you read the Scripture below.

Read: Genesis 41:1–7

Say: **When Pharaoh woke up from his crazy dreams, he was disturbed. Have you ever had a crazy dream?** *(Children respond.)* **Well, Pharaoh knew that his crazy dreams meant something, but none of his wise men or magicians could tell him what they meant. Then his cupbearer remembered a man he knew in prison (two years ago) who, with God's help, could interpret dreams, Joseph.**

Pharaoh had Joseph brought to him to tell him what his dreams meant. Before Pharaoh even told Joseph his dreams, Joseph told him that he couldn't tell him what the dreams meant—but God could. Joseph was faithful to give God the credit instead of pretending to have special powers. Joseph was merely speaking the words God gave him.

After Pharaoh told Joseph the dreams, Joseph told him that both dreams meant the same. God was revealing (to Pharaoh) what he was about to do.

When you are hungry, what do you do? *(Children respond.)* **When you want something to eat, maybe your parents get you some of your favorite fast food as a treat.** *(Hold up fast-food containers.)* **Or maybe someone goes to the grocery store to make a delicious meal at home.** *(Hold up grocery bag.)* **Or you might just grab something out of the refrigerator.**

Note: If the objects you gathered differ from the ones suggested, adapt text to fit the objects you have.

Now imagine you were hungry, really hungry, and there was no food. You didn't have

bread or groceries at home. The fast-food joints have all closed down, and even the grocery stores were out of food. What would you do if there was no food? *(Children respond.)*

This having no food was exactly what God told Joseph would be happening in Egypt. For seven years, their food crops would be really, really good. But then the next seven years, the crops would be really, really bad. There would be a famine for seven years. Famine is when there is no food to eat.

When Joseph told Pharaoh the meaning of his crazy cow and wheat dreams, he also suggested that Pharaoh put a wise man in charge of collecting and storing extra food during those seven good years, so they don't run out of food during the bad years.

Pharaoh knew the exact right person for the job. Who do you guess Pharaoh chose? *(Children respond.)* **Joseph! Joseph was a prisoner no longer. He became Pharaoh's number one helper, in charge of storing food. Pharaoh was the only man in Egypt who had more power than Joseph. Because God revealed his plan for Egypt, Pharaoh and Joseph were able to work together to help the Egyptian people (and God's people) survive the famine!**

It's good that Pharaoh listened to God's word when Joseph told him. It's important to listen to God's Word every day, in everything we do.

Pray: Children spend time quietly before God, asking him to speak to them, and reveal his plan for their lives.

Object Lesson

Act It Out

Materials

- Scraps of paper
- Marker
- Container (hat, box, bin, paper bag, etc.

Preparation: On scraps of paper, print words or phrases for which children can act out a reaction. For example: *run, touchdown, ice cream, not it, fire, baseball, chores, winning, homework,* etc.

Do: Choose a volunteer to choose a paper from the container and act out how they would respond to that word. Remaining children guess the word. Child who guesses correctly gets a turn to choose a paper and act out a reaction. Continue as time and interest allow.

Enrichment Idea: If you have time, ask children to write their own words on pieces of scrap paper to play additional rounds of the game.

Say: **Words can have tremendous power. And nothing is more powerful than God! That's why it's important to listen to God's Word. What God has to tell us can have a POWERFUL impact on our lives. It can have a good impact if we listen and obey, and it can have a bad impact if we don't listen to and instead ignore God's Word.**

Additional Activity Options

Cows and Wheat Tag

Materials

- None

Do: Children divide into two teams and pick silly cow-themed team names. Teams will race to try and tag the other team (MOOOing all the way). Once tagged by the other team, the player sits down and waves arms in the air as if a stalk of wheat. The last team standing answers a question from page 140, recites the memory verse, or tells a sentence about the Bible story. Play additional rounds as time and interest allow.

Say: **What crazy cow dream did Pharaoh have?** (*Children respond.*) **Pharaoh dreamed that seven skinny cows came and ate up the seven healthy cows. But that wasn't just a too-much-pizza before bed dream or something crazy like that. This dream was God speaking to him, revealing his plan. What was God telling Pharaoh?** (*Children respond.*)

Because Pharaoh was willing to listen to God, Pharaoh was able to keep his people and Joseph's family safe during the famine. It's important to listen to God's Word.

Yummy Wheat Snack

Materials

- 3 medium bowls
- 3 serving spoons
- Yogurt
- Granola
- Berries (cut strawberries, blueberries, raspberries, etc.)
- Clear snack cups
- Spoons

Preparation: In separate medium bowls, place the yogurt, granola, and berries. Place a serving spoon in each bowl.

Do: In a clear snack cup, children layer yogurt, granola, and berries, and then enjoy their snack.

Allergy Alert: Children allergic to gluten skip the granola. Or, provide gluten-free granola, even though that's no longer a wheat product.

Say: **Pharaoh's dreams are a great reminder of how it's important to listen to God's Word. God wanted his people safe during the famine. So, he told Pharaoh what to do to keep them safe! Thankfully Pharaoh listened.**

God has a plan for our good, too. Just like Pharaoh, we need to remember it's important to listen to God's Word.

Fact Face-Off Bible Review

Do: Form two teams. Team members face off against each other, one at a time, answering the questions and earning points for their team.

1. **Who was Joseph's father?** (Jacob)
2. **Pharaoh dreamed about ____ fat cows grazing.** (Seven)
3. **What did the seven skinny cows do?** (They ate the fat cows.)
4. **What was in Pharaoh's second dream?** (Seven fat grains of wheat and seven skinny grains)
5. **Who suggested Pharaoh ask Joseph the meaning of his dream?** (The cupbearer)
6. **Who was able to interpret Pharaoh's dream?** (God told Joseph what it meant.)
7. **What did the seven fat cows/heads of grain represent?** (Seven good years of harvest)
8. **What did the seven skinny cows/heads of grain represent?** (Seven years of famine)
9. **What did Pharaoh do to Joseph after he interpreted his dreams?** (He made him second in command of Egypt.)
10. **How were God's people saved?** (Through the grain Joseph helped store before the famine)

Discussion Questions

1. **Why couldn't Pharaoh's magicians and wise men interpret his dream?**
2. **Could Joseph interpret Pharaoh's dream on his own? Why or why not?**
3. **How can God reveal his plans (for you) to you?**

Pharaoh's Dreams Pictures

Chapter 28: King Saul

1 Samuel 8–10

[God said to Jesus,] *"Your throne, O God, endures forever and ever. You rule with a scepter of justice."* **HEBREWS 1:8**

Big Idea

Overview

Say: **Living in Bible times was different when it came to laws. The people didn't get to vote on laws. Countries were ruled by kings. And these kings were constantly trying to fight for more power—or at least to keep what was already theirs.**

Some kings were good, and some were bad. Some cared about their people, while some only cared about power. Even the good kings, though, weren't truly good. That's why God didn't want to give his chosen people, the Israelites, a king. God wanted to be their king, their ruler, and their leader.

If God was your king, why would you want a human king instead? As the Israelites turned away from God, we learn why God wants to be our King.

Opening Activity

King for a Day

Do: Give children about five minutes to write down all of the new laws they would make if they were the king or queen ruling a country. When they are done, children cut a length of yarn or twine, roll their papers into scrolls, and tie the yarn or twine around the scroll. One at a time, children share with the group their rules.

Materials

- Paper
- Markers or crayons
- Variety of yarn or twine
- Scissors

Younger Child Option: Younger children draw pictures of their new laws.

Teaching Tip: If you have a large group, break into small groups to share rules.

Say: **If you were a king or queen ruling today, as much as you might want to have power, you couldn't just make whatever laws you wanted. Most countries, even those with kings and queens, don't allow their royals to rule with absolute authority. There's a reason for this.**

Kings used to be able to rule their country with absolute power. Whatever they wanted, they could do. If your king wanted to go to war with a neighboring country, you fought in the army, whether you wanted to or not. If the king wanted your money, your home, or even your kids, he could take them.

God's people, the Israelites, weren't ruled by a human king, though. God appointed judges and prophets to lead the people; God was their King. But the Israelites wanted a human king to lead them, just like the people in the countries around them.

Bible Story

Israel Wants a King

Materials

- Hat
- Anointing oil (available from your pastor, online, or at Christian bookstores) or essential oil of your choosing

Note: You will also use the hat in the Object Lesson and Leader from a Hat Game on page 144.

Say: **If you looked at everyone around you, and they were all wearing the same shoes, would you want those shoes as well?** *(Children respond.)*

What if everyone around you started doing something silly like wearing a bowl on their head, would you start doing that, too? *(Children respond.)*

Sadly, the people of Israel decided something similar. Israel wasn't ruled by a king, but all of the nations around them were. God was their king and leader, and he appointed judges—men and women that would help him lead the Israelites. I think God is the best possible leader! If you agree, wave your hands up in the air. *(Children respond.)*

Instead of appreciating God as their king, the people of Israel looked around them at all of the other countries being led by kings. They didn't want God to lead them anymore. They wanted a king.

Read: 1 Samuel 8:4–20

Say: **The prophet Samuel warned the Israelites that a human king wouldn't be good for them. They didn't care though. They wanted a king, just like everyone else, so God gave them a king. Samuel didn't think it was a good idea, but God knew it was him the people were rejecting.**

Who would be king, though? And how would they be picked? Israel didn't have a government that voted on things. *(Hold up hat.)* **Did Samuel just pick a name out of a hat, and that person got to be king?** *(Children respond.)*

Read: 1 Samuel 9

(Hold up anointing oil.) **Samuel anointed Saul with oil. Would you like to be anointed with oil?** *(Dab some oil on the foreheads of children who volunteer.)* **This anointing is a blessing. It would show the people that God picked Saul to be Israel's king.**

Later that day, Samuel gathered God's people together and said, "This is the man the Lord has chosen as your king. No one in all Israel is like him!"

All the people shouted, "Long live the king!" *(Lead children to say, "Long live the king!")*

At first, Saul was a good king that followed the Lord. But later, he let jealousy into his heart, and he turned away from God. He didn't lead God's people like he should—just like God warned Samuel (and the people). Saul wasn't a terrible king, but he wasn't as good of a king as God was. God will always be the best choice for leading your life. God wants to be our King.

Pray: Dear God, thank you for always giving us what we need to do the jobs you give us. Help us to always trust in you. In Jesus' name, amen.

Object Lesson

Hats, Hats, Hats

Materials

- Variety of hats, especially hats associated with jobs (chef, firefighter, sailor, police officer, baseball player, construction worker, cowboy, etc.), including a crown

Say: **I've brought in a bunch of hats that people might wear to do different jobs. Let's see if you can identify the type of job that goes with each hat.**

Do: Ask different volunteers to choose a hat to wear. The rest of the group guesses the type of job of someone who would wear that hat. Talk about why the hat might be useful to the person wearing the hat.

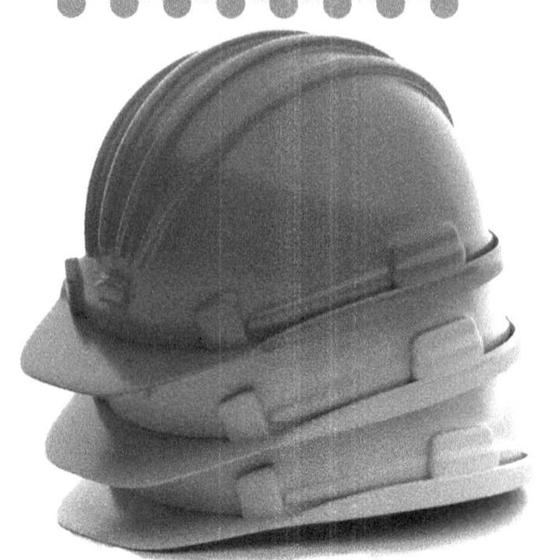

Say: **There are lots of jobs that have hats! Most kings and queens don't go around wearing crowns all the time. It's usually only for special occasions to show how important the king or queen is to the people of their country.**

How do you think Saul felt about suddenly becoming the king of Israel? What feelings might he have had? (*Children respond.*) **Saul must have felt surprised, happy, even a little scared. It would be a tough thing to suddenly become the king of a country that had never had an earthly king before. And it's not like Saul had gone to college to be a king.**

Whenever we feel we have a tough job to do and we're afraid we might not be able to do it, we can always rely on God to help us. God wants to be our King. With God as our King, he will give us the wisdom, strength, and courage that we need to do whatever it is he has called us to do.

Additional Activity Options

Leader from a Hat Game

Materials

- Slips of paper, one for each child
- Pencil or pen
- Hat (from Bible Story and Object Lesson)

Say: **While telling the Bible story, I joked about Samuel picking a leader for God's people from a hat. Well, I have a hat here, and we're going to be picking leaders for our game from that hat!**

Do: Children write their names on separate slips of paper and then place papers in a hat. Choose a slip from the hat. That person becomes the leader of a round of Simon Says. At the end of the round, choose another name from the hat. That child becomes the next game leader.

Say: **We had fun following different leaders in our game. God wants to be our King. That means for our whole lives we can have a leader who loves us and knows what is best for us. What a wonderful leader to follow every day!**

Tic-Tac-Trivia Bible Review

Materials

- Large sheet of paper
- Marker

Do: Draw a Tic-Tac-Toe grid on a large sheet of paper. Children divide into two teams, the *X*s and *O*s. Teams take turns answering one of the questions below. If they answer correctly, they write their *X*s or *O*s in a space on the grid. If they don't answer correctly, the other team has a chance to answer. Draw additional grids as needed.

1. **Who ruled Israel?** (God)
2. **God chose ____ and ______ to help him lead the people.** (Judges and Prophets)
3. **How were other countries led?** (By a king)
4. **What did Samuel warn the people about, when they asked for a king.** (All of the bad things about having a human king)
5. **Who were the Israelites really rejecting?** (God)
6. **How did Israel pick a king?** (God told Samuel [the prophet] who he was to anoint.)
7. **Who was Israel's first king?** (Saul)
8. **Why did God want to be Israel's king?** (Because he is the best leader and king there is)
9. **Jesus is known as the _______ of _______.** (King of kings)
10. **How long is Jesus' reign as king?** (Forever)

Discussion Questions

1. **If you were an Israelite, would you have wanted to have an earthly king or keep God as your king?**
2. **Could a human king do anything better than God could?**
3. **How can Jesus be King in your life, today?**

King vs. King

Materials

- Large sheets of paper
- Markers or crayons

Do: Lead class to compare the characteristics of a human king to Jesus the King.

- How would each act towards other people?
- What words would you use to describe them?
- Where did they live?
- What kinds of work did they do?

Say: **No human king could ever be as good a king as God is.**

- **A human king isn't all-knowing like God is.**
- **A human king isn't all-powerful like God is.**
- **A human king doesn't love you like God does.**
- **A human king is just that—human.**

But **God wants to be our King.** He wants to lead you and me and everyone and to guide us as only he can, forever and ever. Because God knows that's the best life anyone can have!

Amazing Crown Maze: Photocopy Amazing Crown Maze on page 146, making one copy for each child plus extras. Kids complete in class or take home.

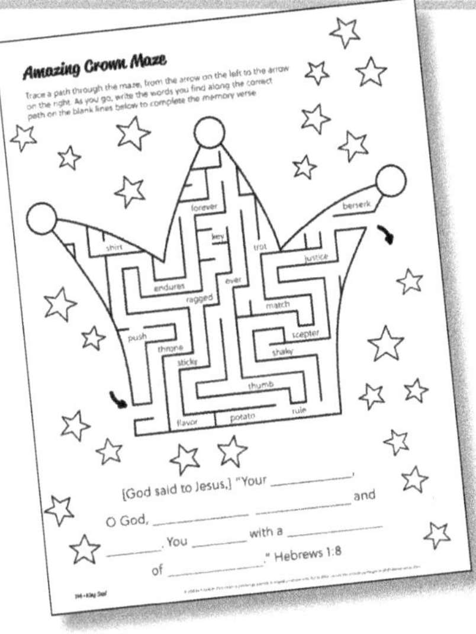

Amazing Crown Maze

Trace a path through the maze, from the arrow on the left to the arrow on the right. As you go, write the words you find along the correct path on the blank lines below to complete the memory verse.

forever
shirt
key
berserk
trot
justice
endures
ever
ragged
match
push
throne
scepter
sticky
shaky
thumb
flavor
potato
rule

[God said to Jesus,] "Your ____________,

O God, ______________ ______________ and

________. You ________ with a ______________

of ______________." Hebrews 1:8

Chapter 29: Ruth

Ruth

Let's not get tired of doing what is good. . . . Whenever we have the opportunity, we should do good to everyone—especially to those in the family of faith. GALATIANS 6:9–10

Overview

Say: **What would it be like if you had no place to live, no one to take care of you, and no way to get a job?** (*Children respond.*)

Females living in the times of the Judges in Israel were dependent on their male relatives to take care of them. Women couldn't have jobs to earn money. Their husbands, fathers, brothers, uncles, or male cousins took care of them.

Because of these rules, a woman named Ruth found herself in a very difficult situation. She and her mother-in-law, Naomi, were widows with no men to take care of them. Until Ruth met a kind man named Boaz.

Through the story of Ruth, we see how caring for others can bless them and others. Our lesson today reminds us that God is the ultimate redeemer!

Opening Activity

Pack Up and Move

Preparation: Use masking tape, rope, or clothesline to make a start line on one side of the playing area. On the opposite side of the playing area, for each team, place a stack of three cardboard boxes.

Do: Children divide into teams of four to six players and line up behind the start line. The first player on each team races to their team's stack of boxes, picks them up and returns to the team. That player hands them off to the next player who hurries to the finish line and leaves the stack of boxes there. Teams continue the relay until everyone has finished. The first team to complete the race recites the memory verse.

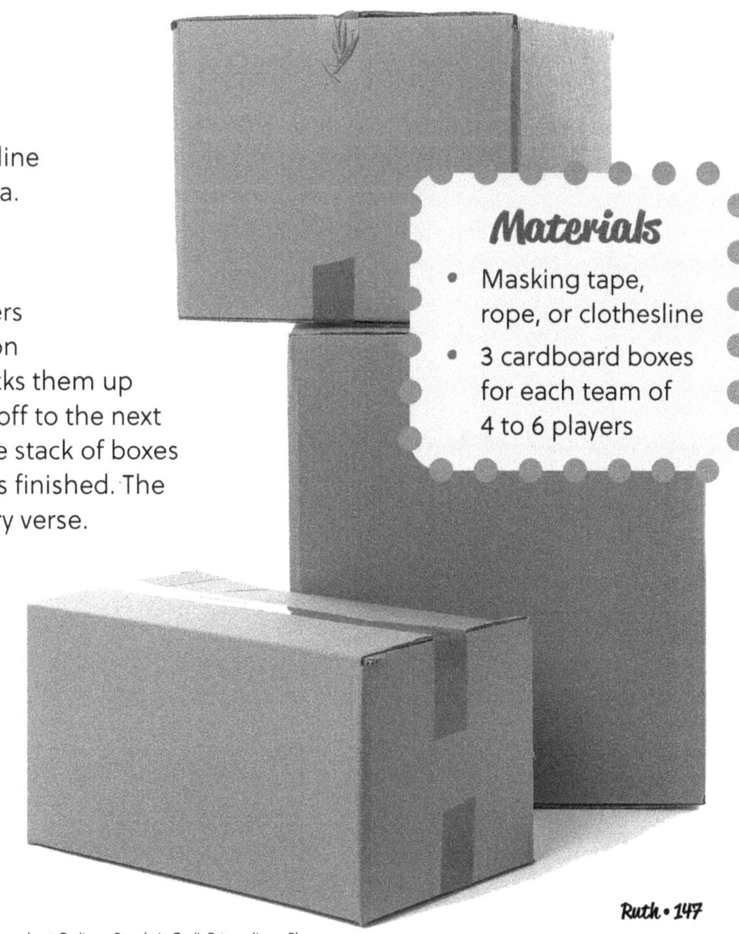

Materials

- Masking tape, rope, or clothesline
- 3 cardboard boxes for each team of 4 to 6 players

Say: **Have any of you ever moved into a new home before?** (*Children respond.*)

Maybe you had to move because of your parent's job. Or maybe you moved to be closer to family, like grandma and grandpa. In today's Bible story, we're going to hear about a very different reason someone had to move to a new home.

Bible Story

Ruth and Boaz

Say: In the days of the judges of Israel, there was a severe famine. A famine is when there is little or no food for people to eat. The famine was so bad that a man named Elimelech; his wife, Naomi; and their two sons packed up and moved to the land of Moab. While there, the two sons married Moabite women—Orpah and Ruth.

Eventually, Elimelech died. And then Naomi's two sons died as well! Naomi, Ruth, and Orpah had lost their husbands and had no one to take care of them. And they couldn't have jobs to care for themselves.

Naomi decided she should move back to Israel where her family was. She told Orpah and Ruth that they should stay in Moab with their families. Orpah decided to stay in Moab, but Ruth wanted to go with Naomi. Ruth told Naomi, "Don't ask me to leave you and turn back. Wherever you go, I will go; wherever you live, I will live. Your people will be my people, and your God will be my God" (Ruth 1:16).

Naomi was touched that Ruth would be so kind not to leave her on her own. So, Naomi and Ruth traveled to Israel. How do you think Ruth and Naomi were able to get food? *(Children respond.)*

Today, if a person is hungry and in need, they can visit a church or food bank and be given a donation of food to help them. They didn't have those in Bible times. But the people of Israel are God's people! And God had instructed them to be kind and care for their poor and widowed—people like Ruth and Naomi. To feed Naomi and herself, Ruth would go into farm fields and pick up grain that was left behind from the harvest. This was a traditional way for the Israelites to care for people in need.

Interactive Storytelling Option: Before class, cut several sheets of wheat-colored paper into strips and scatter them around the classroom. Ask a volunteer to pretend to be Ruth gleaning the fields. Volunteer searches for and gathers the scraps of paper, placing them in a basket.

Ruth was gathering the wheat in the field owned by a wealthy man named Boaz. When he saw Ruth gathering wheat in his field, how do you think he felt? Show me with your face what you think. Was Boaz happy, angry, or what? *(Children respond.)*

Read: Ruth 2:8–20

Say: Naomi was excited to hear about the kindness Boaz showed Ruth. But his kindness turned into more. Boaz became Ruth's "kinsman redeemer." This is a term the Israelites used to describe the men who took care of not just their own families, but their extended family, too. One of the jobs of a kinsman redeemer was taking care of the widowed women in their family. This is one of the reasons Boaz was so helpful to Ruth. But there was another way Boaz could help both Ruth and Naomi—through marriage.

Boaz married Ruth and took care of her and Naomi. Boaz and Ruth had a son named Obed who could care for Ruth after Boaz died. Ruth's story is an example of how **God is the ultimate redeemer!**

Pray: Praise Jesus the Redeemer for dying on the cross to save us from our sins.

Object Lesson

Redeemed

Preparation: Photocopy Treat Redemption Coupons and cut out, making one coupon for each child. Be sure to make extras for visitors.

Do: Pass out the coupons.

Say: **Show me how excited you are about having a coupon.** *(Lead children to respond by jumping up, waving hands in the air, cheering, etc.)* **I want you to take that coupon home and hang it up in your room. It's really special. And I hope it's something you will hang on to forever.** *(Continue talking about how special the coupon is until kids start asking what they get in return for their coupon.)*

Oh! You mean you actually want to redeem your coupon? Get something in exchange for your coupon? *(Children respond.)*

We talked today about Boaz being Ruth's "kinsman redeemer." What Boaz did for Ruth was just a small example of the way someone can provide what someone needs to survive. Jesus is the ultimate redeemer! Jesus' death on the cross redeemed us. He paid the price for the sins we do. He redeems and restores our relationship with God!

Do: Bring out container of treats. Each child exchanges their coupon for a treat.

Materials

- Treat Redemption Coupons, p. 151
- Variety of treats (individually wrapped candies or cookies, stickers, party favors, etc.)
- Container for treats (basket, bin, treasure chest, etc.

Say: **In the same way you didn't have to do anything to receive the coupon I gave you, there isn't anything you can do to earn redemption through Jesus. It's God's free gift to us. If you would like to know more about being redeemed by Jesus, please talk with me or any adult helper today before you go home.**

Additional Activity Options

Sneaky Sneaking Game

Materials

- Masking tape
- 50 sheets of paper

Preparation: Use masking tape to make start and finish lines on either end of the playing area.

Do: Everyone crumples sheets of paper into a ball and places them in the center of the playing area.

Select a player to be "It." The remaining children line up behind the start line.

Players try to sneak past "It," grab a paper ball, and make it to the finish line without getting tagged by "It." If tagged, players return the ball to the center, go back to the start line, and try again. If a player gets to the finish line with a paper ball, they drop the ball there and go back to try and get another.

After several minutes of play, stop the action and count the balls outside the finish line. If there are more balls outside the finish line than in the center, the players answer a question from page 150, or recite the memory verse. If there are more balls in the center, "It" tells or chooses another player to tell a sentence about the Bible story.

Optional: Increase the challenge by having two or three players be "It."

Say: **Was it easy to sneak a paper ball and get back without getting caught?** (*Children respond.*) **Imagine if you were really hungry, and you were trying to sneak food from someone's field. It would be hard to do that and not get caught.**

Ruth didn't have to sneak food from Boaz's field. He took care of her and Naomi by telling his men to drop extra grain for Ruth to pick up. God is the ultimate redeemer!

Beanbag Bible Review

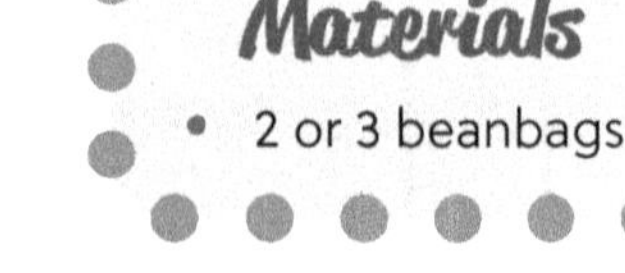

Materials

- 2 or 3 beanbags

Do: Children stand together. Choose a volunteer to stand with their back to the group a few feet away. Volunteer then tosses beanbags, one at a time, to the group. Children who catch the beanbags work together to answer one of the questions below.

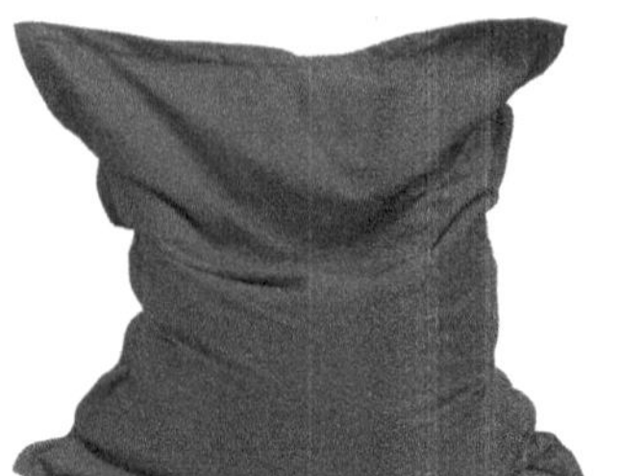

1. **What does it mean to redeem?** (To restore)
2. **Was Ruth from Israel?** (No. She was from Moab.)
3. **Why did Elimelech and Naomi move to Moab?** (The famine in Judah)
4. **What happened to the men in Naomi's family?** (They all died.)
5. **Who moved with Naomi back to Judah?** (Just Ruth)
6. **What was Ruth doing in Boaz's field?** (Gathering leftover grain from the harvest)
7. **How did Boaz show Ruth kindness?** (He told her to come to his field, to have a drink from his well, and he told the men working for him to not just treat her kindly, but to leave extra grain for her.)
8. **Boaz became Ruth's _______ Redeemer?** (Kinsman)
9. **How did Boaz redeem Ruth?** (By taking care of her. By marrying her.)
10. **How did Jesus redeem us?** (By dying on the cross)

Discussion Questions

1. **When is a time someone was kind to you?**
2. **What is something kind you can do for someone today?**
3. **What are some of the reasons someone would want to be redeemed by Jesus?**

Ruth and Jesus

Materials

- Bibles

Do: Groups of children look through the genealogy in Matthew 1 to see how Boaz and Ruth's marriage was important to Jesus' birth.

Say: **Boaz and Ruth's marriage was really important to Jesus' birth. Ruth was the great, great grandmother of David! Why is that important?** (*Children respond.*) **Jesus is from the family line of David! Because Boaz was the kinsman redeemer of Ruth, and Jesus came to Earth to be our Redeemer!**

Treat Redemption Coupons

FREE TREATS!
Exchange this coupon for the treat of your choice.

FREE TREATS!
Exchange this coupon for the treat of your choice.

FREE TREATS!
Exchange this coupon for the treat of your choice.

FREE TREATS!
Exchange this coupon for the treat of your choice.

FREE TREATS!
Exchange this coupon for the treat of your choice.

FREE TREATS!
Exchange this coupon for the treat of your choice.

FREE TREATS!
Exchange this coupon for the treat of your choice.

FREE TREATS!
Exchange this coupon for the treat of your choice.

FREE TREATS!
Exchange this coupon for the treat of your choice.

FREE TREATS!
Exchange this coupon for the treat of your choice.

Chapter 30: Samuel

1 Samuel 1–3

All Scripture is inspired by God and is useful to teach us what is true and to make us realize what is wrong in our lives. It corrects us when we are wrong and teaches us to do what is right. **2 TIMOTHY 3:16**

Overview

Say: **God speaks to his children in many different ways. Some of these are**

- **through the Holy Spirit**
- **through his Word, the Bible**
- **through other people**

The Old Testament prophet Samuel was someone that God used to speak his messages—both good and bad. Just as he used prophets like Samuel, he can use us. We can tell others God's Word!

Opening Activity

Team Telephone

Materials

- None

Say: **Who knows what God's prophets did?** (*Children respond.*) **The prophets were God's messengers. They tell others God's messages. Let's play a game like Telephone and tell others messages.**

Do: Children divide into teams of three to five players and line up. Have the first player from each team come to you and away from the team to receive a message. Players race back to their teams and whisper the message to the next player. Team members continue passing the message down the line.

When all the teams have finished, ask the last person in line for each team to tell the message they heard. The team with the message closest to the original message recites the memory verse.

Say: **Was it easy passing messages?** (*Children respond.*) **What do you think it would be like if you were God's special messenger, a prophet, and it was your job to give people God's messages. Would it be easy or difficult? Why?** (*Children respond.*) **What feelings might you have?** (*Children respond.*) **Even when it's not easy, we can tell others God's Word.**

Younger Child Option: Play the game Telephone in the usual way.

Bible Story

Samuel Was God's Messenger

Say: It's easy to tell people messages like "God loves you!" But what if God told you to tell someone that what they were doing was wrong and to stop? That would be really hard. Today's Bible story is about a kid who had to do just that!

Storytelling Involvement: As indicated in the story, ask children to give you a thumbs up or a thumbs down in response to a question.

Say: There was a lady named Hannah who loved the Lord. She and her husband had no children. How do you think Hannah felt about having no children. Was she happy? Give a thumbs up. If you think she was sad, give a thumbs down. *(Children respond.)* Hannah was very sad that she had no children.

One day, Hannah went to the Temple and prayed to God. She promised that if he would give her a son, she would give her son to work for the Lord. The priest, Eli, saw Hannah praying and told her that God would grant her prayer. And God did! He gave her a son she named Samuel.

Hannah loved Samuel and took care of him. When he was still a young boy, she honored her promise and brought him to Eli in the Temple. Because of Hannah's faithfulness, God blessed her with three more sons and two daughters. How do you think Hannah felt about all her children? *(Children respond with a thumbs up or down.)*

Read: 1 Samuel 1:26–28

Say: As Samuel grew, he helped Eli in the Temple. Every year, Hannah would bring him a new coat she'd made to remind him of her love. Eli took good care of Samuel and Samuel loved and honored God. He was a faithful helper to Eli. How do you think Samuel felt about being a helper to Eli? *(Children respond.)*

Eli had two sons, who were not loving and honoring God. They were taking advantage of the people who came to the Temple by taking more than their share of the sacrifices. They behaved selfishly and badly. Sadly, Eli knew his sons were doing wrong things, but Eli didn't stop them. How do you think God felt about Eli and his sons? *(Children respond with a thumbs up or down.)*

Read: 1 Samuel 3:2–10

Say: God told Samuel that bad things were going to happen as a result of Eli's sons doing bad things and Eli not stopping them. And then God told Samuel that he was the one who would have to tell Eli. How do you think Samuel felt about giving this bad news to Eli? *(Children respond with a thumbs up or down.)* Samuel must have been very worried about bringing such bad news to Eli.

But the next morning, even though it must have been very difficult, Samual obeyed God and told Eli everything God had said. How do you think Eli felt about Samuel's message from God? *(Children respond with a thumbs up or down.)* Eli accepted that God's message was right and fair.

When he grew up, Samuel was the leader of God's people and he was loved and respected by all the people of Israel. Even when it might have been difficult for him, Samuel continued to speak God's words to people all his life. Prophets are men who speak God's words to people and Samuel was one of God's greatest prophets. Like Samuel, **we can tell others God's Word!**

Pray: Ask God to help us tell others his Word, just like Samuel did.

Object Lesson

Spreading the Message

Preparation: Photocopy Paper Airplane Instructions, making one for each child plus extras.

Do: Hand a copy of Paper Airplane Instructions to each child. Children follow instructions to fold a sheet of paper into a paper airplane. After airplanes are folded, children try to fly their airplanes through the hula hoop.

Materials

- Paper Airplane Instructions, p. 156
- Hula hoop suspended from the ceiling or taped between two chairs
- Colored sheets of paper, one for each child.

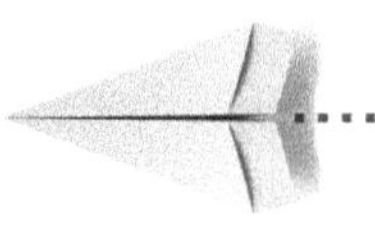

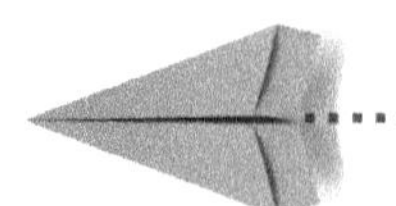

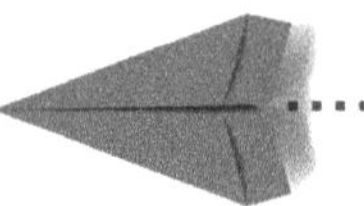

Say: Samuel clearly heard God give him messages, each time. God even woke Samuel up once by calling his name! But many of us have never heard God call out our names. How do we know what messages God wants us to speak to others? (*Children respond.*) **The Bible tells us!**

We kept tossing our airplanes to get them through the hoop. That was the goal. Well, the goal for us as members of God's family is to spread God's messages, the stories of what he has done for us, stories from the Bible, all over the world! We can tell others God's Word.

Additional Activity Options

Relay Ball Pass

Materials

- Playground ball (soccer ball, basketball, etc.)

Do: Children divide into two evenly numbered teams, make two lines, and compete in passing relay races. Before each round, hand the ball to the player at the front of the line and give them an action to do with the ball:

- Pass the ball over your head.
- Pass the ball between your legs.
- Pass the ball with your feet.

Children will have to take a few steps apart to complete the following motions:

- Roll the ball.
- Bounce the ball.
- Gently kick the ball.

At the end of the round, the first team to finish answers a question from page 155, recites the memory verse, or tells a sentence about the Bible story:

Say: No matter what message God had for him, Samuel was obedient and delivered it! Even if it was a difficult or sad message to deliver, Samuel was obedient. We need to be obedient and tell others God's Word, too!

Bible Verse Postcard

Materials

- Blank cards with envelopes or postcards
- Markers or crayons

Do: Children practice spreading God's Word by creating a Bible verse card to mail to someone.

Say: **Samuel delivered God's messages to people. We can tell others God's Word, too! Let's share his message by making a card for someone, telling them what God has done!**

Younger Child Option: Provide cards or postcards with Bible verses already printed on them or use stickers with Bible verses children can put on their cards. Faith that Sticks has a good variety of stickers, some with verses already on them like the John 3:16 stickers shown. The entire line of Faith that Sticks stickers is available at Tyndale.com.

Optional: Turn this into a mission project. Deliver cards to a homeless shelter or local nursing home.

Stand Up If It's True Bible Review

Say: **Stand up if the answer to the question is true but sit down if it is false. If the answer is false, explain what makes it false.**

1. **Samuel was a prophet.** (True)
2. **Samuel didn't start following God until he was older.** (False)
3. **God's message to Eli was a good one.** (False)
4. **Samuel obediently spoke God's messages—good or bad.** (True)
5. **Samuel picked who he wanted to replace Saul as king.** (False)
6. **When God spoke to Samuel, he listened.** (True)
7. **God only speaks to special people.** (False)
8. **God doesn't have messages for us to speak, now.** (False)
9. **Everyone is commanded to share the message of what God has done.** (True)
10. **God can use you to speak his message.** (True)

Discussion Questions

1. **Read Matthew 28:19–20.**
2. **What are we commanded to do?**
3. **How can you be obedient to that command now, while you are still a kid?**

Message Practice

Say: **Today we've been talking about how we can tell others God's Word. What are some messages you'd like to share with others?** (*Children respond.*) **Let's practice telling others God's Word!**

Do: Children form pairs or trios and practice telling someone about God and some of the great things he has done.

Paper Airplane Instructions

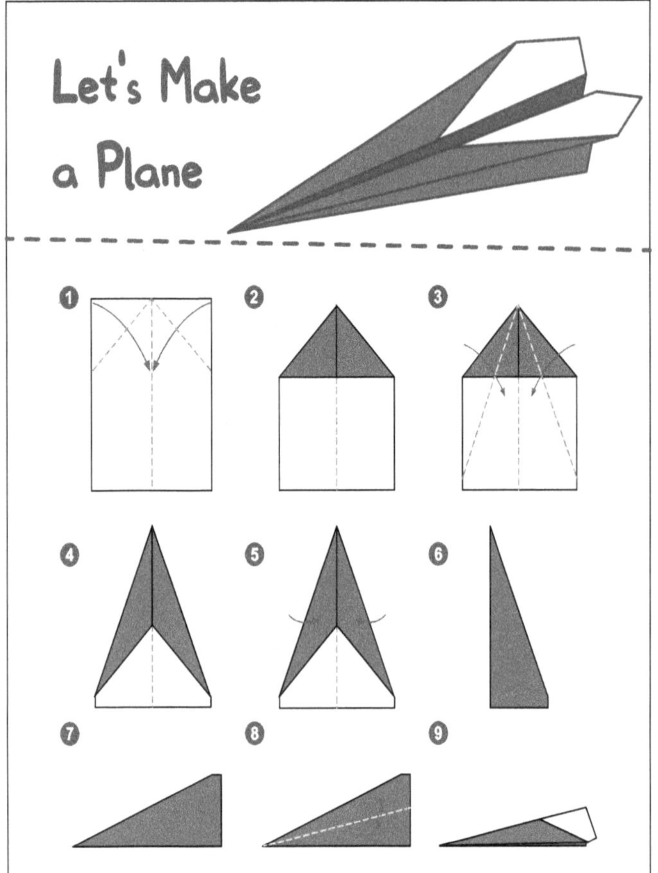

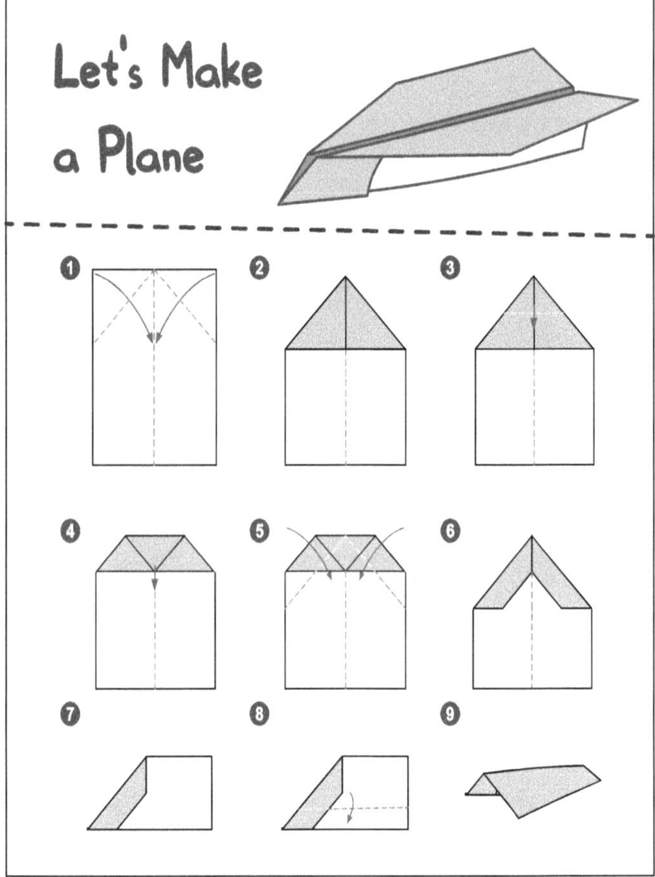

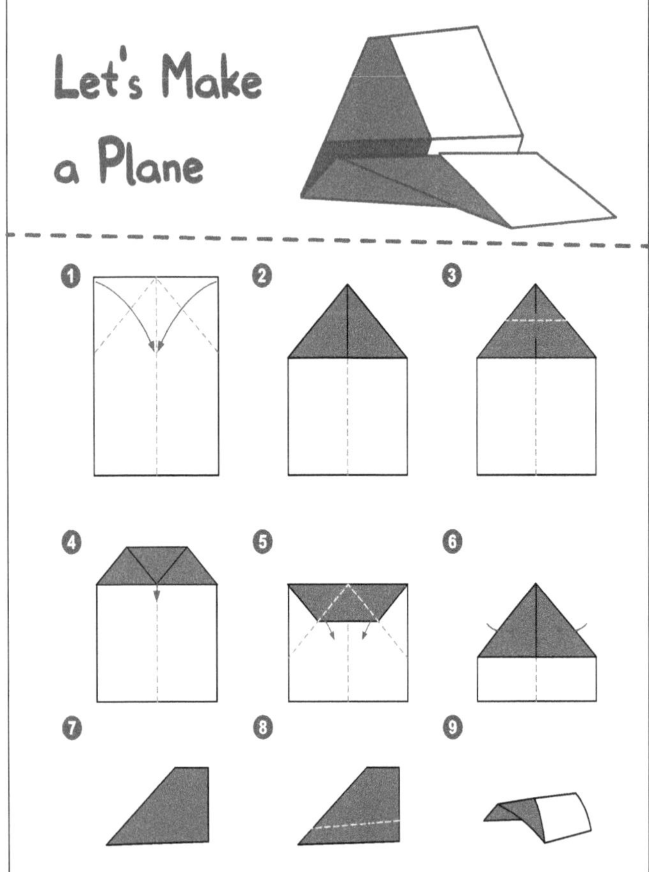

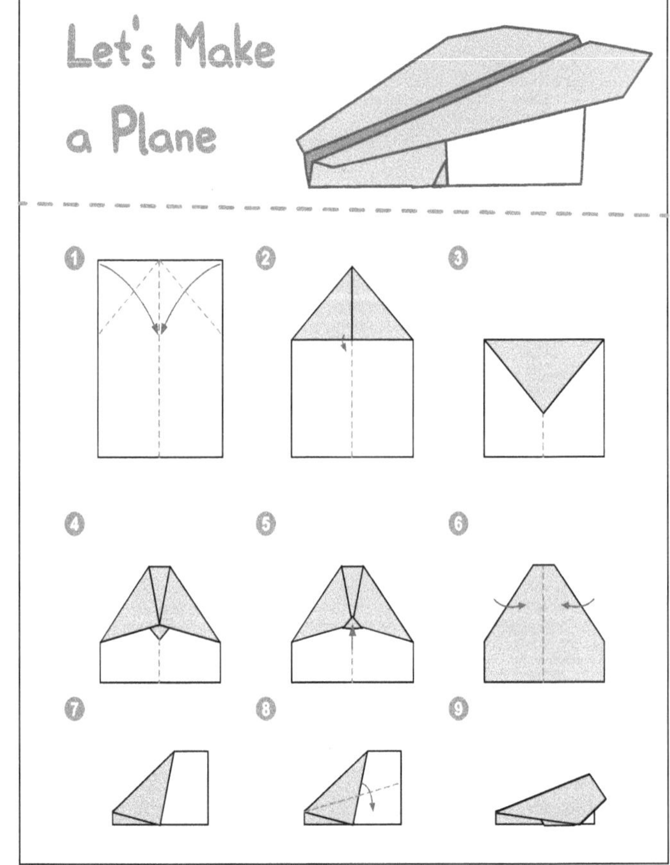

Chapter 31: Noah

Genesis 6:9—9:19

Make me walk along the path of your commands, for that is where my happiness is found. **PSALM 119:35**

Overview

Say: **Sin is a really big deal to God. He wants us to obey him and follow his laws. And because he is a perfect judge and always fair, he punishes sin. In the same way you have consequences when you do something wrong at home or at school, God provides consequences when we do something wrong. That is perfect justice!**

Today's Bible story is about a time when God passed judgment on the people of the world. The people were so wicked and evil that God sent a flood that killed everyone except for one obedient man named Noah and his family. God is a fair judge.

Opening Activity

Follow the Path Game

Materials

- Hula hoops

Do: Place hula hoops in the playing area in a path. Children travel the path by stepping or hopping from one hoop to another. When a player steps out of the hoops, they sit down.

When everyone has completed the path, adjust the path by making the hoops a bit farther apart or removing a hoop or two. Play a few rounds until it is extremely difficult to complete the path without stepping outside of the hoops.

Younger Child Option: Play follow the leader through the hoop path, having children move different ways each time: hopping, crawling, walking backwards, etc.

Say: **Was it difficult to stay in the path?** (*Children respond.*) **Staying in a hoop path may not have been super difficult at the beginning, but it got harder. How about staying in God's path? Is that difficult or easy?**

When we have the choice to tell the truth or lie, God wants us to choose to speak the truth. When we are faced with the choice to steal a candy bar or not, God wants us to choose not to steal.

Sometimes it's easy to make choices that follow him, but other times, it's more difficult. What about if it wasn't a candy bar, but a sandwich and you are feeling very hungry? (*Children respond.*) **Whether it is easy or difficult, God wants us to make the right choice and not sin. God is a fair judge.**

Bible Story

Noah and the Ark

Say: **In the Old Testament, we read that after the world was created, more and more people were born. Over time, the people forgot to love God. They forgot that the best life is one that follows God's Word. The people became more and more wicked. They lied, stole things, and even killed each other.**

God saw what was happening on Earth and was very sad.

There was one man who did love God. Noah obeyed God and talked with God. One day, God told Noah he had decided to wipe the earth clean and start over. God also told Noah about a very special job he had for him.

Read: Genesis 6:13–21

Say: **What would you think if God came to you and told you to build an ark, a very big boat?** *(Children respond.)* **What would you think if God told you that he was going to send a huge flood that would kill every living thing?** *(Children respond.)* **What would you think if God told you to take pairs of all the animals, put them on the ark, and live with them?** *(Children respond.)* **What do you think Noah must have said to God?** *(Children respond.)*

Read: Genesis 6:22

Say: **Noah didn't question God. He simply obeyed. He did everything God told him to do. Noah didn't question God about whether or not it was a good idea to flood the earth and wipe out every living thing. Noah knew God is a fair judge. He trusted that if God believed it was the right thing to do, then it was the right thing to do. Do you always find it that easy to obey God or your parents, teachers, coaches, or other authority figures?** *(Children respond.)*

Noah did everything God told him to do. And it could not have been easy! First of all, that was a very BIG job God gave him to do. It must have taken a very long time. What do you think Noah's friends and neighbors must have thought about him building a huge boat like that? *(Children respond.)* **They must have thought Noah was crazy!**

But they probably really wanted to get on that boat when the rain started and wouldn't stop! They probably wished they had also listened to God as the waters got higher and higher.

Noah and his family and all the animals were all safe on the big boat. When the rain stopped, and the water finally went away and Noah and his family—and the animals—were able to step onto dry ground, Noah built an altar and made a sacrifice to God, thanking God for keeping them safe.

Read: **Genesis 9:**12–15

Pray: Pray, thanking God that he is a fair and just judge and asking for his help to obey his commands.

Object Lesson

Just Judgments

Say: (*Hold up replica or illustration of the ark.*) **We've heard about the time when God looked around at the world and saw that the whole world except for Noah was full of wickedness. So, he judged the world and punished the people of Earth. How did God punish the world?** (*Children respond.*) **God sent a worldwide flood to destroy the wickedness.**

Romans 6:23 tells us that the punishment for our sin is death. That's the judgment for our wickedness, for not obeying him. But while God is a fair judge, he is also merciful. He loves us. And because of that love, (*Hold up cross.*) **God sent Jesus to die on the cross and take our punishment. When we believe that Jesus paid the price for our sins, and accept God's forgiveness for our sins, we can have God's gift of eternal life. Eternal life means that we can live with God and Jesus in heaven forever!**

If you would like to know more about becoming a member of God's family and receiving his gift of eternal life, talk with me or another adult helper.

Materials

- Replica or illustration of the ark
- Cross

Additional Activity Options

Secret Follow the Leader

Say: **We're going to play a game like Follow the Leader. But someone is going to be a guesser and try to guess who the leader is!**

Materials

- None

Do: Children stand in a circle. Name a child to be the Guesser. The Guesser closes their eyes. Touch the head of one of the children, making them the Leader.

Instruct Guesser to open their eyes. Call out a motion for everyone to do, such as swinging their arms. Instruct Leader to take a moment and then change the movement. Leader can change the movement more than once. When players notice the new movements, they copy it. Guesser tries to figure out who the leader is. When they think they know, Guesser says the name of the player they think is the Leader. If they are correct, Guesser chooses the next Guesser. Continue playing rounds as time and interest allow.

Say: **Was it always easy to figure out who was leading?** (*Children respond.*) **Was it always easy to follow when the motions changed?** (*Children respond.*)

In life, we don't always follow the Lord like we are supposed to. But God wants us to follow him and him alone—all the time!

Following the Lord Craft

Materials

- Paint
- Large sheets of construction paper
- Foam brushes
- Baby wipes
- Markers or crayons

Do: On their papers, children create a heart using their footprint (and paint). To make the heart, the heels will touch.

After the footprints have dried, children outline a heart around them with a marker and print the words of the memory verse.

Say: **Why did God send a flood?** (*Children respond.*) **Why did God save Noah and his family?** (*Children respond.*) **God is a fair judge.**

Your picture can remind you that God wants you to follow him, in his paths of righteousness.

Seat Switch Bible Review

Children sit in a circle. Leader or volunteer closes their eyes as children switch seats. When everyone is seated, without opening their eyes, leader or volunteer names a child. That child, plus the children seated on either side of them, answers one of the questions below. Repeat seat switching until each question is answered.

1. **Even though the rest of the world was wicked, who loved and obeyed God?** (Noah)
2. **Why did God send a worldwide flood?** (The world had become overcome with wickedness.)
3. **What are some of the ways Noah obeyed God?** (Built the big boat. Gathered the animals.)
4. **What are some ways kids your age can obey God?** (Help people in need. Be kind to others. Tell the truth.)
5. **What sign did God give us to remind us of his promise not to send another worldwide flood?** (Rainbows)
6. **What is the punishment for our sin?** (Death)
7. **How can our sins be forgiven?** (By accepting the gift of forgiveness Jesus made possible through his death and resurrection.)
8. **How did God show love and mercy for us, even though we sin?** (He sent Jesus to die on the cross to pay the penalty for our sin.)
9. **What does our verse say is the path to happiness?** (Obeying God. Following God's Word.)
10. **How can we know what God's commands are?** (Read the Bible. Ask for God's help.)

Discussion Questions

1. **How does it make you feel to know that Jesus had to die so that our sins can be forgiven?**
2. **Why was Jesus willing to die for us?**
3. **What makes God a fair judge?**

Mystery Word Puzzle

Materials

- Mystery Word Puzzle, page 161
- Markers or crayons

Preparation: Photocopy Mystery Word Puzzle, making one for each child plus extras.

Do: Children follow the instructions to complete the puzzle page.

Mystery Word Puzzle

Discover the Mystery Word by completing the numbered sentences. Write the missing letter of the word on the blank line. Then, write the letter you added on the blank line of the same number in the Mystery Word.

1. God told Noah to build an ___rk.
2. Noah was on the ark because it was ___aining.
3. God is a fa___r judge.
4. Noah ___uilt an altar to thank God.
5. God ___as pleased with the altar Noah built.
6. God made a promise to ___oah.
7. God gave Noah a sign ___f his promise.

The Mystery Word is ___ ___ ___ ___ ___ ___ ___

2 1 3 6 4 7 5

Draw a picture of the mystery word in the space below.

Chapter 32: Daniel

Daniel 6

He rescues and saves his people; he performs miraculous signs and wonders in the heavens and on earth. **DANIEL 6:27**

Overview

Say: **Over and over again, God's people, the Israelites, disobeyed God by worshiping false gods. God sent prophets to warn the people that they would be punished if they didn't turn back to following him. But the people sometimes didn't listen.**

As a result, their land was destroyed and the people were taken captive and made to live in Babylon—a foreign land that didn't follow the one true God.

Daniel was one of the people taken to Babylon. He was a strong young man, and he quickly worked his way up in leadership under the Babylonian kings, even though he was an Israelite. But not everyone liked that Daniel was successful. We will see though, that even living in a foreign land with people wanting to harm Daniel, God was in control.

Just like with Daniel, no matter what happens in our lives, God is in control!

Opening Activity

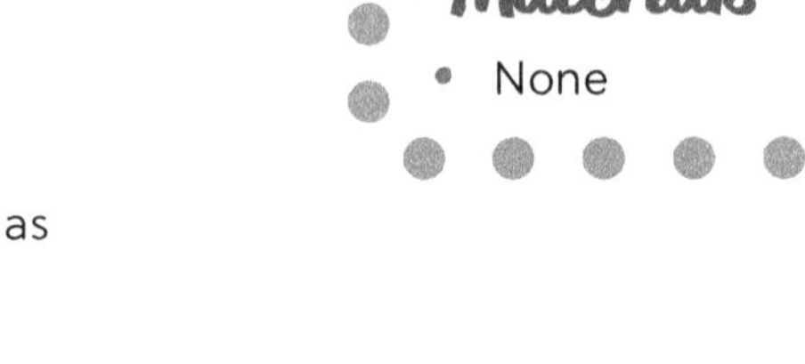

Ridiculous Rules Tag

Do: Play a game like Freeze Tag that includes some ridiculous rules. Select one or more players to be "It." Children begin playing game as usual. Every few moments, call out a ridiculous rule they must follow:

- Keep your right arm behind your back.
- Quack like a duck when you run.
- Hop like a bunny when standing still.
- Lay down when you are tagged.
- Tag with your elbow.

Players not following the rules sit out the rest of the rounds.

Say: **Was it easy to follow all of those ridiculous rules?** (*Children respond.*) **Imagine if all of a sudden there were new and ridiculous rules that you had to follow every day. You might not want to follow them, but if the punishment for breaking those rules was bad enough, you'd follow the rules, no matter how ridiculous they were.**

Today's Bible story is about a young man named Daniel who was expected to follow some ridiculous rules. What do you think Daniel did? *(Children respond.)* Let's find out!

Younger Child Option: Children pretend to be different animals while playing tag.

Bible Story

Daniel and the Lions

Say: **King Darius was the king of Babylon. To help him rule his large kingdom, it was divided into different areas and governors were put in charge. Then King Darius chose a few men to supervise those governors. One of the supervisors he chose was Daniel.**

Daniel wasn't a Babylonian. He was an Israelite who had been taken captive and then forced to live in Babylon. Daniel loved the one true God and sought to follow God. Three times every day, Daniel sat at his window and prayed to God. As a result, God blessed Daniel. Daniel worked harder and better than all of the other supervisors and governors. Because of this, King Darius put Daniel in charge of the whole kingdom.

Imagine you were one of the Babylonian supervisors or governors. How would you feel if someone not even from your kingdom showed you up by working harder and being chosen to lead instead of you? *(Children respond.)*

The other leaders were not happy with Daniel. But Daniel didn't do anything wrong, so there was nothing they could accuse him of to get him in trouble! So they came up with a plan.

Read: Daniel 6:6–9

Say: **King Darius signed the ridiculous law these men suggested. For thirty days, no one could pray to anyone but King Darius! And the punishment for disobeying was being thrown into the lions' den. What do you think God would say about a law like this?** *(Children respond.)*

Daniel knew about this new law. But he also knew God's law said not to worship any other god but the one true God. If Daniel disobeyed the king's new law, he would be thrown into the lions' den, but if he disobeyed God's law he could be punished by God. What do you think Daniel should do? *(Children respond.)*

Read: Daniel 6:10–13

How do you think King Darius felt? *(Children respond.)* **King Darius was so upset! He didn't want to punish Daniel, but there was nothing he could do to change the law. He liked Daniel and was sorry his law ended up punishing Daniel.**

Daniel was thrown into a den of lions. King Darius said, "May your God, whom you serve so faithfully, rescue you." Then a large stone was rolled over the opening to the lions' den. Make a face that shows how King Darius must have felt! *(Children respond.)* **King Darius was up all night worrying about Daniel.**

Imagine you were Daniel. How would you feel to be trapped in a den of lions? Make a face that shows how you'd feel! *(Children respond.)* Daniel must have been frightened, but remember he had tremendous faith in God. Daniel understood that **God is in control!** Even when things are really difficult and bad, **God is in control!**

The first thing the next morning, King Darius ran to the lions' den. He cried out to Daniel, "Daniel, servant of the living God! Was your God whom you serve so faithfully able to rescue you from the lions?" What do you think happened? *(Children respond.)*

Read: Daniel 6:21–27

Say: God knew what would happen when King Darius made that ridiculous law. Because **God is in control.** Not only would Daniel be safe, but Babylon would see who was the one true God. Everyone in Babylon would know **God is in control.**

Pray: Praise God for always being in control, all the time.

Materials

- Penny
- Drinking glass
- Pitcher of water
- Dinner plate

Object Lesson

Disappearing Penny

Say: When Daniel was thrown into the lions' den, things were looking pretty bad for him. Let's check out one reason we shouldn't always believe what our eyes tell us.

(Place penny on a table.) **Can you see the penny?** *(Children respond. Place drinking glass on the penny.)* **Can you STILL see the penny?** *(Children respond. Place dinner plate on the glass.)* **How about now?** *(Children respond. Remove plate, pour some water into the glass, and place dinner plate on the glass again.)* **How about now? Can you see the penny?** *(Children respond.)*

(After children look for the penny without touching the glass or plate, remove the dinner plate and instruct children to look down from the top of the glass. They will see that the penny is still there.) **The reason you couldn't see the penny with the plate on top of the glass is that you were forced to look through the sides of the glass. The water inside the glass causes light to bend and refract the image of the penny upwards not through the sides, making it seem as if the penny disappeared. But when you look straight down from the top, you can see the penny perfectly!**

Remember this the next time you feel afraid. Remember that it all depends on how you look at things. Daniel was safe in the lions' den because God is in control! No matter what scary things we might face, we can trust in God's love and power and know that God is in control.

Additional Activity Options

Materials

- Daniel Coloring Page, page 166
- Markers or crayons

Daniel Coloring Page

Preparation: Photocopy Daniel Coloring Page, making one for each child plus extras for visitors.

Do: Children complete Daniel Coloring Page according to the instructions.

Say: **Lions like to eat meat. So, when Daniel was locked up with them in their den, what was the most likely thing to happen?** (*Children respond.*) **The lions most likely would have attacked and eaten Daniel! But they didn't. God sent an angel to shut the mouths of those lions. God is in control, so Daniel was safe from those hungry lions.**

Lion Clip Craft

Preparation: On orange card stock, photocopy Heart Patterns, enlarging them 150 percent. On yellow card stock, photocopy Heart Patterns, shrinking them to 75 percent. Make one of each heart for each child.

Do: To make the lion's mane, children use scissors to fringe about one inch around the edge of an orange heart. Glue the yellow heart upside down to the center of the orange heart to make the lion's face. Using markers, draw eyes and a heart shaped nose on the lion's face.

Using a glue dot, glue the lion's head onto the clothespin.

Materials

- Heart Patterns, page 66
- Orange and yellow card stock
- Scissors
- Markers or crayons
- Clothespins
- Glue dots

Say: **How did God show that he was in control of Daniel's life?** (*Children respond.*) **God sent an angel to shut the lions' mouths!**

God was in control of the lions, and God is in control in our lives, too!

Optional: Use your hungry lion clip to secure a bag of chips or other snack. Or, glue a magnet to the back of the lion and place it where you will see it as a reminder that **God is in control**.

Stand Up If It's True Bible Review

Say: **Stand up if the answer to the question is true but sit down if it is false. If the answer is false, explain what makes it false.**

1. **God's people were happy to move to Babylon.** (False. They were exiles in Babylon.)
2. **The Israelites were living in Babylon because they were being punished for not following God.** (True)
3. **Daniel was the king in Babylon?** (False. Darius was the king.)
4. **The other supervisors and governors wanted Daniel to be rewarded for the good job he was doing?** (False. They were jealous that Daniel was put in charge over them and that he was so successful.)
5. **King Darius made a law that the people could only pray to him.** (True)
6. **Daniel obeyed the king's law.** (False. He still prayed to God three times a day.)
7. **The punishment for breaking the king's law was to be thrown in a den of lions.** (True)
8. **King Darius was glad Daniel had to go into the lions' den.** (False. He was worried about Daniel.)
9. **God sent an angel to shut the lions' mouths and Daniel was not harmed.** (True)
10. **King Darius made a new law that everyone should pray to Daniel.** (False. The new law said that everyone must fear and respect Daniel's God.)

Discussion Questions

1. **Did God know King Darius would be making a ridiculous rule?**
2. **Why did God shut the lions' mouths?**
3. **How does God show that he is in control of your life?**

Daniel Coloring Page

King Darius made a new law that declared everyone had to worship him. Daniel disobeyed the king by obeying God. Daniel prayed to God. As punishment, Daniel was thrown in the lions' den. God was faithful to Daniel and sent an angel to shut the lions' mouths.

Draw closed mouths and whiskers on the lions. Color the picture.

Chapter 33: The Israelites

Exodus 24, 32

The LORD says, "I will guide you along the best pathway for your life. I will advise you and watch over you." **PSALM 32:8**

Overview

Say: **God wants everyone in his family to obey his laws and to follow the best pathway for life. Sadly, sometimes we stray off of that path and mess up. We do wrong things. The Bible word for doing wrong things is *sin*.**

The Bible tells us that the Israelites were God's chosen people. As he led them out of slavery in Egypt and into the wilderness, they saw God do amazing things. God was with them, leading and guiding them, like he has never been with any other group of people. Yet from time to time, the Israelites would step off of God's path. They would make mistakes and God would have to correct them.

Just like he did with the Israelites, **God shows us the best path**, too!

Opening Activity

Reverse Four Corners Game

Do: Play a game like Four Corners. Select a child to be "It." "It" stands in the middle of the room and slowly counts to ten while the remaining players move to one of the room's four corners. When "It" reaches ten, without opening their eyes, "It" points to one of the corners. Players in the other three corners are out. Players in the correct corner recite the memory verse aloud.

"It" chooses another player to be the new "It" and another round is played. Continue as time and interest allow.

Say: **Was it easy to be in the right corner all of the time?** *(Children respond.)*

In life, it's not always easy to do the right thing all of the time. We know we are supposed to obey our parents when they tell us to clean our room, but maybe we roll our eyes and ignore them. We know that we should be kind to everyone, but sometimes we aren't.

Making the right choices and following God's path one hundred percent of the time isn't easy. But God shows us the best path, just like he did for the Israelites.

Bible Story

The 10 Commandments

Materials

- White board or large sheet of paper
- Dry-erase markers (if using a white board) or regular markers (if using large sheet of paper)

Say: The Israelites were God's chosen people. These are the people that he provided for, protected, and guided. God had a big plan for them and for us!

God wanted his chosen people to follow him and his laws. He instructed the Israelites in how to live the very best life. He even gave them ten special commandments to follow.

Let's see if we can name all ten of God's commandments. (*Print the numerals 1 to 10 down the left side of the white board or large sheet of paper. As children recite commandments, write them next to the appropriate number. When responses slow down, give children hints. Print any commandments that children are unable to name.*)

1. You must not have any other god but me.
2. You must not make for yourself an idol of any kind or an image of anything in the heavens or on the earth or in the sea.
3. You must not misuse the name of the Lord your God.
4. Remember to observe the Sabbath day by keeping it holy.
5. Honor your father and mother.
6. You must not murder.
7. You must not commit adultery.
8. You must not steal.
9. You must not testify falsely against your neighbor.
10. You must not covet.

Say: Which commandment do you think is the most important? (*Children respond.*) Because God said them, they are all important. The first commandment, though, is super important. We must not have any other god but God!

In order to give Moses the Ten Commandments, God had Moses climb up to the top of Mount Sinai. God spoke to Moses there and gave him the Ten Commandments, written on a stone tablet. But it wasn't a quick trip. Moses was up on the mountain for a long time . . . a really long time. He was up there for forty days and nights!

The Israelites who were waiting at the base of the mountain were getting restless.

Read: Exodus 32:1

Say: After everything that God had done to show the Israelites that he alone was God, they decided to make their own, fake and phony god to lead them.

Aaron, Moses' brother and helper in leading the people, agreed. He had the people bring him their gold earrings and melted them down. He formed the melted gold into the shape of a calf and the people worshiped it.

Can you imagine bowing down and worshiping some animal made from gold?

It can't hear you.
It can't answer your prayers.

It can't help you or lead you.
It can't do anything . . . because it's not real!

How do you think God reacted? Would he have been OK with this? (*Children respond.*) **No way! God was angry.**

More than once, God had told his people that they were to worship him alone! The Israelites were not following God's path to the best life. They had chosen to sin instead. As a result, God punished their disobedience. The Israelites were sorry for breaking God's law and went back to worshiping only him once again.

Pray: Praise God for showing us the best path for our lives. Ask for his help to always obey him.

Object Lesson

Spin Test

Materials

- Two marbles
- Dinner plate
- Dinner bowl

Do: Ask two volunteers to come forward. Hand one volunteer a marble and the dinner plate. Hand the other volunteer a marble and the dinner bowl. Challenge both volunteers to spin the marble around and around going as fast as they can. The volunteer with the dinner plate will likely have trouble with the marble falling off, whereas the volunteer with the bowl should have little trouble spinning the marble inside the bowl.

Say: **Looks like one of you is having an easier time than the other. Why is it easier to spin the marble inside the bowl than on the plate?** (*Children respond.*) **The sides of the bowl create a boundary for the marble that allows it to move freely, but it is still safe from falling.**

You can think of God's commands like the bowl. With his rules, God shows us the best path so that we can live the very best life. His rules help us not fall into sin, making a mess of everything.

Additional Activity Options

Wilderness Wandering Course

Materials

- Objects to create an obstacle course (hula hoops, ropes, wooden board or balance beam, carpet squares, play tunnels, etc.)

Preparation: Use objects you gathered to set up an obstacle course.

Do: Players form a line and play a game like Follow the Leader, working their way through the obstacle course. Once everyone has been through the course, choose a new leader to take them through the obstacle course.

Each time the group completes the course, they recite the memory verse, answer one of the questions on page 170, or tell a sentence about the Bible story. Repeat as time and interest allow.

Say: **Unfortunately, the golden calf incident wasn't the only time that the Israelites disobeyed God. They kept disobeying God and moving off the path he had for them. As punishment for their disobedience, God didn't let them into the land he promised them. They had to wander in the desert for forty years!**

God wants to guide us, and God shows us the best path.

Thumbs Up Thumbs Down Bible Review

Say: **Give a thumbs up if the answer to the question is true. Give a thumbs down if it is false. If the answer is false, explain what makes it false.**

1. **The Israelites were God's chosen people.** (True)
2. **The Israelites always followed God.** (False)
3. **The Israelites had never heard about God before Moses told them about him.** (False)
4. **God did amazing things rescuing the Israelites from slavery.** (True)
5. **Moses was only on Mount Sinai for a few hours.** (False)
6. **Only a handful of people made and worshiped the golden calf.** (False)
7. **Aaron was Moses' brother and helped lead the people.** (True)
8. **God was angry with the people's action to worship an idol.** (True)
9. **God just hopes that you will worship only him.** (False)
10. **We are to worship no other god but God.** (True)

Discussion Questions

1. **How does God guide us?**
2. **Why does God want us to only follow him?**
3. **Does God still punish us today?**

What's an Idol?

Say: **Most people today aren't going to bow down and worship a golden calf, but there are things that we make into idols in our life. Anything we put above God in our life becomes an idol.**

Materials

- Length of butcher paper
- Masking tape
- Markers or crayons

Preparation: Tape a length of butcher paper on a wall or table where children can reach it.

Do: Discuss with children some of the things that might come before God and become idols (school or work, sports, friends, social media, video games, substance abuse, etc.). On the sheet of butcher paper, children create a mural by writing or drawing pictures of things people put as idols in their lives.

Say: **God commands us to worship only him. Only God knows the path to our best possible life. God made us and he knows what's best for us. God shows us the best path.**

Code Breakers: Photocopy 10 Commandments Code on page 171, making one copy for each child plus extras. Kids complete in class or take home.

10 Commandments Code

Complete the commandments below by breaking the code. Some of the words are backwards. Print them in the correct order on the blank line.

Some of the commandments aren't commandments from God. Draw a line through them to remember to follow God's rules, not rules others might make up that break God's rules.

1. You must not have any other **dog** ______ but me.
2. You must not make for yourself an **lodi** ________ of any kind or an **egami** __________ of anything in the **snevaeh** ______________ or on the earth or in the sea.
3. You must not **esusim** ____________ the **eman** ________ of the Lord your God.
4. Remember to observe the **htabbaS** ______________ day by keeping it holy.
5. Honor your **rehtaf** ____________ and **rehtom** ____________.
6. You must not **redrum** ____________.
7. You must not commit **yretluda** ________________.
8. You must not **laets** __________.
9. You must not **yfitset** ______________ falsely against your **robhgien** _________________.
10. You must not **tevoc** __________.

Chapter 34: Baruch

Jeremiah 36

Heaven and earth will disappear, but my words will never disappear. **MATTHEW 24:35**

Overview

Say: **Do you have at least one Bible in your house?** *(Children respond.)* **Does your family have more than one Bible in your house?** *(Children respond.)*

It's easy to get a copy of the Bible today. Many people even have several Bibles in their homes. You can go to lots of stores and purchase a Bible or you can even get a free Bible from a hotel room! (See Optional text below.)

After the invention of the printing press in 1440, Bibles began to be mass produced and available everywhere. Before that, though, the Bible had to be handwritten. Scribes had the challenging job of copying the Bible by hand. And they had to be super careful not to make any mistakes.

The Bible scrolls were read out loud for people to hear. But not everyone wanted God's words to be heard. Some people tried to destroy the scrolls containing God's messages. But God's Word can't be destroyed!

Optional: Offer a free Bible to anyone in your class who says they do not have a Bible at home.

Opening Activity

Take Out the Trash Game

Preparation: Use masking tape, rope, or clothesline to make a line down the center of the playing area.

Do: Players divide into two teams and stand on opposite sides of the masking-tape line. Give each group half of the sheets of paper. Players crumple all the paper into balls.

Staying on their own side of the masking-tape line, players try to toss the paper balls onto the other team's side. After a few minutes, signal play to stop. Teams count the paper balls. The team with the fewest paper balls on their side of the line recites the memory verse.

Materials

- Masking tape, rope, or clothesline
- Sheets of paper, four or five for each player
- Trash cans or other containers

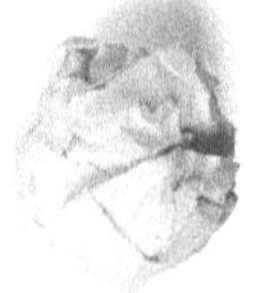

Say: **What a mess! On the count of three, I want everyone to work together to help clean up this mess. 1, 2, 3!** *(Children race to put all of the paper wads into the baskets or trash can.)*

When you have something you want to get rid of, like a used envelope or a picture you messed up drawing, you could just throw it away. It would get taken out with the trash, picked up in the garbage truck, compacted, and eventually decay in the landfill. It would never suddenly appear back in your room.

But what if when you tried to get rid of something, it did come back? *(Children respond.)* Let's hear a Bible story about a time something like that happened!

Bible Story

Baruch and the Scroll

Interactive Storytelling Option: Act out this Bible story by having volunteers pretend to be King Jehoiakim, Jeremiah, and Baruch, while a leader reads the account straight from the Bible.

Materials

- Scroll, made according to Book It! Craft (also used in Object Lesson)

Say: King Jehoiakim was the last king of Judah, and he did not follow the Lord. The Bible tells us that he did evil in the eyes of the Lord. Jeremiah was God's prophet, someone who speaks God's messages to people. Jeremiah had been going to the Temple, telling people God's words. Jeremiah told them that they had to stop doing wrong things. King Jehoiakim didn't like the things Jeremiah was saying. So he banned him from the Temple.

Jeremiah knew God's words were important and he knew God wanted him to tell others. Jeremiah must have wondered how he could tell others God's message if he couldn't go to the Temple. What do you think Jeremiah did next? *(Children respond.)*

God told Jeremiah to write his messages down. Jeremiah called for a man named Baruch, who was a scribe. What is a scribe? *(Children respond.)* Unlike today, when kids can go to schools to learn to read and write, in Bible times, very few people could read or write. Baruch had gone to school and knew how. So he made his living reading for people who couldn't read and writing for people who couldn't write. He was very good at writing.

Jeremiah said the words that God told him to Baruch. Baruch wrote what Jeremiah said on a piece of rolled parchment paper. We call these scrolls. *(Hold up the scroll.)* Day after day, and month after month, Baruch wrote God's words.

Then Jeremiah told Baruch, "I am a prisoner here and unable to go to the Temple. So you go to the Temple on the next day of fasting, and read the messages from the Lord that I have had you write on this scroll. Read them so the people who are there from all over Judah will hear them. Perhaps even yet they will turn from their evil ways and ask the Lord's forgiveness before it is too late."

Baruch did exactly what Jeremiah asked him. Some of the people heard it and told others. And they told others. And on and on it went until eventually some important people heard it and decided they needed to hear God's message for themselves. So they sent for Baruch and asked him to read it to them. Baruch did just as they asked.

Read: Jeremiah 36:16–20

King Jehoiakim decided he needed to hear the scroll for himself. He had one of his men, Jehudi, retrieve the scroll and read it to him. What do you think the king did? *(Children respond.)*

Read: Jeremiah 36:23–25

The king must have thought that everything was done. He'd burned the scroll, certainly that was the end of the matter. Do you think God was done with King Jehoiakim? *(Children respond.)* God doesn't forget that we've done wrong things unless we ask him for forgiveness. King Jehoiakim certainly was NOT sorry for the bad things he had done. So God wasn't finished with him.

God told Jeremiah and Baruch to write the words again. Once more, Baruch spent days, weeks, and months writing down the words Jeremiah told him from the Lord. You can read much of this second scroll in what is now the Bible book of Jeremiah. It also contained the prophecy of what would happen to King Jehoiakim. All of the prophecy came true. Jehoiakim finished his days in defeat because he would not listen to and obey the laws and words of God. He did not know that **God's Word can't be destroyed**!

Pray: Praise God for giving us the Bible.

Object Lesson

God's Word

Materials

- None

Do: Children identify the motion associated with a variety of hand signals.
For example, placing an index finger on your lips means to be quiet. Continue reviewing other hand signals for motions such "come here," "back up," "stop," "go that way," "time out," "OK," etc.

Say: These hand signals tell you what to do without a word being spoken. But the Bible, God's Word, came because God spoke to people like Jeremiah, who spoke the words to Baruch, who wrote them down. The Bible is a unique book, created by God, and miraculously protected for all these years. Even King Jehoiakim burning the Bible scroll couldn't destroy God's Word. **God's Word can't be destroyed**

Additional Activity Options

Spreading the Word Game

Preparation: At one end of the activity area, place six Bibles on a table or chair. Make another stack of Bibles next to the first. On the opposite side of the playing are, place another table or chairs.

Do: Players divide into two evenly numbered teams and form a line that spreads from one side of the playing area to the other. The first player on each team picks up a Bible, passes it to the next player. Players continue passing the Bible all the way to the end of the line. The last player places the Bible on the table or chair, and then runs to the front of the line. That player then picks up the second Bible and passes it down the line in the same manner.

The first team to pass all of their Bibles to the end of their line answers one of the questions beginning on page 175, recites the memory verse, or tells a sentence about the Bible story. Continue playing additional rounds as time and interest allow.

Say: King Jehoiakim didn't like what God's Word said, so he tried to destroy it. But **God's Word can't be destroyed.** God wants us to spread his Word and his message. That's why he calls us to tell people about him and spread his messages!

Book It! Craft

Materials

- About the Bible, page 176
- Brown crayons
- Ribbon or twine
- Scissors

Preparation: Photocopy About the Bible, making one copy for each child plus extras. Remove the paper from the brown crayons.

Do: Children crumple up their About the Bible page, smooth it out, and then crumple and smooth it a couple more times to age the paper. To add more to the effect, rub the sides of the crayons along the papers to highlight the creases.

Then, children roll the papers into a scroll, cut a length of ribbon or twine and tie it around their scrolls.

Say: **Our scrolls remind us what a special book the Bible is and that God's Word can't be destroyed. But the Bible is not a book that is supposed to just sit on a shelf forever. The Bible is meant to be read!**

Pick-a-Side Bible Review

Materials

- Masking tape, rope, or clothesline

Preparation: Use masking tape, rope, or clothesline to make a line down the center of the playing area.

Do: Play begins with children standing along the rope or clothesline.

Say: **As I read each statement, if you believe the statement is true, jump to the right side of the line. If you believe the statement is false, jump to the left side.**

1. **King Jehoiakim was a good king that loved the Lord.** (False)
2. **Jeremiah was a prophet of God.** (True)
3. **Jeremiah wrote whatever message he wanted.** (False)
4. **Baruch was a scribe that added his own words to the scroll.** (False)
5. **King Jehoiakim didn't like what God's Word said.** (True)
6. **When King Jehoiakim threw the pieces of the scroll into the fire, it was gone forever.** (False)
7. **Jeremiah and Baruch were so upset and didn't know what to do after the scroll was burned.** (False)
8. **God told Jeremiah to write his message again.** (True)
9. **God's Word can be destroyed.** (False)
10. **There is no other book like the Word of God!** (True)

Discussion Questions

1. Why can't God's Word be destroyed?
2. Why is the Bible important?
3. Why didn't King Jehoiakim like the message in Jeremiah's scroll?

About the Bible

The Bible is God inspired—humans wrote it, but they didn't just write what they wanted. God told them what to write.

The Bible was written over a span of thousands of years, yet there is one central theme running throughout. The whole Bible tells the story of God's plan of salvation for his children.

Around forty different men wrote the Bible, but there aren't inconsistencies between the books.

The Bible is the number one, all-time bestselling book. More copies of the Bible have been sold than of any other book.

The complete Bible has been translated into over 700 languages.

The oldest copies of the Bible still around (such as the Dead Sea Scrolls found in caves at the Dead Sea) match up with the Bible we read today.

There is no book like the Bible. It's the Word of God, and just like King Jehoiakim found out, **God's Word can't be destroyed**.

Chapter 35: Jesus' Disciples

Matthew 10; 25:31–46

[The King will say,] *"I tell you the truth, when you did it to one of the least of these my brothers and sisters, you were doing it to me!"* **MATTHEW 25:40**

Overview

Say: **When is the last time you helped God?** (*Children respond.*) **You might be wondering how you can help God, because he doesn't actually need our help. He is God and he can do anything; he doesn't need our help. But he lets us help him.**

Jesus even told his disciples exactly how we can help God. God wants you to help him!

Opening Activity

Materials

- 2 buckets for each team of four to six people
- Water
- Plastic cups, one per player
- Ruler
- Towels

Fill It Up! Game

Preparation: Pour an equal amount of water into one bucket for each team. Place the water-filled bucket on one side of the playing area and the second bucket on the opposite side.

Say: **When you are super thirsty, what do you like to drink?** (*Children respond.*) **Water is good for you when you are thirsty. Let's play a game with water!**

Do: Teams line up behind their bucket. Hand each player a cup. One at a time, players dip their cups into the water bucket, race to the other side, pour water into the empty bucket, and then return to team. Players tag the next player on their team and then go to the end of the line.

After a few minutes of play, signal players to stop. Measure the water in each bucket by placing the ruler inside the bucket and measuring the height of the water. The team with the most water in their bucket recites the memory verse. Use towels to clean up spills as needed.

Say: You all worked together to fill up your buckets with water! When we are thirsty, most of us don't have to go to a well or a river and fill up our cups. We can go to the sink to get water or maybe even grab a nice, cold bottle from the refrigerator.

But what if you didn't have water to drink? What if you were really thirsty and had nothing to drink? What would you do? (*Children respond.*) Jesus told his disciples if someone is thirsty, give them a drink!

Bible Story

The Disciples' Command

Say: Jesus chose his twelve disciples. They were the twelve men that traveled around with him for three years.

Read: Matthew 10:2–4

Say: Then, he gave the disciples the command to help others.

> Jesus sent out the twelve apostles with these instructions: "Don't go to the Gentiles or the Samaritans, but only to the people of Israel—God's lost sheep. Go and announce to them that the Kingdom of Heaven is near. Heal the sick, raise the dead, cure those with leprosy, and cast out demons. Give as freely as you have received! (Matthew 10:5–8)

And that's just what they did.

Read: Matthew 25:34–36

Say: Well, this Bible passage makes sense. If someone is hungry, you feed them. If someone is thirsty, you give them something to drink. But in this parable that Jesus is telling to his disciples, they say to the King, "but Lord, when did we see you hungry or thirsty or in prison?"

Jesus says, "I tell you the truth, when you did it to one of the least of these my brothers and sisters, you were doing it to me!"

When we help someone, it's like we are helping God. **God wants us to help him!**

Pray: Children ask God to show them how to help others.

Object Lesson

Doing It for Jesus

Do: Children work together in pairs to make their own ice cream.

- Mix the half-and-half, sugar, and vanilla extract together in a pitcher.
- Pour about a cup of the mixture in each child's sandwich bag.
- Fill a gallon-sized resealable plastic bag about half full of ice. Add ⅓ cup of salt.
- Place two sealed, sandwich bags in a large bag with salt and ice. Seal the large bag firmly.
- Working together, pairs shake the bags for 7–10 minutes.
- After the mixtures have changed into ice cream, spoon into bowls for children to eat and enjoy.

Materials

For every two children

- 1 cup half-and-half
- 2 tablespoons sugar
- ½ teaspoon vanilla extract
- 3 cups ice
- ⅓ cup rock salt or kosher salt
- Sandwich size zipper bag
- 1 gallon-sized resealable plastic bag for every two children
- Plastic spoons
- Plastic bowls
- Large pitcher

Allergy Alert: For children with lactose intolerance, perhaps have lactose-free ice cream to give them when the children are allowed to eat their ice cream. Either that or have a lactose-free recipe to use/make as a substitute.

Say: **You helped each other make a delicious treat just now! But none of you *NEEDED* ice cream. Jesus told his disciples to help others by meeting their physical needs: food, water, clothing, etc. Whenever the disciples helped someone, it was like a gift from God.**

God wants us to help him by helping others. When we help someone, that person learns about God, which was even more important than the food or other things they just received.

Additional Activity Options

Chain of Help Craft

Do: Discuss with children ways that they can help others. In their handprint, children write ways they can help others in the coming week.

Children cut construction paper into strips. On each strip, children write a way to help others. Children form a paper chain by taping strips into interlocking loops.

Materials

- Construction paper
- Scissors
- Markers and crayons
- Transparent tape

Say: **Matthew 25:40 tells us *"When you did it to one of the least of these my brothers and sisters, you were doing it to me."* God wants us to help him** by helping others!

Helper Friends

Do: Children in pairs or groups help each other build a tower out of cups.

Say: **God wants us to help him** by helping others!

Materials

- Plastic cups (100 per group)

Sign-a-Letter Bible Review

Do: Teach children the ASL signs for the letters A and B (see images below).

Say: **Choose one of two ways to complete the following statements, *A* or *B*. If you choose *A*, hold up the ASL sign for *A*. If you choose *B*, hold up the ASL sign for *B*.**

A

B

1. **Jesus had *A*—nine or *B*—twelve disciples.** (*B*—twelve)
2. **The disciple Simon was also called *A*—Peter or *B*—Paul.** (*A*—Peter)
3. **John's brother was *A*—Zebedee or *B*—James.** (*B*—James)
4. **Matthew was *A*—a tax collector or *B*—a fisherman.** (*A*—tax collector)
5. **Jesus told the disciples *A*—to help or *B*—not to help others.** (*A*—to help)
6. **Jesus and the disciples *A*—charged or *B*—did not charge money to heal the sick.** (*B*—did not charge)
7. ***A*—Only the disciples or *B*—all of Jesus' followers were supposed to help other people.** (*B*—all of Jesus' followers)
8. **We are supposed to *A*—help others and tell them about God or *B*—help others but not tell them about God.** (*A*—help others and tell them about God)
9. **When we help someone else, it's like *A*—we are or *B*—we are not helping God.** (*A*—we are)
10. **God wants us to help him, because *A*—he can't do it himself or *B*—it is good for us to help God by helping others.** (*B*—it is good for us)

Discussion Questions

1. **What is more important—giving someone food or water or telling them about Jesus?**
2. **What are some ways you can help others?**
3. **What are some things you could tell others about God?**

Matthew 25:40 Word Search

Find and circle the words of Matthew 25:40 in the word search below. Some words appear more than one in the verse, but they are only in the word-search puzzle once.

[The King will say,] *"I tell you the truth, when you did it to one of the least of these my brothers and sisters, you were doing it to me!"* MATTHEW 25:40

L Q B Q W P T E H H D T J Y T E L L
E Q B Q T Y Z E X W I A N D O I N G
A C D H B D S V O I T O Y C N E L B
S J H H Y B B I P L W M M L G L M M
T J D C T R U T H L Q U B M S M B E
W Y D T Y O Y K K S N R B V V A Z N
H F T H E T P Y T T C G G X O T S A
E X H X X H O B D E Y Y Y T M T A B
N B W E R E D I O J X O F Y Y H Y L
S I S T E R S S O I Z U M K F E B O
E F F R A S L A Z T D A U D Y W X T
Z W J U I I A I U A B P N D O B K N
T I M Z W U X O Z W U G R W O I P C
H H M E I U M Z A S Y F Q E Z U Z N
E B C J L X H L M W K I N G F B S Z
S U O R Y T D A X G D S F F Y E I D
E N N T E G A A L E S N P K E M X K
O S E B E K D I D V M I X W W U J O

Verse Word Search

Preparation: Photocopy Matthew 25:40 Word Search, making one copy for each child plus extras.

Do: Children complete puzzle page according to the instructions on the paper.

Say: **Do you have to have water to live?** (*Children respond.*) **Absolutely! Water is a need—something you have to have. That's why Jesus told his disciples—and us—to give water to the thirsty. God wants us to help him!**

Materials

- Matthew 25:40 Word Search
- Pencils

Matthew 25:40 Word Search

Find and circle the words of Matthew 25:40 in the word search below. Some words appear more than one in the verse, but they are only in the word-search puzzle once.

[The King will say,] ***"I tell you the truth, when you did it to one of the least of these my brothers and sisters, you were doing it to me!"*** **MATTHEW 25:40**

L Q B Q W P T E H H D T J Y T E L L

E Q B Q T Y Z E X W I A N D O I N G

A C D H B D S V O I T O Y C N E L B

S J H H Y B B I P L W M M L G L M M

T J D C T R U T H L Q U B M S M B E

W Y D T Y O Y K K S N R B V V A Z N

H F T H E T P Y T T C G G X O T S A

E X H X X H O B D E Y Y Y T M T A B

N B W E R E D I O J X O F Y Y H Y L

S I S T E R S S O I Z U M K F E B O

E F F R A S L A Z T D A U D Y W X T

Z W J U I I A I U A B P N D O B K N

T I M Z W U X O Z W U G R W O I P C

H H M E I U M Z A S Y F Q E Z U Z N

E B C J L X H L M W K I N G F B S Z

S U O R Y T D A X G D S F F Y E I D

E N N T E G A A L E S N P K E M X K

O S E B E K D I D V M I X W W U J O

Chapter 36: Judas Iscariot

John 13:1–30

Anyone who isn't with me opposes me, and anyone who isn't working with me is actually working against me. **MATTHEW 12:30**

Overview

Say: **God spoke the universe into existence. Jesus commanded the waves to be still and they obeyed. There is nothing that God cannot control, nothing that is out of his power.**

Though God is in control, he doesn't control us. God allows us to choose to follow him or not. In the Garden of Eden, Adam and Eve chose whether or not to obey God's command not to eat the fruit from the tree of the knowledge of good and evil. They choose to disobey. Jonah chose to disobey God's command to go to Nineveh. At least Noah obeyed God and built the ark!

God gives us the choice to follow him or not. Judas Iscariot, one of Jesus' twelve disciples, was given that choice as well. His story and his choices teach us that God lets us choose to follow him.

Opening Activity

Make a Choice

Materials

- 6 to 8 differently colored large hula hoops
- Children's worship music and player
- Individually wrapped candies

Preparation: Place the hula hoops several feet away from each other in the activity area.

Do: Children will walk around the room. When a leader calls "Make a choice" children must stand inside a colored hoop.

Each round, the leader will call out the color of one of the hoops to be the winner, which receives candy. The children in that hoop will receive candy. Play several rounds as time and interest—and your supply of candy—allow.

Say: **Did anyone choose the winning hoop every time?** (*Children respond.*) **Probably not. Without knowing which hoop I would choose, there was no way you could know which hoop to choose.**

In life, each and every day, we have choices. Some are easy choices, like "do I brush my teeth or have stinky breath today?" While some choices are harder like

when you break the rule about throwing balls in the house and you break a window. Do you tell the truth and get in trouble for throwing balls? Or do you lie and say you don't know how the window got broken?**

You don't have to guess what to do to follow God. What are some ways you can know how to follow God? (Read the Bible. Prayer. Talk with others who love and follow God.) **Will we follow God or not?**

Teaching Tip: Don't let anyone feel left out! Make sure each player gets at least one candy.

Bible Story

The Last Supper

Storytelling Option: Tell the Bible story by starting with a foot washing activity, having leaders wash the kids' feet or kids wash each other's feet.

Say: **One evening, Jesus sat down to eat with his twelve closest friends. It had been a whirlwind of a week. He had entered Jerusalem to shouts of praise, visited the Temple and had to throw out people who were there just to make money. He witnessed a poor widow give a generous gift to God of her last two pennies.**

Jesus knew what was going to be happening to him very soon. He had always known. But he wanted to teach and to show his disciples how to follow him.

Read: John 13:4–17

Say: **Jesus was giving his last-minute instructions to his friends before he died. Jesus knew he was going to die. And he knew that one of his closest friends was about to make a terrible, terrible choice.**

Read: John 13:18–30

Say: **Judas Iscariot, who had been Jesus' friend for the last three years, had made the choice to betray Jesus. Judas would leave that dinner and go to the Jewish leaders with an offer to betray Jesus. Even though Jesus had done nothing wrong, Judas's choice would lead to the arrest of Jesus, his being beaten and mistreated, and even his death.**

Judas made a bad choice. And it led to some terrible things for Jesus and for himself. But something good did come out of Judas's bad choice. Because Jesus died and rose again, we can be forgiven of our sins and become members of God's family. As members of God's family, God will help us make good choices. And the best choice is to follow him every day. God lets us choose to follow him.

Pray: Pray over the children, asking God to help them choose to follow him. Invite any children who would like to know more about becoming a member of God's family and following him every day to talk with you or another adult helper.

Object Lesson

Pick a Side

Materials

- Masking tape, rope, or clothesline

Preparation: Use masking tape, rope, or clothesline to make a line down the center of the playing area.

Do: Children line up on the line in the center of the playing area. When asked to choose between two things, children pick a side of the line to show which option they choose.

- Chocolate or vanilla?
- Soccer or swimming?
- Cake or ice cream?
- Summer or winter?
- Christmas or Easter?
- Hamburger or hot dogs?
- Brussels sprout or broccoli?
- Movies or books?
- Ocean or pool?

As you name each choice, point to the side of the rope children should jump to.

Say: **Sometimes we have to make choices. If someone offers you cake or ice cream but you can't have both, what do you choose?** (*Children respond.*) **If you choose cake, that doesn't necessarily mean that you don't like ice cream. You can still like both.**

There is one choice that we all must make for which you can't pick both sides. Scripture tells us in Matthew 12:30 that you are either on God's side or you are against him.

You can't be for God and against him at the same time. You have to choose. You have to choose if you will follow God or if you won't. There's no kinda, sorta, middle choice.

Judas made a choice. When he betrayed Jesus, he chose not to love and follow God.

We won't betray Jesus by selling him for thirty pieces of silver like Judas did, but like Judas, we have to choose whether or not we will follow God with our choices. Jesus knew that Judas would choose to betray him. Instead of forcing him to make the right choice, though, Jesus allowed Judas to choose. He allows us to choose, too. And God wants us to choose to follow him!

Additional Activity Options

Choose to Follow Arrows

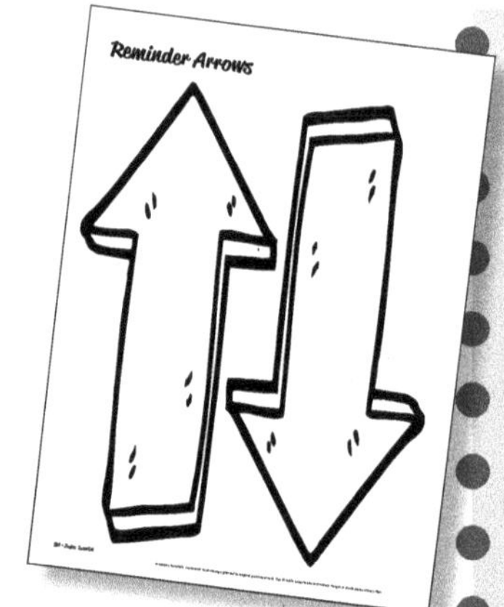

Materials

- Reminder Arrows, page 186
- White card stock
- Scissors
- Markers or crayons
- Decorative materials (glitter glue, sequins, stickers, adhesive-backed craft foam shapes, ribbons and trims, etc.
- Magnetic tape

Preparation: On card stock, photocopy Reminder Arrows, making one arrow for each child plus extras. Cut to separate arrows.

Do: Children cut out arrows, write "Choose to Follow Jesus!" on the arrow and use decorating materials to decorate the arrow. Attach an inch or two of magnetic tape to the back of the arrow.

Say: **Romans 10:9 tells us that we can become a member of God's family by confessing that he is Lord.**

That is a choice we must all make. But we also have to make the choice to follow God daily, all the time. With every action we make and every word we say, we need to choose to act and speak in ways that show we follow God. God lets us choose to follow him, but he wants everybody to do so!

Heads or Tails Game

Do: Children choose what they think the coin will land on—heads or tails. To indicate their choice, children stand for heads and sit for tails.

Materials

- Quarter

Say: **If you didn't make a choice, heads or tails, you couldn't win the game. You had to choose one or the other.**

Jesus tells us the same thing about following him. We can't try to follow him and not follow him at the same time; we must either choose to follow him or not. But God wants you to choose to follow him!

Multiple Choice Bible Review

Materials

- Masking tape

Preparation: Use masking tape to make two lines, dividing the playing area into three sections. Use masking tape to label the sections, *A*, *B*, and *C*.

Say: **For each question, stand next to the letter of the answer you think is correct.**

1. Judas was
- **a.** Jesus' brother.
- **b.** Jesus' friend.
- **c.** Jesus' uncle.

2. How many disciples were there?
- **a.** 10
- **b.** 12
- **c.** 14

3. Which disciple did Jesus know would betray him?
- **a.** Judas
- **b.** John
- **c.** Peter

4. Before eating their meal, the disciples
- **a.** cleaned their feet.
- **b.** asked Jesus to clean their feet.
- **c.** allowed Jesus to clean their feet.

5. After the meal, Jesus told Judas,
- **a.** "Do what you need to do."
- **b.** "Choose what is right."
- **c.** "You will be alright."

7. After Judas betrayed Jesus,
- **a.** Jesus escaped.
- **b.** Jesus was arrested.
- **c.** Jesus disappeared.

6. What wrong thing did Jesus do that got him arrested?
- **a.** Jesus lied to people.
- **b.** Jesus hurt others.
- **c.** Jesus did nothing wrong.

8. Jesus
- **a.** asked Judas to betray him.
- **b.** forced Judas to betray him.
- **c.** allowed Judas to betray him.

9. You can be
- **a.** for God.
- **b.** against God.
- **c.** both for and against God.

10. What good thing happened because Jesus died and rose from the tomb?
- **a.** We can become members of God's family.
- **b.** Jesus made a way for our sins to be forgiven.
- **c.** Both of the answers above.

Discussion Questions

1. How can your actions and words show that you follow God or that you don't?
2. What is the punishment for not following God?
3. How does a person become a Christian?

Reminder Arrows

Chapter 37: Isaiah

Isaiah 8:5–10; 9:1–7

I pray that God, the source of hope, will fill you completely with joy and peace because you trust in him. **ROMANS 15:13**

Overview

Say: When someone asks you, "Which do you want first: the good news or the bad news," which do you pick? (*Children respond.*)

Sometimes the good news and the bad news have to go together. (*Lead children to respond "Yay!" or "Oh, no!" as indicated.*) **You get the day off from school (*Yay!*) because you are running a fever (*Oh no!*). You're not having boiled cabbage for dinner after all (*Yay!*) because that's lunch tomorrow (*Oh no!*).**

The prophet Isaiah was kind of a good news/bad news prophet for the people of Israel. Because of their disobedience, he had some bad news for them. But he also had a message of hope, and a really important message at that. Just like the people of Israel had hope even when dealing with bad news, God gives us hope, too!

Opening Activity

Christmas Tree Race

Materials

- Masking tape, rope, or clothesline

For each team of four to six players

- Artificial Christmas tree
- 4 to 6 Christmas tree ornaments
- Box or other container

Optional

- Christmas music and player

Preparation: Use masking tape, rope, or clothesline to make start and finish lines on opposite sides of the playing area. Place each team's Christmas tree behind the finish line. Place each team's ornaments in a box or other container next to the start line.

Do: Players divide into evenly numbered teams of four to six players and line up next to their team's box of ornaments. On your signal, the first player on each team picks up an ornament, races to their team's tree, places the ornament on the tree, and races back to tag the next player. Play continues until all the team trees are decorated. The first team to finish recites the memory verse.

Optional: Play Christmas music as the teams race.

Say: We've got our trees up, that must mean that Christmas is coming, right? (*Children respond.*) **OK, it may not be Christmastime, but Christmas is our theme for the day! How do you know when Christmas is coming?** (*Children respond.*) **Maybe when you get your Christmas tree up and decorated or when there's Christmas music playing. All of those things, the decorations, the music, the change in the weather even, all bring excitement and hope that Christmas will soon be here!**

The Prophet Isaiah, hundreds and hundreds of years ago, brought bad news to the Israelite people. But he brought the hope of Christmas, too. Just like he did through Isaiah, God gives us hope!

Bible Story

God's Judgment on Israel

Say: The Israelites were messing up . . . again.

Remember, the Israelites were God's chosen people. These were the people that God delivered out of the land of slavery, performing all of these amazing miracles to bring the people to the land he had for them. If God had split the sea in half for you to walk on, made bread fall from heaven, and led you through the wilderness in the form of a column of fire, wouldn't you know that God is real? Wouldn't you only worship the one true God?

But the Israelites didn't. Over and over, they began to worship false gods. They also failed to pass on stories of what God had done to their children and grandchildren. So new Israelites, the generations that came after the generation that God led through the wilderness, didn't always follow God, either.

In Romans 6:23 the Bible tells us that the punishment for sin is death. We know that Jesus took the punishment for our sin. Before Jesus died and rose again, people had to try to be good on their own. And when they sinned, they would go to the Temple and make a sacrifice to show that they were truly sorry.

And whenever we sin, there are consequences. And the Israelites were going to be punished to get them to stop sinning and to start following the Lord again. God sent the prophet Isaiah to the people to tell them what the punishment would be. What do you think is going to happen to the Israelites? *(Children respond.)*

Read: Isaiah 8:5–10

Say: Isaiah warns the people that their enemies, the Assyrians, will defeat them, because of their disobedience. But Isaiah's not just a doom and gloom prophet. He comes with a message of hope—a really important message.

Read: Isaiah 9:6–7

Say: Even though the people were about to be punished for their disobedience, Isaiah was giving them the hope of the Savior—Jesus. Jesus, the Son of God, would come to pay the price for their sins and offer us eternal life. Isaiah was giving hope to the people that their sins could be forgiven. And it's the same hope we have today—Jesus.

Pray: Praise God for the hope we have in Jesus.

Object Lesson

HOPE

Preparation: Place one egg in a mason jar full of vinegar at least 48 hours ahead of time. The vinegar will remove the egg shell and make it rubbery. Place prepared egg and a raw egg in the egg carton.

Say: **Isaiah had a message of hope, and God gives us hope, but what is hope?** *(Children respond.)* **Hope is the expectation of something happening. It's waiting for something to happen. "I hope I get money for my birthday. I hope I got a good grade on my test. I hope I don't get into trouble."**

Sometimes hope can seem like a wish, but true hope, the hope that God gives us, is more than a wish. It's waiting for what we know will happen. *(Hold up the raw egg.)* **If I throw this egg down, what will happen?** *(Children respond.)* **It will break and the egg will go everywhere.** *(Pantomime throwing the egg down.)* **How many of you are hoping I will throw it and make a big mess?** *(Children respond. Throw the egg.)*

Materials

- 2 eggs
- Mason jar
- Vinegar
- Egg carton or other container
- Disinfectant wipes for cleaning up after the Object Lesson

Optional: Instead of throwing the egg on the floor or a table, make it even more exciting by breaking the egg on a leader's head!

There's our mess! You knew what would happen. It was a guarantee! On December 24th, you can go to bed hoping that Christmas comes the next day, and it always will.

But the hope Isaiah spoke of was different. *(Hold up the rubber egg, concealing most of it in your hand so the children can't tell it's different.)* **I am going to throw this egg down, but this time, it won't break. There won't be a mess. I'm telling you that this crazy thing is going to happen. It's not what would normally happen when you throw an egg down, but it will; you can have the hope that it will.** *(Throw the rubber egg.)*

Just like I said, it didn't make a mess. What I said would happen, happened! And the message of hope that Isaiah gave to the people really happened. What was that message of hope? (That a Savior would come and people could be forgiven for their sins.) **That really happened, too! So we know that God gives us hope, too! What he promises will happen, will happen!**

Additional Activity Options

Verse Chorus

Materials

- White board or large sheet of paper
- Dry-erase marker and eraser or marker

Preparation: On white board or large sheet of paper, print the words to the memory verse, Romans 15:13. Place where children will see it easily.

Do: Divide children into three groups. Assign each group a phrase from the verse:

- I pray that God, the source of hope
- will fill you completely with joy and peace
- because you trust in him

Lead the group to repeat the verse, by pointing to each group in turn. After a couple of rounds, reassign the phrases so that each group is saying a different section of the verse. You can also vary the activity by suggesting different ways to say the verse: fast, super-slow motion, while hopping on one foot, in a singsong voice, etc.

Say: **Our verse tells us that God is the source of hope. Without God, we would have no hope! Because of the hope we have from God, we can have complete joy and peace. The last part of our verse tells us the reason we can have hope from God Because we . . .** *(Lead children to complete the verse by saying "trust in him.")* **God gives us hope!**

HOPE Tree Ornament

Preparation: On green card stock, photocopy Christmas Tree Patterns, making one for each child plus extras. Cut to separate the trees. Cut ribbon into approximately 8-inch lengths, creating one length for each child plus extras.

Do: Children cut out trees and use a hole punch to make a hole through the star at the top of the tree. Then, they thread a length of ribbon through the hole and tie a knot to create a loop to hang the ornament.

Children use decorating materials to decorate trees—printing the word HOPE, gluing on pom-poms and sequins as ornaments, shaping pipe cleaners into garlands and gluing to tree, etc.

Optional: To go with the theme of the lesson, play Christmas music as children work.

Materials

- Christmas Tree Patterns, page 191
- Green card stock
- Scissors
- Hole punch
- Decorating materials (markers or crayons, glitter glue, pom-poms, sequins, pipe cleaners, etc.)
- Ribbon

Say: **The promise of Jesus' birth brought hope to the people of Isaiah's day. It brings hope to us today. We don't have to receive the punishment for our sins, like we deserve. Because of Jesus, we can be forgiven if we choose to follow him.**

Jesus is hope, and God gives us this hope!

Alternate Idea: Provide a sheet of Magic Scratch Paper (available online) to each child. Children cut sheets into a tree shape and use scratch sticks (provided with Magic Scratch Sheets) to decorate trees. Punch a hole at the top and thread ribbon through as described above.

Seat Switch Bible Review

Children sit in a circle. Leader or volunteer closes their eyes as children switch seats. When everyone is seated, without opening their eyes, leader or volunteer names a child. That child, plus the children seated on either side of them, answers one of the questions below. Repeat seat switching until each question is answered.

1. **Isaiah was a _____?** (Prophet)
2. **God's chosen people were the _______?** (Israelites)
3. **True or False? The Israelites always followed God.** (False)
4. **Romans 6:23 tells us that the punishment for sin is _____?** (Death)
5. **What kind of message did Isaiah bring the people, good or bad?** (Both!)
6. **What nation would defeat Israel?** (Assyria)
7. **Is hope like a wish?** (No. It's a guarantee.)
8. **What message of hope did Isaiah bring?** (A Savior, Jesus, was going to come.)
9. **Why can we have hope to be forgiven of our sin?** (Jesus took the punishment for our sin.)
10. **What does our verse say we can have because of our hope in God?** (Complete joy and peace.)

Discussion Questions

1. **Why is Christmas such an exciting time?**
2. **How does Jesus take away our sins?**
3. **Did the promises Isaiah made about Jesus come true?**

Optional: At the end of the session, children race to undecorate the trees they decorating in the Opening Activity!

Christmas Tree Patterns

Chapter 38: King Herod

Matthew 2

You know what I am going to say even before I say it, LORD. **PSALM 139:4**

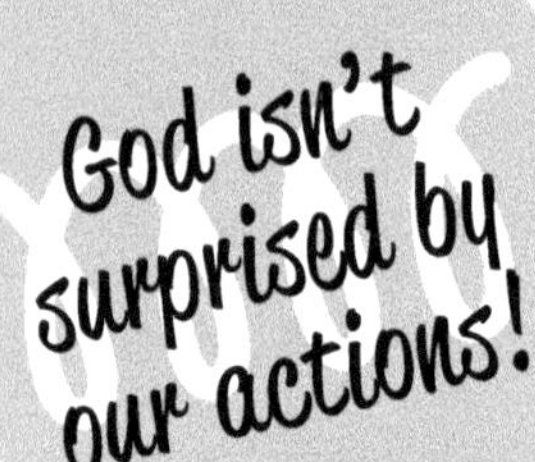

Overview

Say: **Jesus' birth had been prophesied and promised for hundreds and hundreds of years. The Jewish believers knew that the Messiah would be coming one day.**

So how do you think God felt when right after the Messiah, Jesus, was born, the king of the Jewish people decided to kill baby Jesus! (*Children respond.*) **Raise your hand if you think God was surprised.** (*Children respond.*)

Wait a minute! . . . God wasn't surprised at all. God isn't surprised by our actions! King Herod had a terrible plan to kill baby Jesus, but God knew about it. God is all-knowing. God had a plan to keep baby Jesus safe.

Opening Activity

Materials

- Birthday gift box with lid
- Individually wrapped candies or other prizes
- Children's worship music and play

Pass the Parcel

Preparation: Place individually wrapped candies or other prizes in the gift box and place lid on top.

Do: Players sit or stand in a circle. Play music as players pass the box around the circle. After a few moments, stop the music. The player holding the box when the music stops, opens the box and chooses a prize.

Start music again and play continues. If when the music stops, the player holding the box has already received a prize, player passes the box to someone who has not yet received a prize. Play additional rounds until all players have a prize.

Say: **Touch your nose if you love presents!** (*Children respond.*) **Birthdays are so exciting, not just because we are another year older, but because we get presents! It's also customary to give presents, not just for your birthday, but to celebrate your birth!**

Jesus' birth wasn't celebrated like most babies. He didn't have a big baby shower at the synagogue. Mary and Joseph weren't even at home when he was born!

As unique as the circumstances of Jesus' birth were, there was still some celebrating, and even a few gifts.

Bible Story

Baby Jesus' Visitors

Materials

- "Welcome Baby" yard sign

Say: *(Hold up "Welcome Baby" yard sign.)* **Sometimes when a baby is born, parents or friends will put a sign in the yard letting all the neighbors know that the baby was born. What are some other ways people can tell others that a baby was born?** *(Children respond.)*

There wasn't a "Welcome Baby" sign for Jesus, but there was something else that told everyone that the Savior had been born. What was it? *(Children respond.)*

God placed a star over the place where Jesus was. And it wasn't just any star. This star was different. Because of our planet rotating around the sun each day, the position of the stars changes in our night sky. But this star didn't move. It stayed in one spot for a long time. Possibly as long as two years!

There were some wise men, known as Magi, from the East who studied stars. They knew this star was a big deal.

Read: Matthew 2:1–2

But Herod was not happy. These men were coming to worship some baby in his kingdom!

Read: Matthew 2: 4–7

Herod told the Magi that he too wanted to worship the baby Jesus, but that was a lie. Herod didn't want to worship Jesus. He wanted to kill him! He didn't want the people in his kingdom to worship or follow anyone but him. He was jealous of Jesus.

If the Magi came back and told Herod where Jesus lived, he would kill Jesus! Good thing God isn't surprised by our actions.

Read: Matthew 2:12

Say: **God knew exactly what Herod was going to do, so he warned the Magi not to return to Herod. And that wasn't the only angel warning in our story.**

Read: Matthew 2:14–15

Say: **God wasn't surprised at Herod's evil plan. God knows everything. God isn't surprised by our actions! And he had a plan in place to keep Jesus safe.**

Pray: Praise God for never being surprised by our actions!

Fun Fact

There is more than one King Herod mentioned in the Bible! Herod the Great was king when Jesus was born, but it was his son Herod Antipas who had John the Baptist killed.

Object Lesson

Danger Ahead

Materials

- Caution tape or danger sign

Optional

- Warning buzzer sound effect

Say: (*Hold up caution tape or danger sign.*) **What does this tell people?** (*Children respond.*) **It tells people that there is danger! Herod put the baby Jesus in danger, but since the Magi went home a different way after worshiping Jesus, Herod wouldn't know where to find him. Right? So the danger Jesus was in is gone, right?**

Optional: Play warning sound effect.

Unfortunately, not. Herod still wanted to kill Jesus! Jesus was still in danger, but Mary and Joseph didn't know it!

Remember, God isn't surprised by our actions. God knew exactly what Herod was going to do. He knew what Herod was thinking, even before he thought it! God isn't surprised by our actions.

So what did God do to keep baby Jesus safe? (*Children respond.*) **Joseph took Mary and baby Jesus to Egypt and stayed there until King Herod was dead and there was no more danger. God kept Jesus safe so that he could grow up to do what God sent him to do—to die on the cross to save us from our sins.**

Additional Activity Options

Personalized Verse

Materials

- White board or large sheet of paper
- Dry-erase marker and eraser or large marker

Preparation: On white board or large sheet of paper, print the words to Psalm 139:4.

Do: Repeat the verse a couple of times with children. Then, point to a child and repeat the verse, but replace the word *I* with the child's name and fix the verbs so that the verse makes sense: "You know what (Sean is) going to say even before (Sean says) it, Lord."

That child then points to another child, repeating the verse and replacing the words in the same manner. Continue play until each child has had at least one turn to say the verse.

Say: **Our verse tells us that God knows what we are going to say before the words even come out of our mouths! God isn't surprised by our words and God isn't surprised by our actions!**

Surprise Emoji Mask

Preparation: On white card stock, photocopy Emoji Maker, making one copy for each child plus extras.

Do: Children cut out eyes, a mouth, and if wanted, the explosion and glue them to a yellow paper plate to make a surprise emoji mask. Children tape a craft stick to the back of the paper plate to make a handle.

Materials

- Emoji Maker, page 196
- White card stock
- Scissors
- Glue
- Yellow paper plates
- Transparent tape
- Craft sticks

Say: **Was God surprised that Herod lied to the Magi and was planning to kill Jesus? No! Is God ever surprised by what we think, say, or do?** (*Children respond.*) **No!**

Our God is omniscient—he is all-knowing! **Nothing surprises him!**

Optional: Take photos of kids making a surprise emoji face as they look at their Surprise Emoji Masks! Use an instant camera or a printer that works with your cell phone so that kids can take home a copy of their photos.

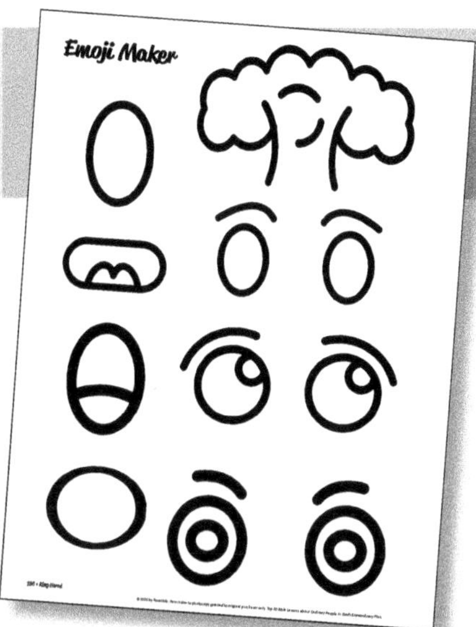

Stand Up If It's True Bible Review

Say: **Stand up if the answer to the question is true, but sit down if it is false. If the answer is false, explain what makes it false.**

1. **Herod was king of the Jewish people.** (True)
2. **King Herod was a super nice king that always told the truth and never planned to kill people.** (False)
3. **Herod read about Jesus' birth in the newspaper.** (False)
4. **Magi were wise men from Macedonia.** (False)
5. **The Magi came to find and worship Jesus.** (True)
6. **Herod wanted to worship Jesus, too.** (False)
7. **The Magi told Herod where to find Jesus.** (False)
8. **God sent an angel to warn the Magi to go home another way.** (True)
9. **After his first plan to kill Jesus didn't work, Herod gave up.** (False)
10. **God kept Jesus safe, because he is all-knowing.** (True)

Discussion Questions

1. **Why is God never surprised?**
2. **How can God know everything?**
3. **If God knows our thoughts, should we still pray to him? Why or why not?**

Emoji Maker

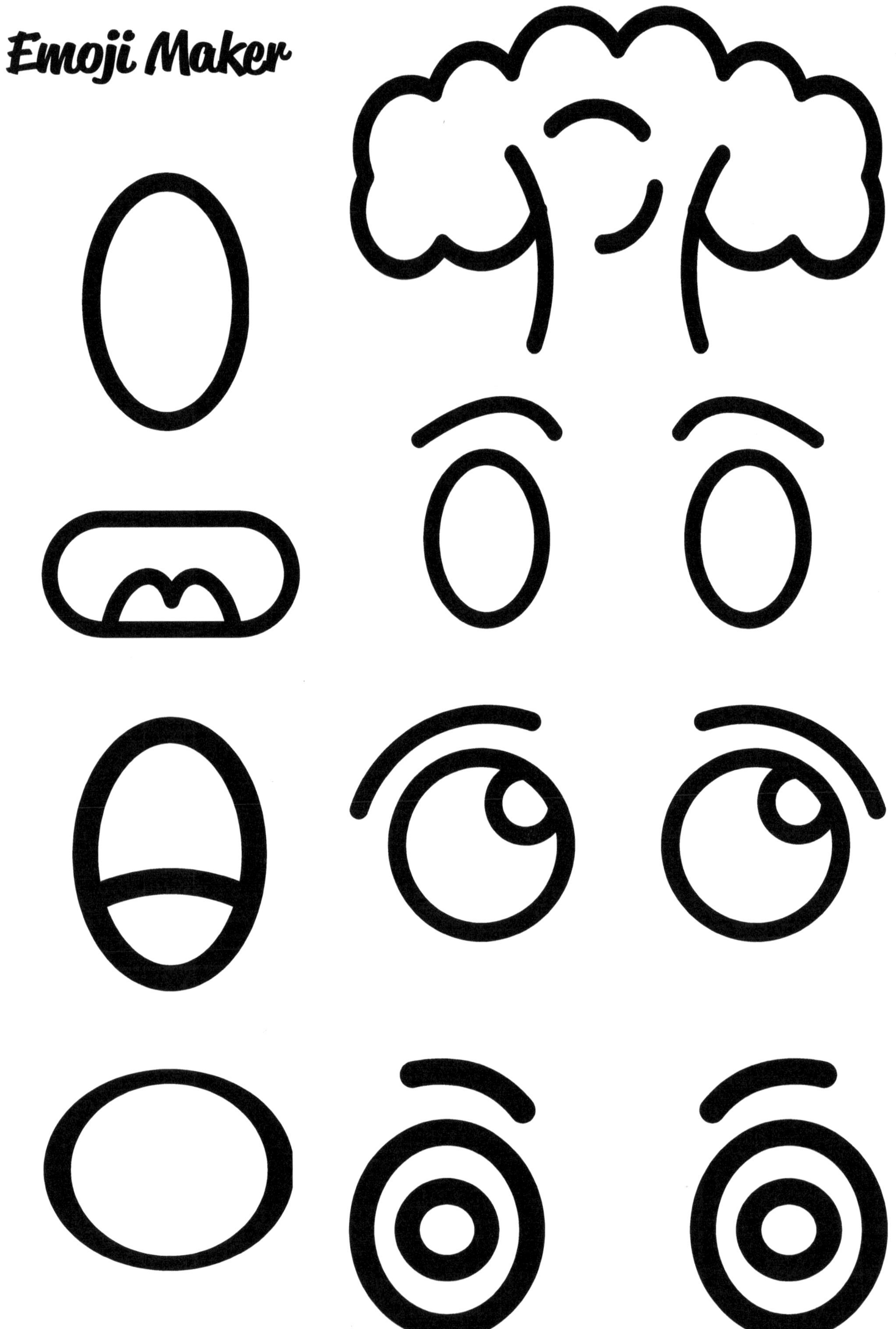

Chapter 39: Lydia

Acts 16:1–15

Let the whole earth sing to the LORD*! Each day proclaim the good news that he saves. Publish his glorious deeds among the nations. Tell everyone about the amazing things he does.* **1 CHRONICLES 16:23–24.**

God wants everyone to be in his family!

Big Idea

Overview

Say: **If you lived in Bible times, what do you think would be different from today?** (*Children respond.*) **Obviously, there weren't cars or computers. No fast-food restaurants. The clothes would have been different. People would have even spoken differently! But if you were a female, things would have been even more different for you.**

Women weren't treated the same as men. At that time, the oldest male in the family was in charge. Women didn't typically have jobs to earn money. Women, like children, weren't always viewed as important. What do you think Jesus thought? (*Children respond.*) **Jesus was different. He recognized women as important—and children too!**

In the book of Acts, the apostle Paul tells us about a woman named Lydia, giving us a lot of detail about her in a short passage. Through her story, we see that God wants everyone to be in his family!

Opening Activity

Materials

- Purple bandanna or fabric square

Steal the Bacon

Preparation: Use masking tape to make two lines on opposite sides of the playing area. Place purple bandanna or fabric square in the center of the playing area.

Do: Players divide into two evenly numbered teams, line up on opposite sides of the playing area, and number off, starting the numbers in opposite directions. (See image at right.)

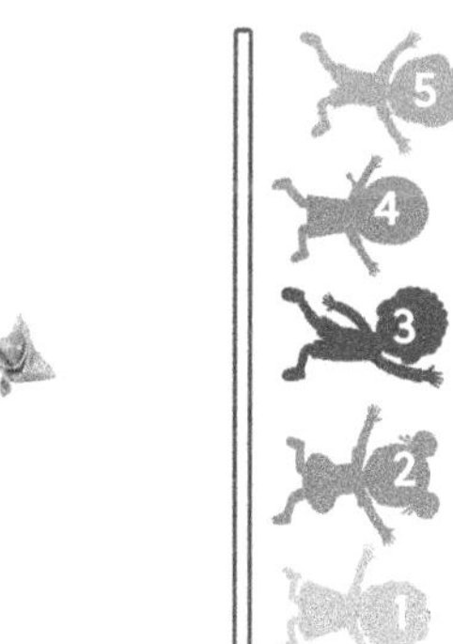

Place the cloth in the middle of the two teams. When leader calls out a number, the player on each team with that number races to grab the bandanna or fabric and take it back across their team's line without being tagged. If successful, the team recites the memory verse. Leader then calls out a different number.

If the player is tagged before crossing the team's line, the bandanna or fabric is returned to the center of the playing area and play continues. Play until all players have had at least one turn or as time and interest allow.

Say: **If I had told you that the cloth from our game was a really expensive cloth, would that have made you try even harder to grab it?** (*Children respond.*) **Nowadays, fabric is mass produced, so there isn't a lot of difference between fabrics.**

Before there were factories and machines to produce fabric, it was made by hand. And you couldn't get it in whatever color you wanted, either. Certain dyes were harder to get and more costly than others, such as purple. Purple cloth—fancier than the kind we used in our game—was an expensive item, a luxury item. And Lydia sold it!

Fun Fact

Wool is the most expensive fabric right now. Alpaca wool is some of the most highly sought after!

Younger Child Option: Play Hot Potato using a purple scarf or bandanna instead of Steal the Bacon.

Bible Story

Lydia

Say: After God changed his life and made him a member of his family, the apostle Paul became a missionary. What is a missionary? (*Children respond.*) For the rest of his life, Paul told people about Jesus and how to have a new life in Jesus by becoming a member of God's family. Sometimes Paul wrote letters to people or churches. You can find these letters in the Bible's New Testament. Other times, Paul traveled to different places, telling people about Jesus.

On his second big trip telling people about God, Paul had a vision from God telling him to go to Macedonia. What would you do if God told you to go to Macedonia or anywhere? (*Children respond.*) Paul obeyed and went to the city of Philippi.

When he first got there, Paul didn't meet up with the men leading the town or the church, he sat and talked with some women. One of these women was a businesswoman named Lydia. Lydia was in the business of selling purple cloths, expensive, luxurious fabric.

The Bible description of Lydia is short, but actually tells us a lot. There's no husband mentioned, so it's possible that Lydia was widowed or divorced. She was the head of her household, which wasn't the norm for women at the time. She was a "God-fearing" woman, but neither Jewish nor a follower of Jesus.

Listen to what happens after Lydia hears Paul talk about Jesus.

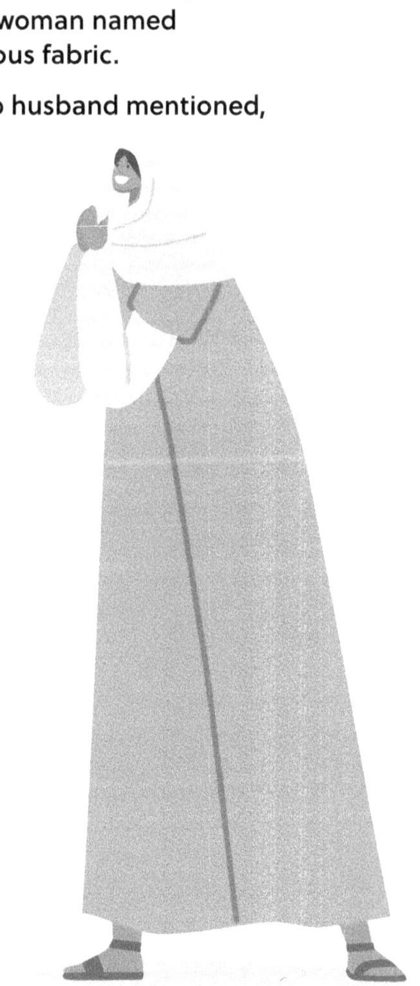

Read: Acts 16:14–15

Say: After listening to Paul, Lydia's heart was opened, and she realized who Jesus was and became a member of God's family.

Paul didn't care that Lydia was a businesswoman. He didn't care that she wasn't Jewish. He wanted to tell her about Jesus!

Lydia believed! But even Lydia knew that the message of Jesus wasn't supposed to be kept to herself. Lydia told her whole household about God, and then they believed! **God wants everyone to be in his family.**

Pray: Ask children to pray for specific people in their life that need to hear about Jesus.

Object Lesson

Materials

- None

Every Nation

Say: **Our verse tells us to go to every nation. But not every nation speaks the same language we do. What other languages can you name?** *(Children respond.)*

Do: Lead children into saying hello in different languages.

- Arabic: *Marhaban* (MARR-hah-bah)
- Cantonese: *Neih hou* (NAY-hoh)
- Catalan/Spanish: *Hola* (O-lah)
- Danish: *Hallo* (HAH-lo)
- Dutch: *Hoi* (HOY)
- Persian: *Salam* (SAH-lahm)
- French: *Bonjour* (bohn-ZJOOR)
- German: *Guten Tag* (GOO-ten tahg)
- Hindi: *Namaste* (NAH-mah-stay)
- Japanese: *Konnichiwa* (co-NEE-chee-wah)
- Russian: *Zdravstvuyte* (ZDRA-stvoy-zteh)
- Swahili: *Jambo* (JHAM-bo)

Say: **Who is allowed to become a member of God's family? Are only certain people supposed to hear about Jesus?** *(Children respond.)*

No! God wants everyone to be in his family! The good news of Jesus' death and resurrection and that we can be forgiven for our sins is for every person from every tribe, tongue, and nation! If you're like me and think that is wonderful, good news, stand up, raise your hands, and shout "Hooray!"

Additional Activity Options

Materials

- None

Optional

- Hats and other props to act out different professions (chef, police officer, firefighter, business person, teacher, actor, rock star, athlete, clown, dancer, etc.)

When I Grow Up Game

Do: One at a time, children silently act out what job they want to have when they grow up.

Optional: Bring in props that children can use to act out their chosen professions.

Say: **Are only businesswomen like Lydia allowed to follow Jesus?** *(Children respond.)* **Is Christianity just for doctors and lawyers? Or only grown-ups?**

No! God wants everyone to become a member of his family, people from every tribe, tongue, and nation!

Beanbag Bible Review

Materials

- 2 or 3 beanbags

Do: Children stand together. Choose a volunteer to stand with their back to the group a few feet away. Volunteer then tosses beanbags, one at a time, to the group. Children who catch the beanbags work together to answer one of the questions below.

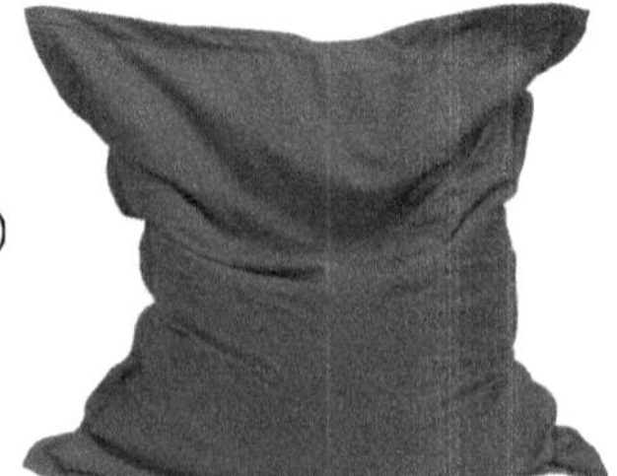

1. **Who was Paul?** (A member of God's family. A missionary.)
2. **How did Paul tell people about Jesus?** (He wrote letters and visited them.)
3. **Why did Paul decide to travel to Macedonia?** (God told him to in a vision.)
4. **Who did Paul first meet in Philippi?** (Lydia)
5. **What job did Lydia have?** (She was a businesswoman.)
6. **What did Lydia sell?** (Expensive purple cloth)
7. **Was Lydia a Christian when she met Paul?** (No)
8. **After Lydia heard Paul's words, what happened?** (God opened her heart and she became a member of God's family.)
9. **Did Lydia keep the message of Jesus to herself?** (No. She told her whole household and they became members of God's family, too.)
10. **Who is the gospel for?** (Everyone!)

Discussion Questions

1. **Why did Paul travel on trips?**
2. **What do you think Paul told Lydia?**
3. **How can we tell others about Jesus?**

Good News Card Craft

Materials

- Card stock
- Markers or crayons
- Decorative materials (glitter glue, beads, stickers, etc.)

Do: Children think of someone in their lives who needs to hear about Jesus and becoming a member of God's family. Children make a card telling that person about Jesus. Encourage them to draw a picture on the front of their card and to include the memory verse.

Say: **When Lydia understood who Jesus was, she didn't just keep it to herself. She told her whole household about him! We shouldn't keep the news about Jesus to ourselves either. God wants everyone to be in his family!**

Optional: Provide cards or postcards with "Good News" and 1 Chronicles 16:23–24 already printed on them. Faith that Sticks has a good variety of stickers with images of Jesus on them like the Life of Christ and Life of Jesus stickers shown. The entire line of Faith that Sticks stickers is available at Tyndale.com.

Lydia Coloring Page: Photocopy page 201, making one copy for each child plus extras. Kids complete in class or take home.

Lydia Coloring Page

Chapter 40: Nehemiah

Nehemiah 1–6

Work willingly at whatever you do, as though you were working for the Lord rather than for people. **COLOSSIANS 3:23**

Overview

Say: **God's chosen people, the Israelites, after a long, LONG walk in the desert, finally were given the land that God had promised to them. In that land, known as Jerusalem, the nation of Israel grew, and they built a strong city to protect their land.**

But the people began to disobey God and started following false gods. They disobeyed God's warnings, given to them through the prophets, so he punished them. Their city was destroyed around 600 years before Jesus was born. The people were either killed or taken captive and became slaves and foreigners in other lands.

God still loved his people and wanted them to have their land again. He chose a man named Nehemiah to help rebuild Jerusalem. Through Nehemiah's example, we learn how God wants us to work hard!

Opening Activity

Destroy the City Game

Do: Teams work together to build a city tower out of cups.

After all of the teams have constructed their city towers, teams crumple up sheets of paper to make paper balls. Throwing the paper balls, teams try to knock down the towers belonging to the other teams.

The team with the tower standing the longest, or the tower with the most cups still standing when you call time, recites the memory verse.

Materials

- 50 cups for each team of 4 to 6 players
- Paper

Say: **If you had fun playing this game, let's hear a loud "Yeah!"** (*Children respond.*) **If these were real buildings, it wouldn't be as much fun. Because there might be shops and homes, the people who owned the shops and lived in the homes would be very, very sad to have them destroyed.**

In today's Bible story, we're going to hear about a time God's people had to live in homes that were half-destroyed.

Younger Child Option: Instead of having children try to knock down others' towers, have groups knock down their own towers.

Bible Story

Nehemiah Rebuilds the Wall

Materials

- Sheets of paper
- Marker

Preparation: On separate sheets of paper, print the words *Hooray! Oh, no! Wah! Boo! WOW!* to make word signs to hold up as indicated during the story. As you do, encourage children to say the words or phrases on each sign.

Say: **Imagine how you would feel if your home was half-destroyed. You could live in your house** *(Hold up "Hooray!" sign.)*, **but there wasn't a door anymore, some of the windows were missing, or there were holes in two of the walls** *(Hold up "Oh, no!" sign.)*. **How do you think your family would feel?** *(Children respond.)* **You'd probably feel pretty sad.** *(Hold up "Wah!" sign.)*

And that's just how the Israelites must have felt when they returned to Jerusalem after it had been destroyed by Babylon. The city wall, in particular, was in bad shape. *(Hold up "Oh, no!" sign.)* **The city wall was very important. It would protect God's people if other armies wanted to attack them.**

Nehemiah was an Israelite who lived in Persia. He was the cupbearer to the king, which meant he was one of the king's most trusted men. One day, Nehemiah's brother and some other men came to visit him from Jerusalem.

Read: Nehemiah 1:3–11

Say: **When Nehemiah heard this, he was upset. He mourned and fasted. He was so upset by this that the King noticed and asked him what was wrong. God had heard Nehemiah's prayer and had softened the king's heart. Nehemiah was given permission to return to Jerusalem and begin the hard task of rebuilding the wall** *(Hold up "Hooray!" sign.)*. . . **but it was going to take a lot of work.**

Nehemiah was going to rebuild the wall around Jerusalem. No big deal, right? *(Children respond.)* **It's just one wall. How hard could that be?** *(Hold up "Hooray!" sign.)*

It was only one wall, but it was a big wall. *(Hold up "Oh, no!" sign.)* **This wall went all around the city. It was almost two and half miles long!** *(Hold up "WOW!" sign.)* **That is the length of about 188 blue whales!** *(Hold up "WOW!" sign.)* **Or two and a half times around the track of a football field!** *(Hold up "WOW!" sign.)*

But Nehemiah didn't just have to rebuild a HUGE broken wall. There were some other obstacles Nehemiah and the others working on the wall had to overcome. *(Hold up "Oh, no!" sign.)*

Read: Nehemiah 4:1–4

Say: **People were mocking them! What does mocking mean?** *(Children respond.)* **But that's not all. Then, the people started attacking the Jewish people and trying to destroy all of the work they were doing on the wall.** *(Hold up "Oh, no!" sign.)*

It might make you want to give up. *(Hold up "Wah!" sign.)* **Nehemiah faced obstacle after obstacle trying to rebuild the wall.** *(Hold up "Oh, no!" sign.)* **Things got so bad that he had to place guards, twenty-four hours a day, to protect both the workers and the wall!** *(Hold up "WOW!" sign.)* **Nehemiah worked hard for the Lord. Nehemiah must have known God wants us to work hard for him! Nehemiah didn't give up when things got hard. He just kept going.**

Read: Nehemiah 6:15–16

Say: In just fifty-two days the wall was built. No obstacle could stop Nehemiah, because he was working hard for the Lord! *(Hold up "Hooray!" sign.)* **And Nehemiah knew the credit belonged to God. He knew all his hard work was successful because he received help from God. That same help is available to everyone who is a member of God's family.**

Pray: Pray over the children, asking God to give them hearts that want to work hard for him. Thank God for helping the members of his family when we have hard work to do. Invite any children who would like to know more about becoming a member of God's family to talk with you or another adult helper.

Object Lesson

Keep Working

Materials

- Balloons
- Funnel
- Tablespoon
- Baking soda
- Empty clear water bottle
- White vinegar

Preparation: Place the end of a balloon over the small end of the funnel. Pour approximately one tablespoon of baking soda into the balloon through the funnel. Remove the funnel and shake the baking powder to the bottom of the balloon. Place the funnel in the mouth of the empty clear water bottle and pour in white vinegar until the bottle is about half full.

Say: Who would like to come up here and blow up a balloon? *(Choose a volunteer or two to come up and blow up a balloon—be sure NOT to give them the balloon with baking soda!)* **That wasn't too hard, was it?**

(Hold up balloon with baking soda.) **What would you say if I told you I could get this balloon to blow itself up?** *(Children respond.)* **That would make the work a LOT easier—especially if I were having a party and needed to blow up HUNDREDS of balloons, right? Well, watch . . .**

Do: Place the mouth of the balloon over the opening of the bottle. Shake the baking soda from the bottom of the balloon into the bottle. The baking soda will react with the vinegar, releasing carbon dioxide gas and filling the balloon.

Say: Today we've been talking about how God wants us to work hard. That doesn't mean we have to break into a sweat every time we do something. But it does mean that even if we face obstacles, we work hard to overcome them.

And we're not in this by ourselves. Who did Nehemiah turn to for help? *(Children respond.)* **When Nehemiah needed to get the king's permission to return to Judah and rebuild the wall, what did he do?** *(Children respond.)* **He prayed! What did Nehemiah do when the workers were being mocked?** *(Children respond.)* **He prayed! And did God help Nehemiah?** *(Children respond.)* **Yes! That's why when the work was finally done, Nehemiah praised God.**

Nehemiah worked hard for the Lord. **God wants us to work hard** for him! Nehemiah didn't give up when things got hard. He prayed to God and with God's help, he kept working hard.

Additional Activity Options

Occupation Charades

Materials

- Occupation Cards, page 206
- White card stock
- Scissors or paper cutter
- Hat, basket, or other container

Preparation: On white card stock, photocopy Occupation Cards and cut out. Place cards in a hat, basket, or other container.

Do: Play a game like Charades, using the cards you prepared. Without looking, a player selects a card and then silently acts it out for the group. The first player to correctly guess the occupation takes the next turn. Continue until each player has had a turn. If you run out of cards, place them in the hat and play again.

Say: **Whether we are doctors or students, God wants us to work hard. All of the things we do, like cleaning our rooms or doing our homework, need to be done like we are doing it for God.**

Verse Wall Art

Materials

- Twigs or dowel rods (1 per child)
- Assorted yarn
- Card stock (1 per child)
- Hole punch
- Scissors

Do: Children wrap a twig or dowel rod with yarn, covering it completely and tying it off. On the card stock, each child writes the memory verse. Punch holes in both top corners. Using a new piece of yarn, thread it through the card stock and tie it to the wrapped twig/dowel. Add another piece of yard to make a loop in which you can use to hang it.

Say: **You did a great job wrapping your twigs! Put this wall hanging up in your room when you get home to remind you of Nehemiah and the wall. Remember that everything we do (even building a wall or wrapping a twig with yarn) should be done like we are doing it for God.**

Fact Face-Off Bible Review

Do: Form two teams. Team members face off against each other, one at a time, answering the questions and earning points for their team.

1. **Who did Nehemiah work for?** (The king)
2. **Why was Nehemiah sad?** (The people in Jerusalem were living with a destroyed city.)
3. **Why was the wall in Jerusalem destroyed?** (God had punished the Israelites.)
4. **How big was the wall?** (2½ miles long)
5. **What obstacles did Nehemiah face?** (People mocked them and harmed the workers.)
6. **How did Nehemiah protect the workers and the wall?** (He had around-the-clock guards.)
7. **Did Nehemiah ever give up?** (No)
8. **How long did it take until the wall was finished?** (52 days)
9. **Who is it that our memory verse says we should be working for?** (God)
10. **What does it mean to work for God instead of people?** (Do our best work all the time to please God, not people.)

Discussion Questions

1. **Why was the wall around Jerusalem important?**
2. **Do kids your age always work like they are working for the Lord? Why or why not?**
3. **If you work for God instead of people, will others be upset or happy? Why?**

Occupation Cards

Chapter 41: Josiah

2 Kings 22–23

Your word is a lamp to guide my feet and a light for my path. **PSALM 119:105**

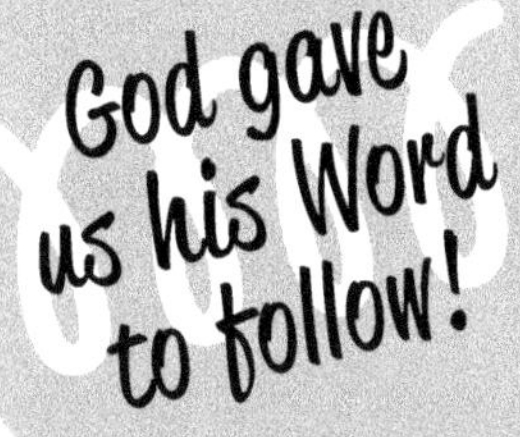

Overview

Say: **For most of the world, it is easy to get your hands on a copy of the Bible. There are churches and organizations that will give you one for free, hotels have them in dresser drawers, and most any store that sells books has copies for sale. But that wasn't always the case.**

Before the Bible was printed in book form (thanks to Johannes Gutenberg's printing press) each individual book was carefully written by hand on a scroll. These were so rare and valuable that the average person didn't have access to them! And sometimes, the scrolls of God's Word were even lost.

That's what happened to the sixteenth king of Judah, Josiah. He loved and followed the Lord, but God's Word had been lost. Josiah discovered, however, that God gave us his Word to follow!

Opening Activity

Bible Believe It or Not

Do: One at a time, read each of the statements below. Children decide whether to believe it or not, and then indicate their choice by standing up for believe it and sitting down for not.

1. **The Bible was written by 40 men.** (Believe it)
2. **The Bible was originally written in English.** (Not—Hebrew, Aramaic, and Greek)
3. **The Bible writers wrote whatever they wanted.** (Not—They wrote what God told them to write.)
4. **It took thousands of years for the whole Bible to be written.** (Believe it)
5. **Paul wrote the most books in the Bible.** (Believe it)
6. **There is an animal that talks in the Bible—other than the sneaky serpent in the Garden of Eden.** (Believe it)
7. **Some of the books in the Bible are letters.** (Believe it)
8. **Every prophecy or promise in the Bible has come true.** (Not—Revelation hasn't happened yet.)
9. **You can choose which parts of the Bible you believe to be true.** (Not—Everything in the Bible is true.)
10. **God wants us to read and follow his Word!** (Believe it)

Did You Know?

In 1455, Johannes Gutenberg printed the Gutenberg Bible, one of the earliest books in the world. It was printed by the first mechanized printing press in Europe, which he invented. He said, "It is a press, certainly, but a press from which shall flow in inexhaustible streams. Through it, God will spread His Word."

Say: **The Bible is an amazing book and we live at such an amazing time in history. The Bible is everywhere, even on our phones!**

But what if you didn't live at a time when there was a Bible? How would you know what God wanted you to do if you didn't have his Word? *(Children respond.)*

Younger Child Option: Play Hot Potato with a Bible. Each time the music stops, read a fact about God's Word from the game.

Bible Story

Josiah Follows God's Word

Say: **Long ago, King Amon was in charge of God's people and he was an evil king. He disobeyed God and allowed his people to worship false gods. He was the same kind of king his father had been. As a result, for many, many years, God's people had not gone to the Temple. It was dirty and run-down. The Temple was where people went to hear God's Word. So no one was listening to or obeying God's Word. Do you think that was a good thing or a bad thing? Stand up if you think that was a bad thing.** *(Children respond.)*

When King Amon died, his son Josiah became king. What do you think is a good age to become king? *(Children respond.)* **Josiah wasn't a grown-up when he became king. He was just eight years old! Raise your hand if you are eight. Would you want to be king?** *(Children respond.)*

Josiah's father was evil just like his father had been. Do you think Josiah was also an evil king? *(Children respond.)* **Josiah was NOT evil! He wanted to honor God. But he didn't really know how because he'd never heard God's Word.**

But there was one thing Josiah knew he could do to honor God. He decided to repair God's Temple. King Josiah hired men to clean and repair God's Temple. They fixed broken walls, cleaned the floors, polished the candlesticks, and did whatever needed to be done to make God's Temple beautiful again.

While the Temple was being repaired, the high priest found something . . . the scroll of the Lord! It had been lost! King Josiah wanted the scroll read to him right away.

Read: 2 Kings 22:11–13

Say: **After hearing God's Word, what do you think King Josiah did? Did he just go back to living the same way he had always been living?** *(Children respond.)* **No way! The Bible, God's Word, tells us that King Josiah pledged to obey God's commands and he led God's people in following the Lord, too!**

King Josiah made sure all the altars that were dedicated to false gods were torn down. He wanted the people to worship only the one true God! He also prepared for a HUGE Passover celebration. The Passover celebration is a time to remember how God led the Israelites out of slavery in Egypt. It had been a long time since God's people had remembered to celebrate the Passover and thank God for caring for them.

Just like King Josiah, the people promised to listen to God's Word and to follow it.

Pray: Give children time to pray, thanking God for his Word and that we can choose to follow God's Word to know how to live the very best life.

Object Lesson

Materials

- Lego kit with instruction book

Read and Do

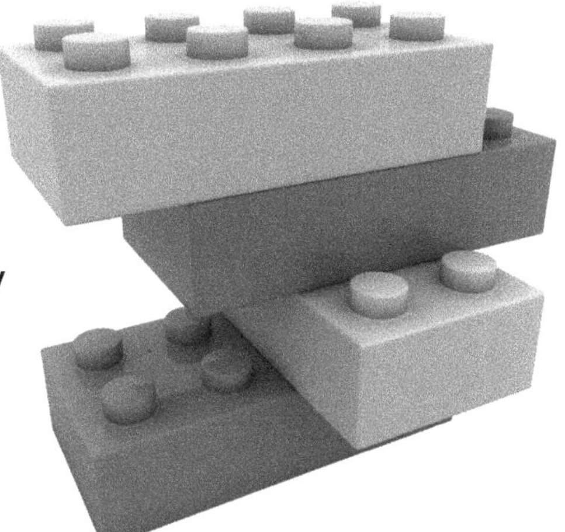

Do: Open up the Lego box, throw out the instructions, and begin assembling. Your Lego creation should look nothing like what was on the box.

Say: **I think that instructions are more like suggestions, don't you? Besides, I have been building with Legos for a really long time. I'm pretty sure I can figure out how to assemble this without any instructions.** (*Show your Lego creation and the picture on the box.*)

OK . . . maybe I should have used the instructions after all. Mine doesn't look anything like it should. If I had used the instructions, I would have known exactly how to build it.

We have an instruction book for life . . . but we don't always use it! God tells us how he wants us to live in his Word. God gave us his Word to follow! But unless we pick up the Bible and read it, we won't know how to live the way God wants us to live.

Additional Activity Options

Find It Game

Materials

- Bibles, one for each group of four or five players
- Masking tape, rope, or clothesline

Preparation: Place Bibles at one end of the playing area. Use masking tape, rope, or clothesline to make a start line opposite the Bibles.

Do: Players divide into teams of four or five players.

Teaching Tip: Place early or reluctant readers in teams with strong readers.

Do: Players divide into teams of four or five players and line up behind the start line. One at a time, read one of the references below and then signal, "Go!" The first player on each team races to their team's Bible, finds the reference in the Bible, and raises their hand. The first player to raise their hand reads, or chooses a volunteer from their team to read, the verse.

Repeat each reference a few times as players try to find it.

- John 3:16
- Philippians 1:3
- Genesis 1:1
- Numbers 6:23
- Colossians 3:23
- Hebrews 13:8
- Romans 10:13
- Matthew 5:14
- Ephesians 4:32
- Psalm 119:105

Say: **The Bible is God's Word. God gave us his Word to follow! We can't follow God's Word if we don't know what it says. What are some ways a kid your age can know what God's Word says?** (Read the Bible. Listen to Bible stories. Memorize Bible verses. Ask teachers, parents, or other caregivers who love God what God's Word says.)

Lantern Lights Craft

Do: Using the foam brushes, children brush on thinned glue or Mod Podge and stick the colored tissue squares on the jars to decorate them.

Optional: When jars are dry, insert a battery-operated tea light.

Materials

- Small glass jars (jelly Mason jars or baby food jars), one for each child
- Glue thinned with water or Mod Podge
- Foam brushes
- Variety of colored tissue paper squares

Optional

- Battery-operated tea lights, one for each child

Say: **Psalm 119:105 tells us that the Bible is a lamp to our feet and a light to our path. Lamps, lanterns, flashlights—they all help us to see which way we need to go.**

Lights may help you see where to physically go, but the Bible is a lamp to follow as you live your life. God's Word helps us to see how to live as God wants us to—the very best life. That's why God gave us his Word to follow.

Tic-Tac-Trivia Bible Review

Do: Draw a Tic-Tac-Toe grid on a large sheet of paper. Children divide into two teams, the *X*s and *O*s. Teams take turns answering one of the questions below. If they answer correctly, they write their *X*s or *O*s in a space on the grid. If they don't answer correctly, the other team has a chance to answer. Draw additional grids as needed.

Materials

- Large sheet of paper
- Marker

1. **How old was Josiah when he became king?** (Eight)
2. **Where was Josiah king of?** (Judah/Israel)
3. **Did Josiah follow the Lord or not?** (Yes!)
4. **What big building project did Josiah start?** (Repairing the Temple)
5. **What was found in the Temple?** (A scroll with the words of the Lord)
6. **After Josiah heard the words on the scroll, what was his reaction?** (He was upset, because the people hadn't been following God like they should have.)
7. **Why didn't King Josiah know what God's Word said before the scroll was found?** (The scrolls were lost. There weren't many copies of God's Word.)
8. **What should we do with the Word of God?** (Read it and follow it!)
9. **Why did God give us the Bible?** (To teach us how to live. So we can follow God's Word. So we can live the very best life.)
10. **When we hear the Word of God, we should . . .** (Do it!)

Discussion Questions

1. **How did people know how to follow God before there were Bibles?**
2. **How do we know what God wants us to do?**
3. **Is it always easy to follow God's laws? Why or why not?**

God's Word Was Followed: Photocopy God's Word Was Followed on page 211, making one copy for each child plus extras. Kids complete in class or take home.

Older Child Enrichment: Read through Psalm 119. Children work together to create a list of what this psalm says about following God's Word.

God's Word Was Followed

2 Kings 22–23

Your word is a lamp to guide my feet and a light for my path. **Psalm 119:105**

The scroll with God's Word written in it had been lost for a very long time. One day, the Temple priest found it and it was brought to King Josiah. Josiah read God's Word to the people. "We will love God and keep his laws. We will do what God wants us to do." God was happy King Josiah wanted the people to hear his Word and follow it.

Color the picture King Josiah reading God's Word to the people.

Chapter 42: Barnabas, Timothy & Silas

Acts 13—16

Go and make disciples of all the nations, baptizing them in the name of the Father and the Son and the Holy Spirit. MATTHEW 28:19

Overview

Say: **After Jesus died, rose to life again, and ascended into heaven, something big began to happen all over the world. Do you know what was happening?** *(Children respond.)*

People all over the world made the decision to follow Jesus!

Jewish people who chose to follow Jesus no longer had to follow the Old Testament laws, because Jesus made a new way to be forgiven. Also, people who weren't Jewish were learning about God and the good news about Jesus, too. Churches began to form and the early church, the group of people who followed Jesus, was growing.

How did all of these people, all over the world hear about becoming members of God's family? *(Children respond.)* **Missionaries, like Paul and his friends, spread the good news!**

Men like Paul, Barnabas, Timothy, and Silas traveled the world telling people about Jesus. We can share the good news about Jesus, too!

Opening Activity

Mixed-Up Messages

Preparation: On each sheet of paper, photocopy Matthew 28:19 Verse Cards. Cut each set of cards apart and shuffle them. Scatter cards around the playing area. Use masking tape, rope, or clothesline to make a start line several feet from the scattered cards.

Do: Children divide into teams of four or five players and line up behind the start line. Assign a different color of card to each team. On your signal, the first player on each team searches for their team's color of cards to find the first words of the verse. When the correct card is found, the player returns to the team and tags the next player who takes a turn to find the next verse card. Play continues until all teams have completed their verse. The first team to finish reads their verse aloud.

Materials

- Matthew 28:19 Verse Cards, page 216
- Different colored sheet of paper for each team of four or five players
- Scissors
- Masking tape, rope, or clothesline

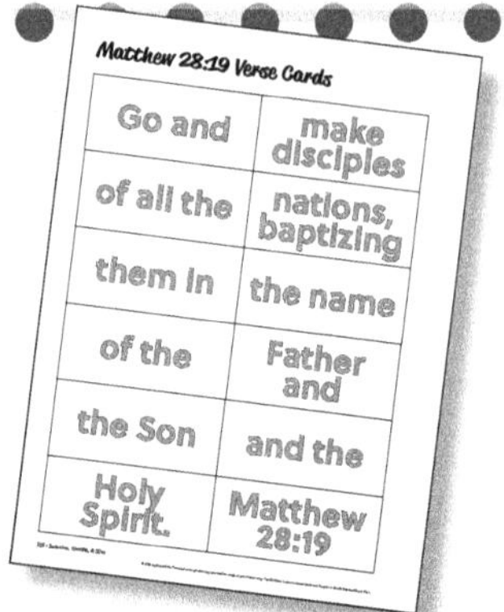
Matthew 28:19 Verse Cards

Go and	make disciples
of all the	nations, baptizing
them in	the name
of the	Father and
the Son	and the
Holy Spirit.	Matthew 28:19

Say: Before returning to heaven, Jesus gave his disciples one last command: to share the good news of how to become members of God's family. This wasn't just a command for Jesus' disciples though. This command was for everyone who follows Jesus. **We can share the good news about Jesus.**

Younger Child Option: Divide younger children into three groups. For each group, write the verse on a differently colored piece of poster board. Cut each poster board into three puzzle pieces. Hide puzzle pieces in room for teams to find and put together.

Bible Story

Spread the Gospel

Say: Do you remember Jesus' twelve disciples' names? I'm going to give you a name, and you tell me if they were a disciple or not.

- **Matthew?** (Disciple)
- **John?** (Disciple)
- **Lazarus?** (Not)
- **Peter?** (Disciple)
- **Moses?** (Not)
- **James?** (Disciple)
- **What about Paul?** (Not)

Jesus had only twelve disciples. These were the men who traveled around with him as Jesus taught about God, healed, and helped others for three years. But there were lots of other people who followed Jesus. Paul wasn't one of Jesus' original twelve disciples, but he was a follower of Jesus. And Paul obeyed Jesus' last command to spread the good news—the message of Jesus' birth, death, and resurrection.

But Paul didn't do it alone.

Read: Acts 13:2–4

Say: This passage talks about Saul, not Paul. Why? (*Children respond.*) Saul and Paul are the same man! After deciding to follow Jesus, Paul started traveling with his new friend Barnabas to spread the good news about Jesus.

Timothy traveled with him, too.

Read: Acts 16:1–3a

Say: And so did Silas.

Read: Acts 15:40

Say: These men traveled together telling people the good news about Jesus. And they traveled by themselves, too. They spread Jesus' messages in their hometowns and far away from home. Everywhere they went, they told people how to become a member of God's family, living with Jesus forever in heaven. **We can share the good news about Jesus,** too!

Pray: Pray over the kids, asking God to give them boldness to tell people about him!

Object Lesson

Materials

- Bag
- Embarrassing object to hide in bag (teddy bear, blankie, etc.)

Secret Bag

Preparation: Place object in bag to conceal it.

Say: *(Hold up the bag.)* **OK, I brought something really cool to show you all today.** *(Look into the bag and act very embarrassed.)* **Oh . . . um . . . this is really embarrassing. I must have accidentally put this in here by mistake this morning.** *(Look in the bag and act embarrassed again.)* **Ugh! I can't show you this.** *(Peek in again and then close the bag quickly.)* **No. No way! Much too embarrassing.**

(Continue like this until the children are going crazy to see what's inside.) **Fine! I'll show you if you promise not to laugh at me. It's really embarrassing.** *(Pull object—teddy bear or blankie—out of the bag.)*

There. Now you know. I still sleep with a (teddy bear)! And I'm a grown-up! Do you see why I was so embarrassed? *(Children respond.)*

OK . . . I don't REALLY sleep with a (teddy bear), but if I did, I might be ashamed of it and not want you all to know. Did you know that some people feel like that about Jesus? They are ashamed of following him.

But we shouldn't be. In 2 Timothy, Chapter 1, Paul encouraged his friend Timothy to not be ashamed of the gospel. Paul told Timothy that he shouldn't keep the message of Jesus to himself, like he was ashamed of it, but that he should boldly go and tell everyone about Jesus!

We should too! Our relationship with Jesus and the message of the gospel isn't something to be ashamed of. We can boldly go and share the good news about Jesus!

Additional Activity Options

Materials

- None

Traveling Tag

Do: Play a game like Tag. Instead of running, a leader calls out different ways for children to move: fly, ride a horse, walk, swim, etc.

Say: **How do you think Barnabas, Timothy, and Silas traveled telling people about Jesus? Did they take a train or airplane?** *(Children respond.)* **They walked or maybe rode a donkey or camel. Paul took some boat rides to visit people.**

How can we travel to share the good news about Jesus? *(Children respond.)* **Any way we want! We can tell people in our neighborhood about Jesus or people on the other side of the world, even!**

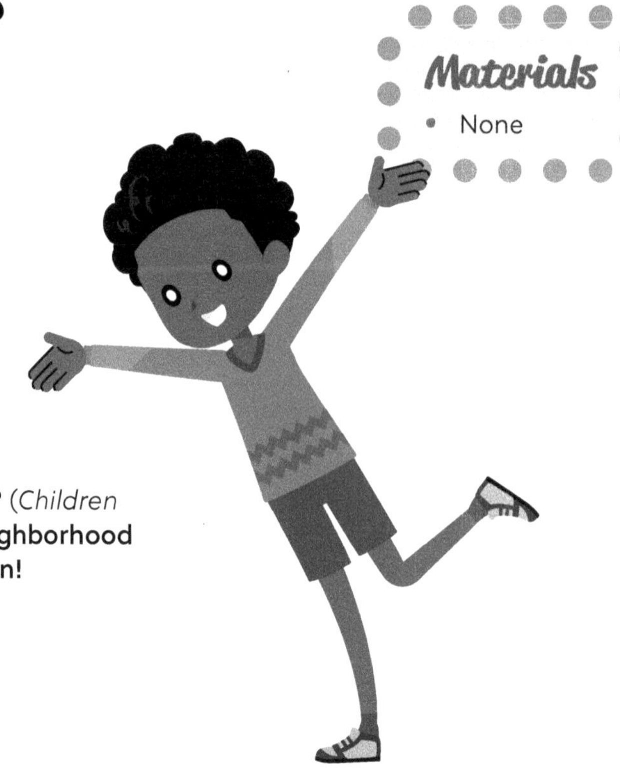

GO! Craft

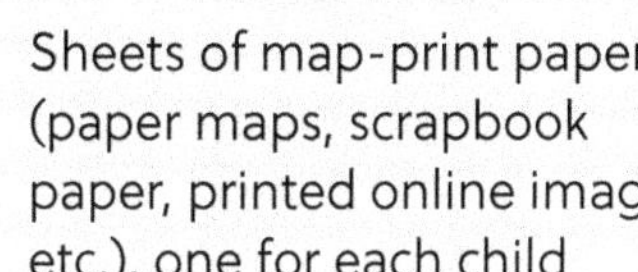

Materials

- Sheets of map-print paper (paper maps, scrapbook paper, printed online images, etc.), one for each child
- Cardboard squares or rectangles, one for each child
- Pencils
- Scissors
- Glue
- Colorful card stock
- Markers or crayons
- Stringing material (yarn, twine, thin ribbon, etc.)
- Tape

Do: Children turn a sheet of map-print paper facedown and place a cardboard square or rectangle on top. Pencils are used to trace the cardboard shape onto the paper sheet which is then cut out and glued to the cardboard.

Children cut out a colorful card-stock arrow and print the word *GO!* in large letters on it. Also, on either the arrow or map-print paper, children print the reference to the memory verse, Matthew 18:19.

Children cut a length of stringing material and tape each end to a top corner on the back of the cardboard.

Say: **Our wall art reminds us of our Bible story, our memory verse, and Jesus' call to go into the world like Barnabas, Timothy, and Silas. We can share the good news about Jesus wherever we go!**

Pick-a-Side Bible Review

Materials

- Masking tape, rope, or clothesline

Preparation: Use masking tape, rope, or clothesline to make a line down the center of the playing area.

Do: Play begins with children standing along the rope or clothesline.

Say: **As I read each statement, if you believe the statement is true, jump to the right side of the line. If you believe the statement is false, jump to the left side.**

1. **Jesus didn't want anyone to know he came back from the dead.** (False)
2. **Jesus returned to heaven without telling anyone.** (False)
3. **Before Jesus returned to heaven, he left one last instruction to his disciples.** (True)
4. **Jesus wanted ONLY his twelve disciples to spread the message of the gospel.** (False)
5. **Jesus wants everyone to tell people about him.** (True)
6. **Paul only traveled alone telling people about Jesus.** (False)
7. **Barnabas, Timothy, and Silas all traveled with Paul at one time.** (True)
8. **These missionaries never traveled by themselves preaching the gospel.** (False)
9. **We should never be ashamed of our relationship with Jesus and the gospel.** (True)
10. **Everywhere we go we should tell people about God!** (True)

Discussion Questions

1. **What is the gospel?**
2. **How would you tell someone how to get to heaven?**
3. **Why would someone (maybe) be ashamed of the gospel, like Paul warns against?**

Matthew 28:19 Verse Cards

Go and	make disciples
of all the	nations, baptizing
them in	the name
of the	Father and
the Son	and the
Holy Spirit.	Matthew 28:19

Chapter 43: Matthew

Matthew 9:9–13

Jesus said to his disciples, "If any of you wants to be my follower, you must give up your own way, take up your cross, and follow me." **MATTHEW 16:24**

Overview

Say: **We know the names of Jesus' twelve disciples, and we know that they gave up their lives to follow him. However, we don't know a lot of details and facts about all of the disciples' lives. We do know that Jesus called each man by name to follow him.**

Just like Jesus called his disciples to follow him, Jesus wants US to follow him, too!

Opening Activity

Come Over, Rover

Do: Play a game like Red Rover. Play begins with players in the middle of the playing area and two leaders, one on each side of the playing area. One of the leaders takes a turn to call players over to their side by calling out, "Come over, come over, anyone wearing red." Players wearing red join that leader.

Next, the leader on the other side takes a turn to call over players with different characteristics: wearing sneakers, with red hair, boys, girls, etc. After each turn, the leader names a new leader from the players on their team and then plays in the additional turns.

After several rounds, play is stopped, the players on each team are counted, and the team with the fewest players recites the memory verse.

Teaching Tip: If you have a large group, play with three or four leaders in a triangle or square formation.

Say: **It was fun being called by descriptive things about us. It's always special when we get called by name. When are some times you might be called by name?** (When you've been picked for a team. When you've won a prize. When it's your turn to be the line leader.)

Now imagine how it would have felt to live in Bible times and hear Jesus call your name! How exciting! You may not be able to hear Jesus call your name, but you can know that Jesus wants us to follow him.

Bible Story

Jesus Calls Matthew

Say: **Jesus had twelve disciples; some we know a lot about, and there are some that we know very little about. How many of Jesus' disciples can we name?** *(Children respond.)* **When Jesus called his disciples and invited them to follow him, each of them left his job and his family to follow Jesus—not just the way WE follow Jesus by obeying him and acting the way he acted, but by LITERALLY following Jesus as he traveled from town to town, telling people about God's love and helping others.**

There were four disciples who all had the same job. Guess what that job was. *(Children respond.)* **Peter, Andrew, James, and John were all fishermen. It was a common job for that time and at that place.**

Matthew, however, wasn't a fisherman. Matthew had a different, less popular job. He had a job that made most people not like him.

Read: Matthew 9:9

Say: **What job did Matthew have?** *(Children respond.)* **Matthew, also known as Levi, was a tax collector.**

The tax collectors in Jesus' day would charge some people extra taxes. What do you think they would do with all that extra tax money? *(Children respond.)* **They kept it for themselves!**

As you can imagine, it made people angry. Tax collectors were thought of as thieves, and people didn't really like them.

But Matthew was a tax collector! Jesus chose a man to follow him that had a job in which it was common to steal from people.

When Jesus was having dinner at Matthew's house with some of his tax collector friends, the Pharisees got upset. They fussed and fumed, "How could Jesus eat with sinners? How could Jesus choose a sinner to be one of his twelve closest friends?" What do you think Jesus said about that? *(Children respond.)* **Let's hear what Jesus had to say about that.**

Read: Matthew 9:12–13

Matthew's past didn't matter to Jesus. It wouldn't have mattered if Matthew was the most crooked tax collector that had ever lived. Jesus invited Matthew to follow him. Jesus called him. And right away, Matthew followed.

Pray: Praise Jesus for inviting us to follow him, like he invited Matthew. Invite any children who would like to know more about becoming a member of God's family to talk with you or another adult helper.

Object Lesson

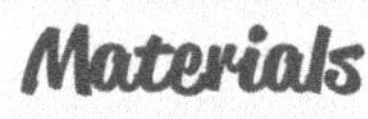

Candy Tax

Materials

- Individually wrapped candies, 2 for each child
- Bucket, box, or other container

Say: **I'm handing out some candies, but you can't eat any until you pay your candy tax!**

Do: Pass out two pieces of candy to each child. One at a time, call the children up by name to pay their candy tax. Each child must pay one piece of candy as their tax by placing it in the bucket, box, or other container. To demonstrate the unfairness of the tax collectors in Jesus' day, choose some children to pay you both pieces of candy. Take some of the candy out of the container to keep for yourself.

Say: **Was it very fair if you had to pay double the amount of candy tax that everyone else had to pay?** *(Children respond.)*

Teaching Tip: Make sure all children end up with two pieces of candy to eat or take home at the end of the activity!

Additional Activity Options

Compass Magnets

Materials

- Compass Cards, page 221
- White card stock
- Scissors or paper cutter
- Markers or crayons
- Glue
- Magnets, one for each child

Preparation: On white card stock, photocopy Compass Cards, making one card for each child. Cut out cards.

Do: Children color their Compass Card and glue a magnet on the back.

Say: **Over and over throughout the Bible, Jesus wants us to follow him! He wants each and every person to be his follower, to be his disciple. Put your Compass Magnet on your refrigerator or another place at your home to remind you to follow Jesus every day. You could also give your Compass Magnet to a friend so that they will know that Jesus wants them to follow him.**

Who's It?

Materials

- None

Do: Play a game like Tag. Depending on the size of your group, choose one to three taggers. Every once in a while, change who is "It" by calling out different names of children to be new taggers. Continue play as time and interest allow.

Say: **It was fun being chosen by name to be "It." Jesus chose his disciples and called them by name. Jesus has chosen you** *(Point to a child and say their name.)* **and you!** *(Continue pointing to and naming each child by name.)* **Jesus wants us to follow him!**

Beanbag Bible Review

Materials

- 2 or 3 beanbags

Do: Children stand together. Choose a volunteer to stand with their back to the group a few feet away. Volunteer then tosses beanbags, one at a time, to the group. Children who catch the beanbags work together to answer one of the questions below.

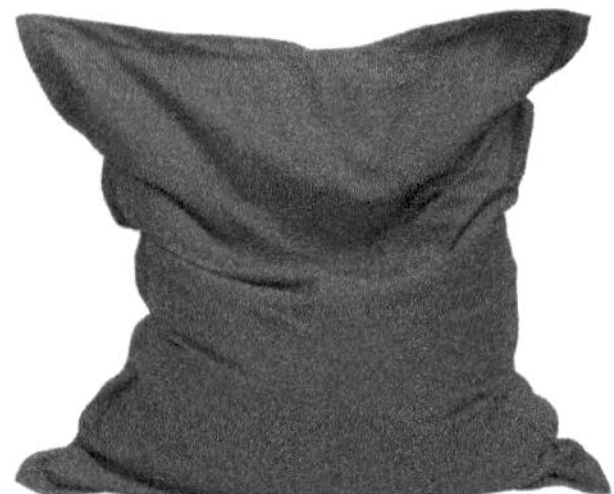

1. **How many disciples did Jesus have?** (Twelve)
2. **What was the most popular profession of the disciples?** (Fisherman)
3. **Which four disciples were fishermen?** (Peter, Andrew, James, and John)
4. **What did Matthew do for a living?** (Tax collector)
5. **Why didn't people like tax collectors?** (They would steal money from people by charging extra.)
6. **What did the Pharisees think of tax collectors?** (They thought they were sinners.)
7. **Did Jesus hang out with sinners?** (Yes! He had dinner at Matthew's house with other tax collectors.)
8. **Did Jesus know Matthew was a tax collector before he called him?** (Yes!)
9. **What did Matthew do after Jesus invited him to follow him?** (He followed Jesus immediately.)
10. **Does Jesus invite us to follow him?** (Yes!)

Discussion Questions

1. **Did Jesus only want the best, most God-fearing men to be his disciples?**
2. **What sort of people does God invite to follow him today?**
3. **What does it mean to be a follower of Christ?**

Twelve Friends

Materials

- Bibles

Do: Read about Jesus calling his disciples.

Read: Mark 3:13–19

Say: **How did these men respond when Jesus invited them to live for him? How have you responded?**

Compass Cards

Jesus said to his disciples, "If any of you wants to be my follower, you must give up your own way, take up your cross, and follow me." MATTHEW 16:24

Jesus said to his disciples, "If any of you wants to be my follower, you must give up your own way, take up your cross, and follow me." MATTHEW 16:24

Jesus said to his disciples, "If any of you wants to be my follower, you must give up your own way, take up your cross, and follow me." MATTHEW 16:24

Jesus said to his disciples, "If any of you wants to be my follower, you must give up your own way, take up your cross, and follow me." MATTHEW 16:24

Chapter 44: The Roman Officer

Mark 15:33–39

These were written so that you may continue to believe that Jesus is the Messiah, the Son of God, and that by believing in him you will have a life by the power of his name. **JOHN 20:31**

Overview

Say: **Before Jesus came to Earth, sins could only be temporarily forgiven by animal sacrifices. Jesus' death would change that, however. Jesus would be the one and only way to be forgiven of your sins once and for all and granted eternal life.**

While this is an amazing gift God gives us, not everyone in the time when Jesus was on Earth was happy with this. The religious leaders, the Pharisees, didn't like Jesus and what he was teaching. They didn't want others to listen to Jesus, either.

For many people, Jesus' death and coming to life again helped them to realize that Jesus is the Son of God, the Messiah, and that God offers eternal life through Jesus.

Opening Activity

Jail Tag

Materials

- Masking tape, rope, or clothesline

Preparation: Use masking tape, rope, or clothesline to mark off a large square in the playing area to be the "jail."

Do: Select one or two children to be "It." When a child gets tagged, they must go to the jail. Only a leader can release children from the jail by tagging them.

Say: **In our game, you only went to jail for a little while. Imagine, though, if you were arrested and sent to jail when you were innocent! But that shouldn't be too bad, right? When you go to trial, they'll figure out that you are innocent, and you'll be released in no time. Except what if you weren't?**

This is what happened to Jesus. Even though he hadn't committed any crimes or broken any

laws, he was arrested. Because he admitted to being the Son of God, some of the religious leaders had him sentenced to die. Jesus was crucified on a cross.

After his death, some people began to realize who Jesus was and what his death meant. Today, we're going to hear about a Roman officer who, after Jesus died, realized that **God offers eternal life through Jesus.**

Bible Story

Jesus the Messiah

Say: Jesus' death wasn't an ordinary death, because Jesus wasn't an ordinary man. When someone dies, their family is sad, but the earth itself doesn't start going crazy.

Jesus had been telling people for three years that he was the Son of God. Most people either didn't understand or didn't believe him. And when Jesus, the Son of God, died . . . Well, things got a little crazy.

As I read from the Gospel of Matthew, listen for the four, crazy things that happened.

Read: Mark 15:37–38

Say: What four crazy things happened when Jesus died?

- Darkness fell throughout the day for three hours.
- The Temple curtain was torn in two.
- The earth shook.
- Graves split open and the dead walked again.

Not only did things go crazy, but after he died, a lot of people realized that Jesus was exactly who he said he was. Jesus had been saying for years that he was the Messiah, the Son of God and that he was going to make a way for people to become members of God's family. It wasn't until after he died that many, like the Roman officer, realized that he had been speaking the truth all along.

Read: Mark 15:39

The Roman officer said it best, "This man truly was the Son of God!" Jesus came to seek and to save the lost. **God offers eternal life through Jesus.** We can't have this eternal life, except through Jesus.

Pray: Thank Jesus for dying on the cross for us so that we can be forgiven of our sins and become members of God's family. Invite any children who would like to know more about becoming a member of God's family to talk with you or another adult helper.

Object Lesson

Materials

- Clear glass with water
- Metal pie pan
- Empty toilet-paper tube
- Large egg

Believe It or Not

Preparation: Set the clear glass with water on a table. Center the metal pie pan on the top of the glass. Place the toilet-paper tube in the center of the pie pan. Set the egg on top of the tube.

Before children arrive, practice knocking the egg into the glass of water by keeping your hand flat, swinging it back a few inches and then smacking the pie pan forcefully. The pie pan will slide off the glass, knocking away the toilet-paper tube and the egg will fall directly into the glass of water. Practice a few times until you are comfortable with the action before demonstrating it to the children.

Say: *(Place the pie tin on the glass, the tube on the pie tin, and the egg on the tube.)* **What would you say if I told you that I can get this egg into the glass of water without touching the egg, the toilet-paper tube, or the glass? Would you believe me?** *(Children respond.)* **Any ideas how I can do that?** *(As children offer theories, remind them you can't touch the egg, the tube, or the glass. After a few moments of theorizing, smack the pie tin as practiced.)*

I told you exactly what I was going to do, but some of you didn't believe me. That's the same thing that happened to Jesus, both in his time and today. But like the Roman officer from today's Bible story, we can know Jesus was the Savior God had promised. We can know that God offers eternal life through Jesus.

Additional Activity Options

Guards!!! Game

Materials

- None

Do: Select one to three players to be the Guards. The remaining players move around freely as you play music. When you stop the music, the players freeze. The Guards' job is to make sure no children move while the music is not playing.

Children can try to move as much as possible without being caught. If a player is caught moving, they become a Guard and the Guard who caught them moving becomes a regular player. After a few moments, start music again. Play additional rounds as time and interest allow.

Say: **The Roman officer was a solider, and one of the jobs of soldiers was to guard things. The officer was likely at the crucifixion of Jesus to keep an eye on everything and make sure that everyone was behaving themselves. He might have been assigned to keep control of the crowd, but he got something amazing in return. He realized who Jesus was that day! He learned that God offers eternal life through Jesus.**

Cross-Marks Craft

Materials

- Cross-Marks Patterns, page 226
- White card stock
- Scissors
- Markers or crayons
- Hole punch
- Variety of thin ribbbon

Preparation: On card stock, photocopy Cross-Marks Patterns, making one cross pattern for each child plus extras. Cut to separate the crosses.

Do: Children use markers or crayons to decorate their crosses and then cut them out. They punch a hole at the top of the cross, cut a length of ribbon, and thread the ribbon through the hole to make a bookmark.

Say: **Jesus' death on the cross was a really big deal. Since we have the Bible, God's Word, we can read about it and realize just how big of a deal Jesus' death and resurrection was. We still need to be reminded, though.**

Jesus wasn't just any ordinary guy. He was, and still is, the Son of God. Because Jesus died on the cross and rose again, we can accept the gift of eternal life. God offers eternal life through Jesus.

Younger Child Option: Pre-cut the paper into cross shapes. Assist children to punch holes and thread ribbons through the holes.

Thumbs Up Thumbs Down Bible Review

Say: **Give a thumbs up if the answer to the question is true. Give a thumbs down if it is false. If the answer is false, explain what makes it false.**

1. **Jesus was a criminal.** (False)
2. **Jesus claimed to be the Son of God.** (True)
3. **Jesus was (and is) the Son of God.** (True)
4. **The religious leaders, the Pharisees, understood that Jesus was God.** (False)
5. **It was a surprise to everyone that Jesus was actually God, because he never said anything about it.** (False)
6. **Jesus was innocent of any crimes.** (True)
7. **Jesus was crucified on a cross.** (True)
8. **Jesus' death was a normal, nothing-weird-about-it death.** (False)
9. **Dead people came back to life when Jesus died.** (True)
10. **Jesus is the only way to have your sins forgiven.** (True)

Discussion Questions

1. **Is Jesus God or the Son of God?**
2. **Are there any ways (other than through Jesus) to be forgiven?**
3. **How can a person be saved?**

Jesus Is God

Materials

- Bibles and Bible storybooks
- Large sheet of paper
- Markers or crayons

Do: Using the Bibles and Bible storybooks for reference, children make a chart or diagram listing the ways Jesus had shown people who he was during his earthly ministry.

Cross-Mark Patterns

Chapter 45: Nicodemus

John 3:1–21

This is how God loved the world: He gave his one and only Son, so that everyone who believes in him will not perish but have eternal life. JOHN 3:16

Overview

Say: **Think for a minute: What's something you really love? When I count to three, say that thing really loud. One . . . Two . . . Three!** (*Children respond.*) **You all had a lot of really good ideas. I heard a lot of great answers there!**

Maybe you said you love ice cream or baseball. You might really love your mom or your best friend. But there is a love that's even greater than that.

Nicodemus, a man who lived at the time Jesus was here on Earth, went to Jesus one night and learned about the greatest love ever, the love that would make a way for people to be freed from their sins. That night, Nicodemus learned just how much God loves us!

Opening Activity

Have a Heart Game

Preparation: Print each word from John 3:16 on a separate paper heart. Before children arrive, hide the hearts around the room.

Do: Children search for the hearts and work together to put them in order.

Materials

- Paper hearts
- Marker

Say: **Let's say the verse all together.** (*Lead group to recite John 3:16 aloud.*)

Younger Child Option: Lead children to repeat the verse after you, one phrase at a time.

This verse might be one of the most popular and well-known verses in the Bible. It's also a very important verse. In one verse—in one sentence—Jesus told Nicodemus all about God's extraordinary plan for the salvation of all people. God made this plan because God loves us!

Bible Story

Nicodemus Visits Jesus

Do: Start the lesson off by lowering the lights. Lead children to sneak from one area of the room to another to gather for the Bible story.

Say: **Today we're going to hear about a man who must have felt like he had to sneak around to talk to Jesus. Nicodemus was a Pharisee—one of the Jewish religious leaders of Jesus' day. Most of the Pharisees where angry with Jesus. They didn't want the people to make Jesus their leader instead of them. It was the Pharisees who plotted to have Jesus killed.**

But Nicodemus was different. He wanted to know more about Jesus. So, one night, after it was dark and he wouldn't be seen, he went to visit Jesus. Nicodemus called Jesus *Rabbi*, which means teacher, so Nicodemus must have respected Jesus. "Rabbi," Nicodemus said, "we all know that God has sent you to teach us. Your miraculous signs are evidence that God is with you."

Read: John 3:3–4

Nicodemus didn't understand what Jesus was talking about. He asked Jesus, "How can an old man like me be born again?"

Jesus wasn't saying that person had to become a baby again. Jesus explained that he was talking about our spirits being born again. Our spirits are the inside part of us that think and feel and make decisions. When we become part of God's family, God gives us the Holy Spirit to change the way we think and feel and make decisions. God's Spirit helps us have good attitudes and make good decisions so that we can live the very best life. The changed spirit inside us is what Jesus meant by being born again.

Read: John 3:3–4

Say: **What did Jesus compare the Holy Spirit to?** (*Children respond.*) **Can you see the wind?** (*Children respond.*) **If we can't see the wind, how do we know it is there?** (*Children respond.*) **Even though we can't see the wind, we can see what it does: trees bend, leaves fall, kites fly, etc. In the same way, even though you can't see the Holy Spirit in someone, you can see how the Holy Spirit changes them.**

Jesus explained that it is because God loves us that he wants our spirits to change so we can have the right thoughts, the right feelings, and make the right decisions.

Read: John 3:16–17

Say: **God was willing to send Jesus to Earth to die for us because God loves us!**

Pray: Thank God for sending Jesus so that we can become members of his family and that our spirits can be born again. Ask children interested in learning more about how to become a member of God's family to speak with you or another adult leader or helper.

Object Lesson

Baby Talk

Say: *(Show the baby-care objects you gathered. Children identify each one. Discuss how each one is used to care for a baby.)* **Why do parents and caregivers bother buying so much stuff to take care of a baby?** *(Children respond.)* **Parents and other caregivers want to take care of babies because they love them! And the babies can't take care of themselves. That's why so much time, money, and attention is given to caring for babies.**

God loves us. That's why Jesus was sent to Earth—to make a way for us to become members of God's family. We can't save ourselves any more than a baby can take care of itself. Only Jesus was able to be the perfect sacrifice to pay the price for our sins. We can never be good enough to earn our place in God's family. It's only by accepting forgiveness through Jesus that we can be born again into God's family and live with him in heaven forever.

Materials

- Variety of baby-care objects (blankets, bottles, baby food, car seat, baby wipes, etc.)

Additional Activity Options

God's Love Rocks Craft

Do: Children use permanent markers to decorate rocks with messages about God's love. Suggestions:

- God's Love Rocks!
- God Loves Us!
- John 3:16

Children draw other decorations:
hearts, swirls, polka dots, flowers, lightning bolts, etc.

Materials

- Clean, flat fist-sized rocks, one or more for each child
- Black and colored permanent markers

Say: **John 3:16 is a perfect reminder of just how much God loves us! Every time you see your rock, remember that God loves you so much that he sent Jesus to die for you!**

Enrichment Idea: Encourage children to place their rock somewhere in their neighborhood for someone to find and learn that God loves them.

Fact Face-Off Bible Review

Do: Form two teams. Team members face off against each other, one at a time, answering the questions and earning points for their team.

1. **What group was Nicodemus a part of?** (The Pharisees)
2. **Did the Pharisees like Jesus?** (No. They wanted to kill him.)
3. **When did Nicodemus visit Jesus?** (At night)
4. **Why did Nicodemus visit Jesus?** (To ask him questions)
5. **Jesus told him that a person had to be ______ ______.** (Born again)
6. **Did Jesus mean that a person had to become a baby again or to be born again spiritually?** (Spiritually)
7. **Because God ______ us, he sent Jesus.** (Loved)
8. **How can a person be saved from their sins?** (Through Jesus)
9. **Can we save ourselves from our sins?** (No)
10. **In your own words, what does John 3:16 say?** (*Answers will vary. Call on two or three children.*)

Discussion Questions

1. **How did Nicodemus know about Jesus if the Pharisees hated him?**
2. **What does it mean to be born again?**
3. **How many ways are there to get to heaven?**

Shark Attack Game

Do: Children sit on the ground in a large circle with a parachute spread out in the middle of the circle. Select one child to be the Shark and one to be the Lifeguard. The Shark goes under the parachute, while the other children sit with their legs under the parachute.

Materials

- Large parachute

The Shark will try to pull the other children under the parachute. The Lifeguard tries to rescue any children being pulled under the parachute by grabbing their hands and saying, "I've saved you!" The Shark immediately stops pulling the child and finds someone else to pull under the parachute. If the Shark successfully pulls a child under, they become another Shark and plays continues.

Say: **You couldn't rescue yourself from the shark attacks in our game. Can you save yourself from sin?** (*Children respond.*) **Because God loves us, he sent Jesus to Earth so that we can be forgiven from our sins and become members of God's family. Only Jesus was able to make it possible for us to be with him in heaven forever.**

John 3:16 Word Search

Find and circle the words of John 3:16 in the word search below.

M G Q O S I H N M U L Z Z B E
X A D Z G U D N D N P N C R F
L L I W E I E E E I X C S E M
G O D Y W Y V N H S I R E P R
O E R P S R O O S K N Z P V J
V T U B O N L Y O M I H D Y B
R E M K G O H R N A L X T K W
N R X R A D A E O N E G Q U O
R N W C V R V V U P E E O G R
T A H T E W E E S E K L X K L
H L W U P H S Z Z J S I A N D
E I D K E O E F I L T H P C M

Chapter 46: John the Baptist

Matthew 3

"John saw Jesus coming toward him and said, 'Look! The Lamb of God who takes away the sin of the world!'" **JOHN 1:29**

Overview

Say: **If you knew a giant robot was going to destroy your house in two days, what would you do?** (*Children respond.*) **You wouldn't just sit in your house waiting for it to be destroyed. Because you have time, you'd likely try to figure out a way to stop the robot or at least make sure that you aren't in your house when the robot comes! At the very least, wouldn't you tell someone?** (*Children respond.*)

We don't have to worry about any giant robots destroying your house, but we do know that everyone needs to get right with God. The word *repent* means to feel sorry about the wrong things you do and decide to STOP doing them. Jesus' cousin, John the Baptist, was chosen by God to tell people that if we repent, God will forgive us.

Opening Activity

Heads or Tails

Materials

- Coin

Do: Instruct children to stand if they think the coin will land on heads and sit if they think it will land on tails. Flip coin. Children who guess incorrectly recite the memory verse.

Flip the coin several times, playing several rounds of the game. Vary the motions kids do to show heads or tails: touch their nose or touch their ear, put hands on their hips or over their head, stand on one foot or tiptoes, etc.

Say: **Could you know for certain if the coin would land on heads or tails?** (*Children respond.*) **No! Coin flipping is a game of chance. There is no way you could know what it would land on. If you did, you could have picked the right answer every time.**

Has God given any clues about how to get to heaven? (*Children respond.*) **Yes! Throughout the Bible, over and over, God has told his people about heaven and how to get there. Our story is about John the Baptist and how he prepared the way for people to know that they need to stop doing wrong things and that Jesus is the way to be forgiven.**

Bible Story

John Baptizes Believers

Storytelling Option: Select a volunteer to dress up like John the Baptist by wearing a faux fur robe or vest (explain this was as close as you could get to camel's hair!) and a leather belt. While you talk about his eating locusts, make the volunteer think they are going to have to eat locust, but give them gummy bugs instead.

Say: **Long before John the Baptist was born, the prophet Isaiah wrote about him.**

Read: Matthew 3:3

Say: **God was promising that a messenger would come. This messenger would prepare people for Jesus to teach them about God. This messenger would tell the people that they need to repent of their sins and be forgiven. This messenger was Jesus' cousin, John the Baptist.**

John the Baptist was a very interesting person. He lived in the hot, dry desert and wore rough clothes made from camel's hair. And John had a very interesting diet. He ate honey and locusts! Locusts are insects like grasshoppers!

Naturally, people were very curious about John. They came from their homes and traveled from different cities to hear him preach. John spent most of his days talking to crowds of people. He told them to stop doing wrong things and that God's Son, the promised Savior, would be coming soon.

Many of the people believed what John told them. They wanted to show God that they were sorry for their sins. How do you think the people showed God they were sorry and wanted to repent? *(Children respond.)*

John would take the people who were sorry for doing wrong things to the river and he would baptize them. This is why John was called "John the Baptist!"

One day while John was preaching and baptizing people, some of the religious leaders came to listen to him. John told them that they needed to repent from their sins, just like everyone else. The religious leaders didn't like hearing that. They preferred to think of themselves as better than other people.

Read: Matthew 3:11

John told them that his job was to prepare the way for the great person still to come. John knew that Jesus was the Messiah, the Savior of the world. And only through Jesus can we be forgiven of our sins and live forever in heaven.

John told his message to everyone he could. He didn't know when people would die or when the world would end. Just like we don't know, either. So, just like John, we can tell people that if we repent, God will forgive us.

Pray: Pray that the boys and girls will repent from their sins and accept God's forgiveness!

Object Lesson

One Way

Say: **Is there just one way to get into our church building?** *(Children respond.)* **No way! There are different doors, plus you can travel to this building by different roads, too.**

How many ways are there to get to heaven?

Can you get to heaven by being really, really good? *(Children respond. Hold up No sign.)* **No!**

Can you go to heaven by believing in whatever you want to believe in? *(Children respond. Hold up No sign.)*

(Hold up the One Way sign.) **There is only one way for us to get to heaven—through Jesus! He is the one and only way for us to have our sins forgiven and receive eternal life.**

John knew this because God had revealed it to him! That is why he spent his life telling people that they needed to repent of their sins and follow Jesus. Jesus is the only way to get to heaven! If we repent, God will forgive us.

Materials

- One Way Object Lesson Signs, page 236

Additional Activity Options

Sweeter Than Honey Snacks

Do: Children take turns measuring and adding ingredients to mixing bowl and then take turns mixing ingredients together. Divide the mixture evenly and pass out to children on a waxed paper square. Children roll their dough into bite sized bites and then enjoy.

Say: **John the Baptist didn't just live off of locusts in the wilderness. Scripture tells us that he ate honey, as well. Honey is sweet. Like a natural sugar!**

Psalm 119:103 tells us that God's words are even sweeter than honey.

In Jesus' day, God sent John the Baptist to warn people that the Kingdom of Heaven was near and that they needed to follow Jesus. Today, God has given us his words—words that are sweeter than honey—to tell us to repent and follow Jesus. If we repent, God will forgive us.

Yield: This recipe makes approximately 24 bite-sized snacks.

Materials

- 3 cups quick cooking oats
- 1 cup smooth nut or seed butter
- ½ cup honey
- ⅓ cup mini chocolate chips
- Measuring cups and spoons
- Mixing bowl
- Spatula
- Waxed paper

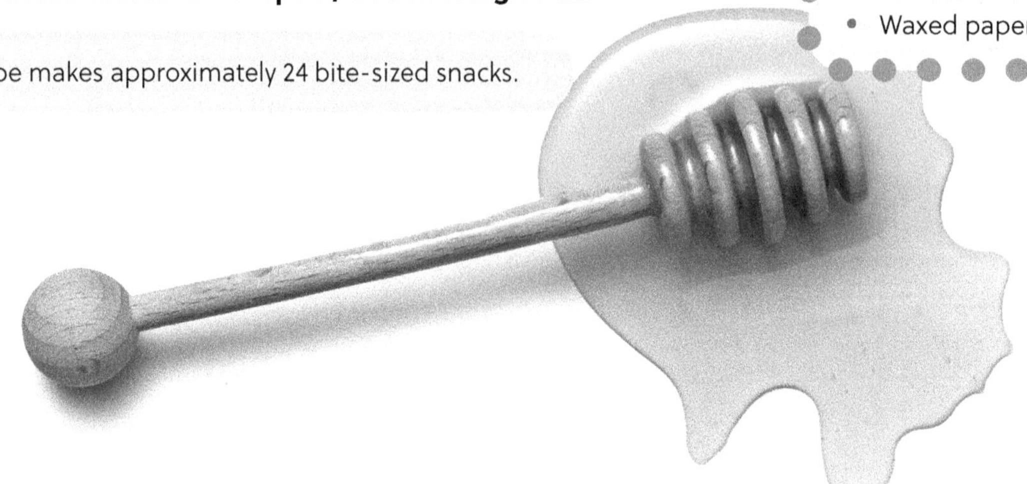

A Voice in the Desert Game

Do: Choose a volunteer to be John. Place blindfold on John. Remaining players move freely around the playing area while John calls out, "Repent for the Kingdom of Heaven is near!"

When John stops speaking, other players all freeze. John tries to tag another player. He can take five steps in any direction as he reaches with both arms to find a player to tag.

Say: **After John started preaching in the wilderness, people came from all over Jerusalem, Judah, and the Jordan Valley to hear him. What he was preaching about the Kingdom of Heaven was an important message that people needed to hear. People need to know that if we repent, God will forgive us.**

Beanbag Bible Review

Do: Children stand together. Choose a volunteer to stand with their back to the group a few feet away. Volunteer then tosses beanbags, one at a time, to the group. Children who catch the beanbags work together to answer one of the questions below.

Materials

- 2 or 3 beanbags

1. **John was Jesus' cousin.** (True)
2. **John had no clue who Jesus was.** (False)
3. **John had a nice house in the city.** (False)
4. **John ate locust and honey in the wilderness.** (True)
5. **John prepared the way for Jesus.** (True)
6. **John told people that they needed to repent from their sins.** (True)
7. **Following Jesus is not needed to go to heaven.** (False)
8. **Jesus is the only way to heaven.** (True)
9. **John said that Jesus would baptize people in the name of the Holy Spirit.** (True)
10. **We need to repent from our sins, too.** (True)

Discussion Questions

1. **How did John know that the Kingdom of Heaven was near?**
2. **What is heaven like?**
3. **What is the difference between being saved and being baptized?**

Additional Time-Filler: Read Revelation 21–22 aloud. Children write or draw what they think heaven is like. When children are finished, they share with each other what their vision of heaven is like.

One Way Object Lesson Sign.

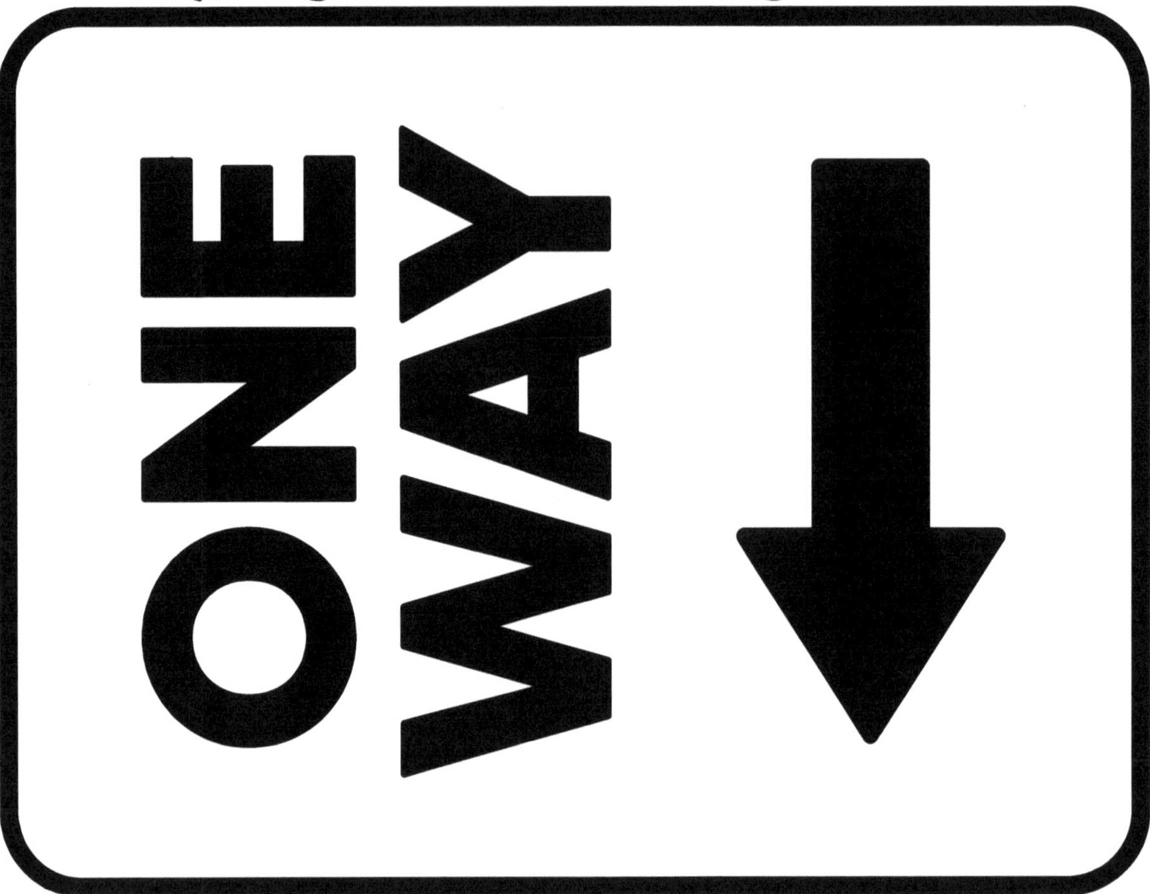

Chapter 47: Jeremiah

Jeremiah 29

"I know the plans I have for you," says the Lord. *"They are plans for good and not for disaster, to give you a future and a hope."* **JEREMIAH 29:11**

Overview

Say: **What are some things you hope for? When you have a stomach bug? When it's Christmastime? When you have a math test?** *(Children respond.)*

Hope feels good! When something bad is happening in life, hope keeps you going. God knows this. Our verse tells us one very good reason we can have hope at all times. God's plans are good.

God's plans are good.

Big Idea

Opening Activity

Face Off!

Say: **On the count of three, I want you to show me with your face how you are feeling today—happy, sad, angry, worried, or even hungry! Let's see if your face matches my face! One . . . two . . . three!** *(Children show how they feel. If their face matches the one you made, give them a high five. Repeat a few times, instructing children to choose a different face.)*

Since we are human, we have happy days and sad days. We have days when we are feeling silly, cranky, or upset. We feel all sorts of emotions. But what if you were known by others because of the way you always felt?

How would you feel if people called you "the weeping kid?" *(Children respond.)*

The prophet Jeremiah is known as "the weeping prophet" because in a lot of his writings, he was sad. He was sad because things weren't going well for God's people. But there was still reason for hope because God's plans are good! Let's hear more about Jeremiah.

Bible Story

Hope for Israel

Do: Before telling the story, instruct children to build a home out of cardboard building blocks or boxes. After a few minutes, a leader comes and destroys the children's homes, telling them they have been "exiled" from their home and must move to the Bible storytelling area.

Materials

- Variety of cardboard building blocks or boxes

Say: Wow! Your home was destroyed, and you were sent to live somewhere else. If this really had happened to you, if your home was destroyed and you were exiled, how would you feel? *(Children respond.)* You might be like Jeremiah and weep.

Things were rough for God's people, the Israelites. They had disobeyed God, over and over, so God allowed their land to be taken over by another country and the people were exiled. They had no country they could call their own. Guess how many years they had been in exile. *(Play a game telling children to guess higher or lower until they land on the correct answer, seventy years.)* They were in the first year of their seventy-year exile when God gave them hope. Listen to the message God gave his prophet Jeremiah.

Read: Jeremiah 29:10–14

Say: Life was not easy for the Israelites while they were in exile. And they would have seventy years of it! But they had hope. God gave them the promise that he was with them and that he had a plan for them. No matter how bad life seemed at the moment, they had hope that God would bring good to their lives again.

Pray: Give children time to pray for their futures.

Object Lesson

Materials

- Magic 8 Ball or faux crystal ball

A Hope and a Future

Say: *(Hold up Magic 8 Ball or faux crystal ball.)* If you know what this is, put your hands on your head. What is it used for? *(Children respond.)* If you had a magic ball to tell you what was happening in the future, do you think you'd be sad? If so, stand up. *(Children respond.)* How about worried. Would you worry? If you think you might worry, stand on one foot. *(Children respond.)* What are some other things a magic ball could tell you? (What you were getting for your birthday. If you passed your spelling test. If you made the swim team.)

Perhaps the magic ball would make the bad times in life seem not so bad, because you'd know exactly when it would end and what would happen.

But magic balls aren't real. Magic isn't real.

God IS real. And his Word, the Bible, is true. We know that what the Bible says will happen, will happen. And the Bible tells us that **God's plans are good**. In his Word, over and over, God gives us promises for our future. And it's always GOOD!

- He promises to be with us always, through the good times and the bad.
- God promises that he is in control of our lives and that he has a plan for our lives, as well.
- God promises that this life isn't the end. Heaven is waiting for all the members of his family.

We don't know the future, but we have hope. We know **God's plans are good!**

Additional Activity Options

Materials

- 5 hula hoops
- 5 sheets of construction paper

Hope Hop

Preparation: On separate sheets of paper, print a phrase of the memory verse:

- "I know the plans I have for you"
- says the LORD.
- "They are plans for good and not for disaster
- to give you a future and a hope."
- Jeremiah 29:11

Place hoops in activity area, a few feet apart in a random design. Inside each hoop, place one of the verse papers you prepared.

Do: One at a time, players hop from hoop to hoop, in verse order, saying the memory verse aloud. Play additional rounds, rearranging the verse papers before each round.

Say: Jeremiah 29:11 reminds us that as believers in Christ, we have hope. We know that God is in control. He has a plan for our future! God's plans are good!

Pick-a-Side Bible Review

Materials

- Masking tape, rope, or clothesline

Preparation: Use masking tape, rope, or clothesline to make a line down the center of the playing area.

Do: Play begins with children standing along the rope or clothesline.

Say: Choose one of two ways to complete the following statements, *A* or *B*. If you choose *A*, jump to the right side of the line. If you choose *B*, jump to the left side.

1. **The Israelites *A*—obeyed God all of the time or *B*—disobeyed God.** (*B*—disobeyed God)
2. **Jeremiah was a *A*—prophet or *B*—king.** (*A*—prophet)
3. **Jeremiah was known as the *A*—weeping prophet or *B*—happy prophet.** (*A*—weeping prophet)
4. **He wept because *A*—his dog died or *B*—God's people were being punished.** (*B*—God's people were being punished)
5. **Where were the Israelites exiled to? *A*—Babylon or *B*—Judah** (*A*—Babylon)
6. **The Babylonian Exile lasted for *A*—seventy years or *B*—seven years.** (*A*—seventy years)
7. **Through Jeremiah God reminded the people *A*—that they deserved their punishment or *B*—that he was still with them.** (*B*—that he was still with them)
8. **God promises *A*—that bad things won't happen to his people or *B*—that he will be with his people.** (*B*—that he will be with his people)
9. ***A*—God's plans are good or *B*—knowing the future is good.** (*A*—God's plans are good)
10. **The hope of heaven is for *A*—all who believe or B—everyone.** (*A*—all who believe)

Discussion Questions

1. **What hope did God give to the Israelites living in Babylon?**
2. **What hope does God give us?**
3. **How does God give us hope?**

Frame It!

Preparation: Photocopy Beautiful Plans, making one copy for each child plus extras.

Do: Children color pictures and glue to pieces of lightweight cardboard that are larger than the picture. Then, using scissors, children cut the cardboard into a frame around their picture.

Children lay strips of colored or patterned duct tape around the edges of the frame to decorate it.

Finally, children punch a hole in each of the two top corners of their framed picture. Children cut a length of stringing material long enough to form a hanger for their framed picture, thread each end through a hole in their framed picture and tie knots to secure the hanger.

Say: **God's plans are good.** **But sometimes, like the Israelites, we need a reminder. Our verse today is a great reminder that God has a plan for our futures and that plan gives us hope!**

Materials

- Beautiful Plans, page 241
- Markers or crayons
- Scissors
- Lightweight cardboard (such as a cereal box) or poster board
- Glue
- Variety of colored and patterned duct tape
- Hole punch
- Stringing material (yarn, twine, thin ribbon, etc.)

Hope Cards

Do: Children write cards with messages of hope about God's plan to give to others.

Encourage them to include the memory verse, Jeremiah 29:11, and to remind people that **God's plans are good**!

Materials

- Cards and envelopes
- Markers or crayons

HE'S GOT
big plans
for me
JEREMIAH 29:11

Beautiful Plans

Jeremiah 29:11

Chapter 48: Balaam

Numbers 22–24

My sheep listen to my voice; I know them, and they follow me. **JOHN 10:27**

Overview

Say: **The Bible tells us about a lot of the crazy things that have happened here on Earth. When you think about all the crazy things that we read about in the Bible, what do you think is the CRAZIEST thing?** (*Children respond.*) **A worldwide flood was pretty crazy. The dead coming back to life was pretty crazy. All of the miracles—like the splitting of the Red Sea or when Jesus multiplied the bread and fish—were crazy. They were crazy, but they really happened!**

Today we're going to hear about a time something really crazy happened with an animal. Can you guess what it might be? (*Children respond.*)

In the Bible, we read how God spoke to a man named Balaam, but Balaam didn't listen. So God had a DONKEY talk to him! Before we hear what happened with Balaam and the donkey, let's play a game where we need to listen carefully.

Opening Activity

Listen Closely!

Do: Players walk around the playing area while music plays. When a leader calls out a number, players race to form groups of that many children.

The last child or group to form recites the memory verse. Repeat, calling out different numbers as time and interest allow.

Materials

- Children's worship music and player

Say: **What happened if you weren't listening for the numbers in our game?** (*Children respond.*) **Listening is important.**

When are some times it is important to listen? Why is it important? (*Children respond.*) **We need to listen to the fire alarms warning us of danger. We need to listen to the bell telling us when we are late for class. We need to listen to teachers, coaches, parents, and most importantly, we need to listen to God. God speaks to us. But we have to listen.**

Bible Story

Balaam and His Donkey

Storytelling Option: Bring in a king's costume, a Bible-times robe and headdress, a donkey costume, and an angel costume. Volunteers put on the costumes and act out the action as you tell the story.

Say: **King Balak the Moabite king was worried. He saw the Israelites traveling throughout Moab and he was worried. There were a lot of Israelites. He felt threatened by them, fearing that because there were so many of them, they would devour everything in the land . . . HIS land. They might even try to take his land away from him.**

So, King Balak sent messengers to ask Balaam to come and curse the Israelites. Balaam was not one of God's true prophets. Instead, he was someone who could be paid to make prophesies or bring blessings or curses on others. He was not one of the Israelites who worshiped the one true God. Instead, Balaam would worship and speak for any god he was paid to speak for.

Read: Numbers 22:4–6

What do you think Balaam said? (*Children respond.*) **Balaam told the men to wait and he would ask God what to do first. This sounds like a good idea, right?** (*Children respond.*) **But the Bible doesn't tell us that Balaam prayed to God to ask him what he should do. Instead, the Bible tells us that Balaam went to sleep! What do you think happened next?** (*Children respond.*)

Since Balaam didn't come to him in prayer, God came to Balaam! God told Balaam, "You are not to curse these people, for they have been blessed!"

So the next morning, Balaam told the men, "God said not to curse the people, so I won't do it. You can just go home."

Read: Numbers 22:14–20

God was angry. The Bible doesn't tell us why God became angry. But God knows everything. God may have known that Balaam was planning to take all the money and curse God's people.

Let's read what happens next.

Read: Numbers 22:21–38

Say: **How amazing—and crazy—was that? A talking donkey . . . God found a very interesting way to get Balaam's attention! God speaks to us, and when he does, we need to listen and obey.**

Pray: Pray that the boys and girls will listen to God's voice and obey.

Object Lesson

Materials

- Sound effects for an earthquake, wind, and fire; and player (Free sound effects MP3s are available online)

Listen Up

Say: **Balaam heard God speak directly to him. Has God ever spoken to you that way?** *(Children respond.)* **Most people haven't heard God speak out loud to them. What do you think God's voice would sound like?** *(Children respond.)*

Balaam wasn't a true prophet of God. But Elijah was a true prophet of God. In 1 Kings 19:11–13, the prophet Elijah was listening for God's voice. An earthquake came *(Play earthquake sound effect.)*, **but God's voice wasn't in the earthquake. A mighty wind tore through** *(Play wind sound effect.)*, **but God's voice wasn't in the wind, either. Finally, there was fire** (Play fire sound effect.), **but God's voice wasn't in the fire.**

When God spoke to Elijah, he spoke to him in a still, small voice—like a whisper. Elijah heard him because he was listening for him.

God speaks to us. If we listen, God speaks to us through his Holy Spirit and he speaks to us through his Word. Sometimes God speaks to us through the wise words of people who love God. But in order to hear God speak to us, we have to be listening!

Additional Activity Options

Listen, Balaam

- None

Do: Play several rounds of a game like Simon Says. Instead of beginning commands with "Simon says" the leader says, "Listen, Balaam." If the leader says "Listen, Balaam" players have to do the command mentioned until another command is given. If the leader does not begin a command with "Listen, Balaam," then any players who do the command have to sit on the ground and wait for the next round.

When there is one player left, remaining players and the leader answer one of the questions beginning on page 245, recite the memory verse, or tell a sentence about the Bible story.

The last remaining player then becomes the new leader and a new round is played. Continue playing rounds as time and interest allow.

Say: **In order to win at our game, you have to do more than just listen carefully. You have to do what you're told!**

God speaks to us. But like with Balaam, just hearing what God says isn't enough. We have to listen to him and obey.

Donkey Headband Craft

Materials

- Donkey Headband Patterns, page 246
- White card stock
- Scissors
- Markers or crayons
- Stapler

Preparation: On card stock, photocopy Donkey Headband Patterns, making one pattern for each child plus extras. Cut to separate patterns. Cut several strips of card stock that are 1- to 2-inches wide.

Teaching Tip: Paper cutters make quick work of cutting out the card-stock strips!

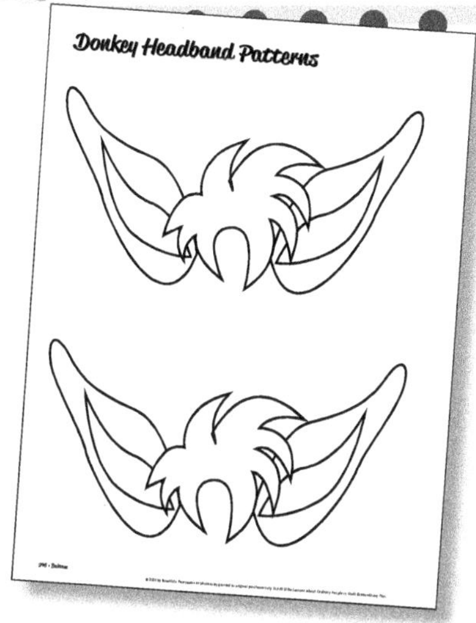

Do: Children color and then cut out their donkey pattern. Help each child wrap the card-stock strips around their head and staple the ends of the strips together to make a headband. Staple the colored donkey pattern to the front of the headband.

Say: God spoke to Balaam, but he didn't obey God. God speaks to us, too. We can choose not to be like Balaam and listen to and obey God.

Seat Switch Bible Review

Do: Children sit in a circle. Leader or volunteer closes their eyes as children switch seats. When everyone is seated, without opening their eyes, leader or volunteer names a child. That child, plus the children seated on either side of them, answers one of the questions below. Repeat seat switching until each question is answered.

1. **Balaam was a prophet of the Lord—True or False.** (False)
2. **Where was King Balak king of?** (Moab)
3. **What did King Balak ask Balaam to do?** (To curse the Israelites)
4. **Why was King Balak afraid of the Israelites?** (There were so many of them)
5. **What did God say to Balaam?** (Not to curse the Israelites)
6. **Did Balaam listen to God?** (No—he went with the king's men.)
7. **Which of his donkey's actions made Balaam angry?** (The donkey lay down and even ran him into a wall.)
8. **Why was the donkey acting strange?** (It saw an angel with a sword.)
9. **What was the angel there to do?** (To kill Balaam for his disobedience.)
10. **What amazing thing happened to the donkey?** (God opened up its mouth to talk.)

Discussion Questions

1. **Why did God speak to Balaam?**
2. **How did Balaam's donkey talk?**
3. **Does God speak today? How?**

Be Still

Do: Give children time to be still before the Lord, pray silently to him, and listen to him.

Donkey Headband Patterns

Chapter 49: Prison Guard

Acts 16:16–40

We know that our old sinful selves were crucified with Christ so that sin might lose its power in our lives. We are no longer slaves to sin. **ROMANS 6:6**

God frees us from sin.

Big Idea

Overview

Say: Right after Jesus' resurrection and return to heaven, it was common for Christians to be imprisoned for telling others the good news about Jesus. Imagine being locked up in prison and beaten just for telling people about Jesus! This happened to Paul. This happened to Paul more than once!

Today's Bible story is about a time Paul was set free from prison in a very unusual way. More importantly, Paul was set free from sin. Paul knew what we are learning today: God frees us from sin!

Opening Activity

Prison Guards

Materials

- Masking tape, clothesline, or rope

Preparation: Use masking tape, clothesline, or rope to form a large square at one end of the playing area to make a "holding cell."

Do: Choose a volunteer to be a Prison Guard. The Prison Guard stands next to the holding cell with their back to the other players. The rest of the players move freely, bending, walking, stretching, etc.

When the Prison Guard turns around, players must freeze. If the Prison Guard catches anyone moving, they must go to the holding cell. Prison Guard turns around and again, players are free to move around, but they can also choose to free anyone in the holding cell by tagging them.

Play continues until there are two or three players left. Remaining players recite the verse and then choose a new Prison Guard. Play additional rounds as time and interest allow.

Say: Once you were caught moving and sent to the holding cell, was there anything you could do to unfreeze yourself? *(Children respond.)* **No! You had to wait until someone came to free you. Most of us will never be stuck in jail in real life. But we are all born stuck in slavery to sin. We are trapped in sin and there is nothing we can do on our own to get free from it. We can be free, though. God frees us from sin!**

Bible Story

Paul and Silas in Prison

Storytelling Option: Provide Bible-times costumes for volunteers to wear as they act out the action as you tell the story.

Say: **Paul and Silas had come to the city of Philippi to tell people about Jesus. Things were going well, until a day when a slave girl started following them around. The girl had an evil spirit inside her that helped her tell people's futures. Her owners made a lot of money from the girl's fortune-telling abilities.**

Paul commanded the evil spirit to leave the girl, and it did! How do you think the girl felt after being freed from the spirit? (*Children respond.*) **The girl was happy to be free of the evil spirit, but the men who owned her were very angry. Now they couldn't make money off of her fortune-telling.**

The angry men took Paul and Silas to the city authorities and had them arrested. Even though Paul and Silas had done nothing wrong, they were beaten with whips and locked up in jail. Their feet were clamped into stocks—two heavy blocks of wood with holes for a man's legs. They couldn't walk or move! What do you think Paul and Silas were feeling? (*Children respond.*) **What do you think they did while they were in jail?** (*Children respond.*)

Read: Acts 16:25–29

Say: **Instead of being sad or angry, Paul and Silas sang songs of praise to God! They knew that God would take care of them. And God did! What did God cause to happen that set all the prisoners free?** (An earthquake.)

The jailer was amazed! And the first thing he wanted to know was how he too could be saved. The jailer took Paul and Silas to his home to have their wounds washed and bandaged. And the prison guard and his whole household were baptized as members of God's family.

When Paul and Silas were put into the prison guard's custody, it seemed like they were the ones who needed to be set free. But the prison guard learned that he needed to be set free, too. He needed to be free from his sins. He learned that God frees us from sin!

Pray: Pray that the children understand that God frees us from sin, and that they will accept God's gift of freedom. Tell children interested in knowing more about being freed from sin and becoming a member of God's family to speak with one of the adult helpers today before they go home.

Object Lesson

Trapped

Do: Hand each child a Chinese finger trap to explore.

Materials

- Chinese finger traps, one for each child plus extras (available at party supply store or online)

Say: **Chinese finger traps aren't actually a trap. It's not all that hard to get your fingers free once you know the trick.**

We are all born trapped in sin; we are slaves to sin. We can try all we want, but there is nothing that we can do to free ourselves.

Paul knew this. Even the prison guard knew this. That's why he asked Paul, "What must I do to be saved?" The answer is that God frees us from sin!

Jesus is the one who saves us from our sins. Not because of anything we did, but because of what he did on the cross. We can be forgiven of our sins and freed from the punishment and power of sin. And all we have to do is put our trust in Jesus and follow him.

This was the message that Paul was put in prison for preaching. The prison guard became a follower of Christ that day. But not just him. His whole household was saved and freed from their sins!

Additional Activity Options

Musical Cans

Materials

- Children's worship music and player
- Clean and empty soda can, one for each child

Do: Play a game like Musical Chairs. Players grab an empty soda can and form a large circle, placing the can at their feet. Remove one of the cans from the circle.

Play music. Players walk around the circle as the music plays. When you stop the music, players grab the nearest soda can. Player left without a can chooses two other players to join them in reciting the memory verse, answering one of the questions on page 250, or telling a sentence about the Bible story.

Say: **Our sin separates us from God. But we can be freed from our sins. God frees us from sin!**

He sent Jesus to die on the cross to take the punishment for our sins so that we can be forgiven and become members of God's family. If we choose to accept his gift of forgiveness, we can be free from sin!

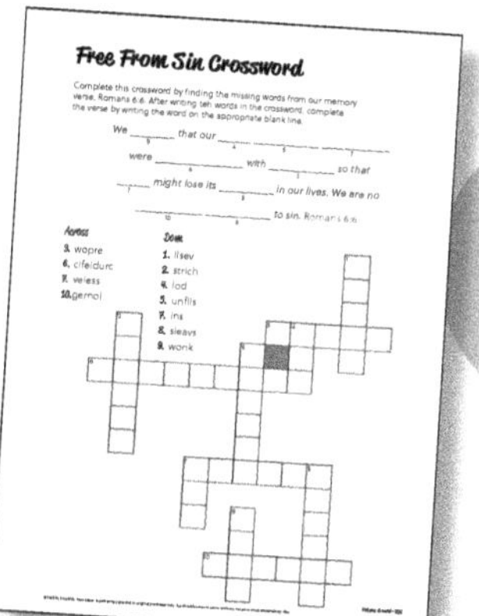

Free From Sin Crossword: Photocopy the Free From Sin Crossword on page 251, making one copy for each child plus extras. Kids complete in class or take home.

Freedom Chain

Preparation: Use scissors or paper cutter to cut construction paper into strips one or two inches wide. Make about thirty strips for each child.

Materials

- Construction paper
- Scissors or paper cutter
- Markers or crayons
- Tape

Do: Children write each word of today's memory verse, Romans 6:6, on separate strips of paper, and then tape them together to create a paper chain.

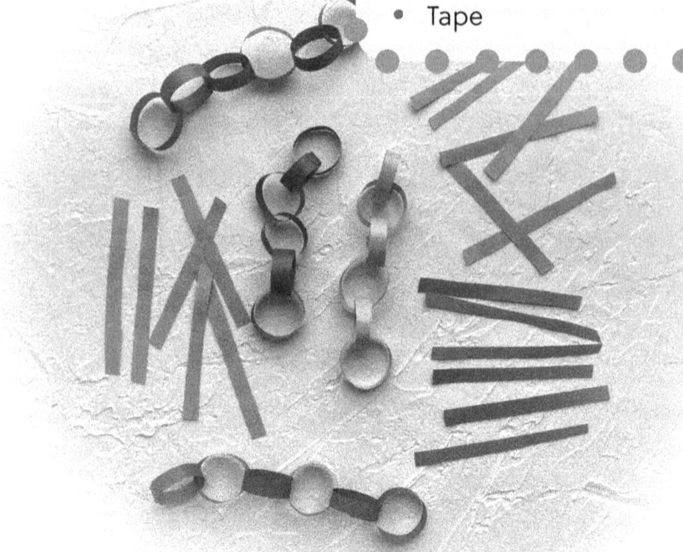

Say: **Paul and Silas were chained up in prison. But God broke those chains and they were set free! We can be set free, too, because of what Jesus did on the cross. God frees us from sin!**

Stand Up If It's True Bible Review

Say: **Stand up if the answer to the question is true but sit down if it is false. If the answer is false, explain what makes it false.**

1. **Paul kept quiet about the message of Jesus.** (False)
2. **Paul and Timothy were put in prison.** (False)
3. **Silas was beaten and imprisoned with Paul.** (True)
4. **The guard was commanded to watch Paul and Silas to make sure they didn't escape.** (True)
5. **At midnight there was a tornado.** (False)
6. **At midnight there was an earthquake that broke open the cell doors.** (True)
7. **The guard helped the prisoners dig out from the earthquake and escape.** (False)
8. **Paul stopped the guard from killing himself.** (True)
9. **All of the prisoners except for Paul and Silas escaped.** (False)
10. **The guard asked Paul how he could be saved.** (True)

Discussion Questions

1. **What does it mean that we are slaves to sin?**
2. **How can we be freed from sin?**
3. **Does being free from sin mean that we don't sin ever again?**

Free From Sin Crossword

Complete this crossword by finding the missing words from our memory verse, Romans 6:6. After writing the words in the crossword, complete the verse by writing the word on the appropriate blank line.

We ________ *that our* ______ __________ __________
9 4 5 7

were ______________ *with* __________ *so that*
6 2

______ *might lose its* _________ *in our lives. We are no*
7 3

__________ __________ *to sin.* Romans 6:6
10 8

Across

3. wopre
6. cifeidurc
7. veless
10. gernol

Down

1. ilsev
2. strich
4. lod
5. unfils
7. ins
8. sleavs
9. wonk

Chapter 50: Mary

Luke 1–2

[God said,] *"My grace is all you need. My power works best in weakness." So now I am glad to boast about my weaknesses, so that the power of Christ can work through me. . . . For when I am weak, then I am strong.* 2 CORINTHIANS 12:9–10

Overview

Say: **Merry Christmas! Even though today isn't Christmas, we are celebrating Christmas. We are going to learn about a very important person in the Christmas story. Who do you think we are learning about?** (*Children respond.*) **We are learning about Jesus' mother, Mary.**

Mary is important to the Christmas story. She is important to God's plan. But . . . she was just an ordinary person. She was an imperfect person, just like you and me. But through her story, we see how God chooses ordinary people!

Opening Activity

Deck the Halls Game

Do: Players divide into teams of four to six players. Teams race to turn a teammate into a Christmas tree using the supplies. The first team to completely use their roll of crepe paper and tape on all five decoration pieces answers one of the questions beginning on page 255 or recites the memory verse.

Optional: Play Christmas music as the game is played.

Materials

For each team of 4 to 6 players

- Roll of green crepe paper streamer
- 1 large paper star
- 5 paper circles
- Tape

Say: **What is your favorite thing about Christmas?** (*Children respond.*) **Those are all wonderful things about Christmas! Christmas is such a wonderful time. There are decorations and lights. There are yummy treats everywhere and special music. Plus, there are presents!**

But imagine if you were at the very first Christmas—at the birth of Jesus. Today, all around the world people celebrate Jesus' birth at Christmastime, but at that first Christmas (on the day of his birth), there weren't decorations and lights.

Younger Child Option: Using large sheets of paper, draw the outline of a Christmas tree. Younger children decorate it by gluing on paper ornaments.

Bible Story

Mary Is Chosen

Say: **We know that Christmas is when we celebrate Jesus' birth. Because of God's love for us, he sent his son, Jesus, to Earth as a tiny baby. Jesus would grow up to eventually die on the cross so that we can be forgiven of our sins and become members of God's family.**

Jesus is one hundred percent God which makes him the only perfect and final sacrifice for our sins. But Jesus is also one hundred percent human and had a human mother. Who was Jesus' mother? *(Children respond.)*

What kind of mother do you think God would want for his son? *(Children respond.)*

Mary was a young woman about to be married. The Bible doesn't tell us what kind of person she was or what her family did for a living. We just know what God favored her. God chose her, even though she was a sinner. You and I are sinners, too.

Read: Luke 1:28–38

Say: **Mary was given a big job, an important job. God chose her to be the mother of Jesus. There is nothing in the Bible that tells us Mary was anything but an ordinary person. But just as God chose Mary to do an important job, God chooses us to serve him, too. God chooses ordinary people—people like you and people like me.**

Pray: Children praise God for his love and that he chooses ordinary people like us.

Object Lesson

What's Inside?

Materials

- 2 gift boxes: a beautifully wrapped and decorated gift box containing an old pair of socks or similarly distasteful gift, and a plain brown box, tied with twine, in which there are individually wrapped candies, enough for all the children.

Say: *(Hold up the two gift boxes. Choose a volunteer to come forward.)* **Which of these two gifts would you like to have?** *(Volunteer chooses.)* **Why did you choose this gift?** *(Volunteer explains why they wanted that gift.)*

(Whichever gift they choose, open the beautifully decorated box first to show the unpleasant gift. Then, open the plain box and distribute the candy to all of the children.)

When God chooses us to do his will, he doesn't expect us to be perfect and beautiful. God didn't choose Mary to be the mother of Jesus because she was a perfect person. King David wasn't known as

a "man after God's own heart" because he never did anything wrong, because he did make mistakes and sin. Even the disciple Peter, who had true faith in Jesus the Messiah, had moments of weakness and sin.

Throughout the Bible, we see that **God chooses ordinary people**.

Our memory verse tells us that God's power works best in people who are weak. That's because if we were strong and perfect, we might try to do things with our own strength, our own abilities. But the best person in the world doesn't have the same power as God. We do our best when God's power works through us. That's why God chooses us ordinary people to serve him.

Additional Activity Options

Pass the Ornament

Materials

- Christmas music and player
- Christmas ornament

Do: Sitting in a circle, children pass the ornament around while music plays. After a few moments, stop the music. Whoever is holding the ornament and the players on either side recite the memory verse, answer one of the questions on page 255, or tells a sentence about the Christmas story.

Continue to play as time and interest allow.

Say: **What's your favorite part of Christmas?** (*Children respond.*) **Decorating a Christmas tree, singing Christmas songs, having family and friends over to celebrate Christmas are all fun traditions. So is getting gifts! But the greatest gift of all was when God sent Jesus to be born, so that we can become members of God's family.**

Stained Glass Decoration

Materials

- Christmas Stained Glass Art, page 256
- White card stock
- Markers or crayons
- Scissors
- Hole punch
- Ribbon

Preparation: On white card stock, photocopy Christmas Stained Glass Art, making one copy for each child plus extras.

Do: Children color their stained glass art, cut out the shape, and then punch a hole at the top of the shape. After cutting a length of ribbon approximately six to eight inches, children thread the ribbon through the hole and tie to form a hanger.

Optional: Before cutting out shape, children cover their stained glass art with clear Con-Tact paper.

Say: **What was Mary supposed to name her son?** (*Children respond.*) **Mary's baby was named Jesus! He would have a lot of other names, too: Savior, Messiah, King of kings, Lamb of God, Good Shepherd—Jesus is all of these things and more! Mary's baby, the Son of God and the Savior of the world, would grow up and make a way for us to be saved from our sins—Jesus!**

Mary and Joseph were just ordinary people that God chose to raise his Son, Jesus, here on Earth. Your stained glass art can remind you that God chooses ordinary people like you and me to do extraordinary things!

Fact Face-Off Bible Review

Do: Form two teams. Team members face off against each other, one at a time, answering the questions and earning points for their team.

1. **Who was Jesus' mother?** (Mary)
2. **Is Jesus human or God?** (100% human and 100% God)
3. **Why did God choose Mary?** (She was favored by God, but the Bible doesn't tell us why.)
4. **Who visited Mary to tell her of God's plans for her?** (The angel Gabriel)
5. **Who picked out Jesus' name?** (The angel told Mary to name him Jesus.)
6. **Did everything happen to Mary just as Gabriel told her?** (Yes)
7. **Was Mary a perfect, sinless person?** (No)
8. **Can a person be sinless?** (No)
9. **Where do we read about Gabriel visiting Mary?** (In the Bible, Luke Chapter 1)
10. **Why did Jesus come to Earth?** (So that we can be forgiven from our sins and become members of God's family.)

Discussion Questions

1. **How do we know that Mary wasn't perfect?**
2. **Why would God choose sinners to do his will?**
3. **Can God use you to do his will?**

Prayer Journal

Materials

- Blank notebook or book, one for each child plus extras
- Markers, crayons, or pens
- Decorating materials (stickers, craft-foam shapes, glitter glue, sequins, etc.

Say: **The angel Gabriel came and spoke to Mary to tell her God's plan for her life. Through prayer, God speaks to us, too! We know he has a plan for each and every one of us. We know this because God's Word, the Bible, tells us so!**

Your prayer journals can be a tool you use as you spend time praying to God the Father. Allow him to speak to you and tell you his plans for your life. Never forget that God chooses ordinary people to do his work here on Earth. Pray for God to show the extraordinary things he wants you to do for his kingdom.

Christmas Stained Glass Art